Exploring Music

Teacher's Reference Book

Eunice Boardman
Beth Landis
Barbara Andress

Consultants

Milton Babbitt
Keith E. Baird
Louis W. Ballard
Chou Wen-chung
Dorothy K. Gillett
Hope Heiman
Alan Lomax
Kurt Miller
Elena Paz
Virginia Stroh Red
Fela Sowande
Kurt Stone
Nelmatilda Woodard

HOLT, RINEHART AND WINSTON, INC.
New York, Toronto, London, Sydney

Contents

Acknowledgments

Grateful acknowledgment is given to the following authors and publishers.

• American Book Company for the words to "Grinding Corn." From *The American Singer*, Second Edition, Book 2, by Beattie, Wolverton, Wilson, and Hinga. Used by permission.
• Beacon Press for "Since Others Do So Much for Me" by Vincent B. Silliman from *We Sing of Life*. Copyright © 1955 by The American Ethical Union. Used by permission.
• Behrman House, Inc., for "In the Window." Reprinted from *Gateway to Jewish Song* by Judith K. Eisenstein. Used by permission.
• The Bodley Head for "Aunt Hessie's White Horse" from *The Children's Song Book* by Elizabeth Poston. Used by permission.
• Milton Bradley Company for the poem "Like a Leaf," originally entitled "Whirl About," from *Songs of a Child's Day* by Emilie Poulsson. Used by permission.
• Cooperative Recreation Service, Inc. for "On a Monday Morning" from *Sing a Tune*, copyright © 1966, and "The Lion Game" from *The Score*. Used by permission.
• E. P. Dutton & Company for the poem "Stars" ("Bright Stars, Light Stars") from *Stories to Begin On* by Rhoda W. Bacmeister, set to music by Irving Lowens. Copyright 1940 by E. P. Dutton & Co., Inc. Used by permission.
• E. P. Dutton & Company, Associated Book Publishers Ltd., and Methuen & Company, Ltd. for "Pooh's Song" from *The House at Pooh Corner* by A. A. Milne. Copyright 1928 by E. P. Dutton & Co., Inc. Renewal © 1956 by A. A. Milne. Used by permission.
• Leo Feist Inc. for "Santa Claus is Coming to Town." Words by H. Gillespie; music by J. Fred Coots. Copyright 1934, renewed © 1962 by Leo Feist Inc. Used by permission.
• Sam Fox Publishing Company, Inc. for "Animal Crackers in My Soup." Words by Ted Koehler, Irving Caesar; music by Ray Henderson. Copyright 1935 by Movietone Music Corp., New York. Used by permission.
• Friendship Press for "The Magic Tom-Tom" from *The Whole World Singing* by Edith Lovell Thomas. Copyright 1950. Used by permission.
• Gulf Music Company for "All Things Bright and Beautiful" by William Tyndale, "Shake the Papaya Down," and "Welcome Spring." Collected and adapted by William S. Haynie. Used by permission.
• Harcourt Brace Jovanovich, Inc. for "I Wish I Was a Little Bird" from *The American Songbag* by Carl Sandburg. Copyright 1927, by Harcourt Brace Jovanovich, Inc. Renewed © 1955 by Carl Sandburg. Used by permission.
• Highland Music Company for "Kuma San" from *Favorite Songs of Japanese Children* by Hana Fukada. Used by permission.

• Instructor Publications, Inc. for the words to "For the Tiny Child." Lyrics by Elva S. Daniels, published in *Instructor*, copyright © December, 1964 Used by permission.
• Macmillan Publishing Co., Inc. for "Swinging," originally entitled "When You Go Up," from *Summer Green* by Elizabeth Coatsworth. Copyright 1948 by Macmillan Publishing Co., Inc. Used by permission.
• Edward B. Marks Music Corporation for "The Moon Is Coming Out" from *Children's Songs from Japan*. Copyright © Edward B. Marks Music Corporation. Used by permission.
• David McKay Company, Inc. for lines from "Summer Morning" from *Christopher O!* by Barbara Young. Copyright 1947 by Barbara Young. Used by permission.
• Oxford University Press, Inc. for "Three Bears' Song," "Goldylocks' Song," and "Baby Bear's Song" from *The Golden Voice of Songs* by Roger Fiske. Copyright 1952 by Oxford University Press, London. Used by permission.
• Peer International Corporation for "I Love My Shirt." Copyright © 1969 by Donovan (Music) Ltd. Sole Selling Agent Peer International Corporation. Used by permission.
• Joseph and Nathan Segal for "If I Were a Flower." Copyright © 1971 by Joseph and Nathan Segal. Used by permission.
• Shawnee Press, Inc. for "Hey Lidee." Words by James Leisy, music adapted from a traditional melody. Copyright © 1973, 1966 by Shawnee Press, Inc., Delaware Water Gap, Pa. 18327. Used by permission.
• Stackpole Books for "Anton Firulero" from *The Unicef Book of Children's Songs* by William Kaufman. Used by permission.
• Systems for Education, Inc. for the music of "Summer Morning" by William S. Haynie from *Headstart with Music* by William S. Haynie and Buryl A. Red. Used by permission.
• The United Synagogue of America for "Hakof" from *Songs of Childhood* by Judith K. Eisenstein and Frieda Prensky. Used by permission.
• The University Press of Virginia for "It Rained a Mist" from *Traditional Ballads of Virginia* by Arthur Kyle Davis. Copyright © 1969, University Press of Virginia, Charlottesville. Used by permission.
• Wonderland Music Company, Inc. for "Step in Time." Words and Music by Richard M. and Robert B. Sherman. Used by permission.
Additional copyright acknowledgments and photo credits appear with the materials used.

Exploring Music

The teacher sets the environment for learning through which the child may explore the music of mankind. As he discovers this rich heritage, the child will grow in his ability to understand and organize, as well as interpret and express, musical ideas.

It is the teacher's challenge to help the child

in order that he may:

• realize that music is an expressive art and thus value his own involvement as a music maker and knowledgeable listener.

• understand that one may interpret another's music and express one's own through the communicative tools of language (written or spoken) and musical notation (devised or traditional).

• develop the ability to use nonverbal skills, including movement and visual imagery, to reveal his awareness of the musical totality when other forms of communication prove inadequate.

• grow in his understanding that the same components of music have been combined in many ways to produce music of many styles, time periods, and cultures of man.

• develop a bank of knowledge, based on many sensory experiences, which will enable him to make valid judgments about his own musical efforts, as well as those of others.

• realize that understanding the relationship of music's components to its totality may deepen the esthetic experience.

Each child should have this opportunity so that he may develop his own set of values regarding the kinds of music he will find satisfying and the place music will fill in his own life.

MUSICAL BEHAVIORS · 5-7 YEAR OLD

Given an opportunity to explore music through performing, describing, and organizing, the five- to seven-year-old will demonstrate the following musical behaviors after completing the first level of musical experience.

		TIMBRE	DURATION
PERFORMS	SINGS · PLAYS · MOVES	Play instruments in various ways to produce different qualities of sound. Be able to play common classroom instruments skillfully in ways which will produce satisfying qualities of sound. Demonstrate progress in the ability to produce a pleasing vocal quality. Use his body as a musical instrument to produce different timbres by such actions as clapping, tapping, and stamping.	Control, with voice or when playing instrument, the relative duration of tone (**longer-shorter-same**). Perform chants in relation to a basic beat, using appropriate rhythm patterns. Sing familiar songs with rhythmic accuracy. Echo rhythmic patterns on percussion instruments, or using body sounds such as slaps or taps.
DESCRIBES	MOVES · VERBALIZES · VISUALIZES	Develop movements that reflect various qualities of sound. Recognize contrasts in timbre by changing movements to match change in sound. Group sound categories according to quality (rasping, clicking), or method of playing (rattling, ringing, scraping). Associate the names with the sounds of representative classroom instruments. Associate pictures of selected orchestral instruments with their names and sounds.	Distinguish between sounds that are sustained and those that are not sustained. Indicate awareness of duration (longer, shorter) with appropriate body movements. Use motions, such as clapping and stepping, to reveal recognition of rhythmic pattern, beat, and accent grouping. Develop own vocabulary to describe rhythmic ideas. Verbalize differences between pattern and beat. Reproduce rhythmic patterns from line notation, interpreting the patterns in terms of longer-shorter duration. Transfer recognition of line notation to interpretation of simple rhythm patterns in traditional notation (2-1 relationships).
ORGANIZES	IMPROVISES · COMPOSES	Select appropriate timbres to communicate his musical and extra-musical ideas. Provide contrast in own compositions by selecting instruments of contrasting timbres.	Develop patterns of his own, using both longer and shorter sounds, and incorporate them into his own compositions. Improvise rhythm patterns in relation to other patterns or to a basic beat. Use line notation (or notational schemes of own) to record his musical ideas.

MUSICAL CONTROLS

Volume • Tempo • Articulation

Reveal sensitivity to musical controls by singing with appropriate dynamic level, tempo, and articulation.

Develop ability to control volume levels when playing instruments.

Use appropriate volume changes when chanting poems.

Expand ability to chant, sing, and play instruments with appropriate changes of tempo.

Become aware of the possibilities of varying articulation (*legato, staccato*) when chanting, singing, and playing.

Develop a repertoire of movements with which to show contrasts in loud and soft, fast and slow, and *staccato-legato*.

Use visual imagery (ikons) to reflect volume and tempo changes in music.

Gain a vocabulary with which to describe contrasts in musical controls and indicate reasons for the differences, such as source of sound and method of performance.

Use different articulations, contrasts of volume, and tempo changes, when planning own compositions.

When improvising, demonstrate awareness that loud and soft contrasts may be a result of the method of performance, of adding or subtracting sounds to the totality, or of varying the distance of the sound source from the listeners.

Devise notational schemes to indicate volume, tempo, and articulation in own compositions.

PITCH

Melody • Harmony

Develop ability to sing accurately within a limited range.

Sing with a contrasting accompaniment, indicating awareness of multiple sounds.

Play one or more appropriate instruments to indicate understanding of relative highness and lowness.

Perform patterns on pitched instruments (such as bells, xylophones) to demonstrate understanding of melodic direction (up-down, same) and type of movement (step-skip).

Produce harmony by playing simple accompaniments on pitched instruments.

Echo simple melody patterns with voice or on limited number of bells.

Possess a repertoire of songs he can sing with tonal accuracy.

Reflect melodic contour with appropriate body movements.

Indicate recognition of chord changes on autoharp or piano by responding with changes of movement.

Associate a visual image (ikon) with a melodic shape.

Devise own visual images to indicate recognition of melodic shapes.

Play melodies on bells in response to visual clues.

Group some common orchestral instruments into high or low categories.

Use an expanded vocabulary to describe overall highness or lowness (squeaky, growly) and melodic contour (climbing, or stepping, close together or far apart.)

Make judgments as to choice and organization of pitches when planning his own music.

Improvise accompaniments, given a limited number of pitches with which to work.

Work with others to create compositions using multiple sounds based on pentatonic, whole-tone, or devised scales.

STRUCTURE

Design • Texture • Form

Identify same and different sections by using same or different instruments or patterns for song accompaniments.

Demonstrate awareness of the phrase by singing or playing each as a "complete musical idea."

Show recognition of pattern by echoing rhythmic or tonal patterns accurately.

Respond to phrase with appropriate body movements.

Demonstrate, with movement, the recognition of same or different sections.

Use terms such as **phrase, same** or **different, part,** and **whole,** to describe musical design.

Select appropriate visual image from several choices to match design of music. Develop other visual aids to describe same or different sections.

Verbalize understanding that "pictures" of music (including traditional notation) that look alike will sound alike.

Demonstrate awareness of several strands of sound by moving appropriately.

Organize compositions into same and different sections. Consider ways that same and different melodies, rhythms, timbres, and expressive controls help to give structure to composition.

v

THE CHILD WILL
Synthesize musical explorations

EXPRESSIVE TOTALITY

Reflect a growing sensitivity to the contributions of timbre, musical controls, rhythm, melody, harmony, and structure to the expressive totality in the manner in which he sings and plays.

Select instruments and organize patterns for song accompaniments appropriate to the mood or feeling of the song. Move in ways which show sensitivity to the expressive totality of music.

Show awareness of the expressive nature of music by developing visual images to express his responses to music.

Create compositions that communicate musical ideas, or suggest extra-musical feelings or objects.

Acquire vocabulary to describe ways music is organized expressively.

Show his enthusiasm for.and interest in music as an expressive medium by seeking opportunities for musical involvement in and out of the classroom.

TIME AND PLACE

Perform chants and songs of many times and places as the child builds its own repertoire.

Play simple accompaniments using percussion instruments that reflect the origin of the song.

Respond to music in various times and places through traditional dance and expressive movement.

Begin to recognize that each group of people combines musical components in a unique way to express the music of a time and culture.

Reveal awareness of time and place by using terms such as "music of long ago" or "far away."

Plan compositions that reflect awareness of musical sounds of his own time.

Musical Behavior: Planning for Learning

Who has not entered a classroom during music time to see children who are highly motivated, excited and obviously enjoying the musical experience? Continued observation, however, may reveal that these experiences are not really meeting the educational needs of the children. Each child has the right to a classroom experience that will not only be momentarily exciting, but will also help him develop the behaviors he will need for satisfying and continued musical involvement.

Parents and administrators also have the right to hold the teacher accountable for the musical growth of the children. It is each teacher's responsibility to know the yearly objectives for the class and to plan learning activities that will help children move towards these objectives. Each music session must be planned with this responsibility in mind. In order to be certain that the children's experiences are not only exciting events, but also learning events, the teacher should:

1. identify the musical concept (see page viii) to be emphasized;

2. assess the children's present level of musical understanding and skill;

3. set the behavioral objective for the session in terms of one of the three modes of musical involvement: performing, describing, organizing (see pages iv-vi);

4. select appropriate materials from textbooks or other sources;

5. determine the level at which children are now representing their understanding: enactive, ikonic, or symbolic (see this page);

6. decide on the level of thinking children will be involved in using: recall, translation, analysis, synthesis, valuing (see this page);

7. design introductory activities, problem-solving situations, questions, and instructions based on decisions made when completing steps 1-6 (see individual lessons throughout book);

8. plan ways of evaluating the session in relation to the desired objectives (see **Extend** section of individual lessons).

Learning is not only the ability to recall knowledge; it is also growth in the ability to use other modes of thinking. The teacher must plan activities that will stimulate the children to make use of higher levels of thinking so that they may become independent in their ability to apply their understandings to new situations.

How will you encourage the children in your class to use different levels of thinking as they work?

To encourage recall and translative skills, guide them to
> **label**
> **list**
> **imitate**
> **define**

To encourage analytic skills, guide them to:
> **compare**
> **describe**
> **discriminate**
> **interpret**

To encourage synthesizing skills, guide them to:
> **perform**
> **compose**
> **improvise**
> **create**

To encourage valuing skills, guide them to:
> **choose**
> **reject**
> **evaluate**
> **accept**
> **prefer**

As children conceptualize, they demonstrate their understanding of the knowledge they are acquiring in many ways. How will you recognize the level at which children are conceptualizing? If at the **enactive level** they will be:

- **demonstrating** their understanding through **active** physical involvement.
- **performing** music by imitating what they hear.
- **describing** what they hear with gesture or dance movements.
- **organizing** their own musical ideas by improvising, on instruments or vocally.

If at the **ikonic level,** they will be:

- growing in ability to retain a mental image and to associate that image with visual images ("ikons") that "look like the music sounds."
- **performing** music by interpreting what they see (the ikon).
- **organizing** their own musical ideas and communicating them through ikons of their own invention.
- **describing** what they hear by choosing appropriate ikons, developing their own, or by using their own verbal images.

If they are at the **symbolic level,** they will be:

- growing in their ability to associate their aural concepts of music with traditional symbols (words or notation).
- **describing** music by turning sound into symbols, or by using musical terms.
- **performing** music by turning symbols into sound.
- **organizing** their own musical ideas and recording them with traditional musical notation.

As teachers plan, they must constantly remember that music makes a unique contribution to the child in the **affective** area—sensitivity and feeling. No matter how well objectives are stated and music lessons planned, the experience is successful only if each child leaves the music class richer not only in musical knowledge, but also with a feeling for the beauty and sensitivity which the music has added to his being.

The Young Musician Performs

The young child performs by singing, playing instruments, and using his body as a musical instrument. Through performing, he expresses his understanding of music and his feelings about it. The teacher will find the suggestions in this unit helpful when guiding the child as he develops the appropriate Musical Behaviors (see pages iv-vi) projected for his early experiences.

The Young Musician Sings

Children will enjoy singing many of the songs in this book throughout the year. The song material includes nursery rhymes and other songs on topics of interest to young children: holidays, time of day, the weather, people, and animals. Help children build a repertoire of favorite songs that they can sing at home with their friends, or with other classes.

Use the songs to help children become sensitive to expression in music, to melodic contour, rhythmic movement, and phrase structure. As children listen and sing, guide them toward awareness of basic concepts about melody, rhythm, design, expression, and harmony as outlined in the Musical Behavior charts, pages iv-vi.

Most little children love to sing. They participate enthusiastically and are quick to learn new words and melodies. When involving children in song activities, the teacher should understand the "instrument": a child's voice should not be measured against the quality or volume of the adult voice.

Sometimes, the children's enthusiasm may take them beyond the point of singing and into shouting. The teacher must be alert to this and not allow children to strain their voices. They should be encouraged to sing with a natural vocal quality that is in no way "forced." At times the voice will be louder, at other times softer, reflecting the expressive intent of the song. The children's voices on the recordings with this book provide examples of a type of voice quality toward which a teacher might realistically help pupils strive.

When teaching a song to young children, the teacher should use a variety of approaches. Children are used to learning songs by listening. The following approaches will aid the child when learning a song in this manner.

- The teacher sings the words of the song, either phrase-by-phrase or in its entirety. Children listen first, then echo.
- Discuss the words to insure understanding. If the child is not certain of the words, he will have difficulty in following the melodic line.
- To help children remember the sequence of words, the teacher might use visual aids such as pictures, charts, puppets, and masks.
- Add pantomime or finger plays to songs to help children remember the words.
- Repeat songs many times. Children learn through repetition, and are delighted to sing familiar songs time and again.

Many musical learnings are acquired while singing. The child will discover the characteristics of melody. He may move his hands to indicate direction as he sings. He may discover that words and melodies of specific lines repeat or that melody lines may repeat with different words. The child is developing a feeling for voice placement. His voice can be "in his throat" or higher "in his head." Games which will help the child feel the placement of his voice are included in the book. (See page 106)

The use of hand movement coupled with vocal production provides a kinesthetic approach to "feeling" the voice. Whether specific hand signals are assigned to each tone, or children demonstrate general melodic direction with their hands, the use of movement with singing can promote greater tonal accuracy.

Help children become aware that they must also listen as they sing. Develop the child's sensitivity to how his voice may blend with others and contribute to a group musical experience.

All of the songs in this text are recorded in styles and instrumentation that reflect their musical characteristics and origins. The recordings can thus serve as more than mere accompaniments. Discuss the instruments used and why these particular ones were selected for the song. Help children become aware that the song material reflects many different cultures. When the young child leaves your classroom, he will take with him a musical instrument (his voice), certain understandings about how to use his voice, and the many songs you have introduced. He will be very aware that the joy of singing does not belong only in the music classroom but can be with him anywhere.

Tone Games

Little children have few problems when singing independently. They will sing freely on the playground using simple two- and three-tone chants, usually very much in tune with themselves. It is when the child joins a group and is required to match his voice with others that he becomes aware of the need for greater pitch accuracy. A good place to begin is with the child's present "style" of singing. Bring his two- and three-tone chants into the classroom. Instead of singing the traditional teasing words of these chants, however, use the same tones as echo games for a variety of classroom procedures:

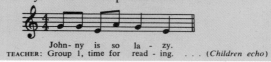

John- ny is so la- zy.
TEACHER: Group 1, time for read-ing. . . . (*Children echo*)

As the child participates in these games, he discovers that he must listen and compare the sound of his voice with that of others. He may be asked to join the musical conversation with a solo answer or as a part of a group response. Some approaches for aiding the child's tone-matching responses follow.

1. Echo sing: teacher sings, children answer with the same words and tune.

TEACHER: Good morn - ing . . . (*Children echo*)

2. Question and answer.

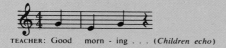

TEACHER: How are you? CHILDREN: I'm fine.___

3. Combine ideas for children's responses. Call the roll using this sequence:

TEACHER: Where is Jo - sé?

CLASS: Where is Jo - sé?

JOSÉ: Here I am.

These tonal call-responses should permeate daily activities, making music a functional part of the child's life. Since the child's tonal range should be increased, the teacher will want to use a variety of short melodic ideas which pose increasing tone-matching challenges.

4. Sing fragments of familiar songs, but make up new words.

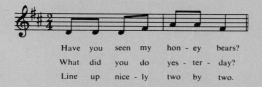

Have you seen my hon - ey bears?
What did you do yes - ter - day?
Line up nice - ly two by two.

5. Use short scale or chordal patterns as children play tonal games.

TEACHER: Mon - ey for milk; Who has mon - ey for milk?
CLASS: Mon - ey for milk; I have mon - ey for milk.

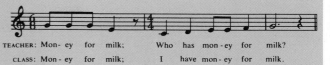

TEACHER: Time to go home.

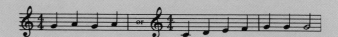

TEACHER: Who is sit - ting in the sun?
CLASS: I am sit - ting in the sun.

6. Match pitches of instruments. Play echo games using instrumental sounds. Children may echo tones which you dictate on bells or piano using "loo" or words:

Choose sides and have a "Tonal Spell-Down." This will be an exciting time for children, as they must listen carefully for each response and judge its accuracy. Use a limited range of tones in the beginning, then increase the challenge to the children's listening and performance skills as the game progresses. Use more pitches in the patterns and increase the length and complexity of the patterns.

Children will need many experiences to gain the necessary skills for singing as a group. Some children will have more problems than others. Plan moments to work with individuals within a group activity so that most children are not aware that you are singling out a particular child.

Involving the child in tone-matching activities is an important developmental step in helping the child move toward successful singing experiences.

The Young Musician Plays Instruments

The teacher of primary music should make every attempt to obtain instruments of good quality which produce valid musical sounds. At this state in their development, children are becoming aware of the timbres of musical instruments and are beginning to make choices about how they can be used for making music. If such choices are to reflect the characteristic sounds of instruments, then one cannot rely on an inexpensive imitation that may look like a percussion instrument but sound like a tin pan.

The teacher's goal should be to provide a variety of good sound sources that will enable the children to make up appropriate accompaniments for songs and create compositions, rather than to provide one instrument of lesser quality for every child. An adequate selection of classroom instruments might consist of small percussion instruments such as jingle bells, jingle clogs, maracas, claves, rhythm sticks, triangles, wood blocks, finger cymbals, larger cymbals, and assorted drums. A collection of "sound starters," such as hard and soft mallets, sticks, drum brushes, and metal beaters, is most important. Have available several sizes of the same instruments to provide a source of contrasting pitches. These instruments can be used for activities involving pitch as well as rhythm. The teacher thus might request a large and small triangle, rather than two identical triangles, when ordering supplies.

Melodic percussion instruments are important sound sources in the classroom. There are many varieties from which the teacher may choose.

Resonator bells will be very useful in the classroom. They may be used to discover

. . . melodic concepts such as movement from high to low and low to high.
. . . movement of melodies by steps and skips.
. . . simple harmonies and accompaniments.

Resonator bells make it possible to limit the child's choices of tones by putting out only those bell blocks needed for a given activity.

Many **xylophone**-like instruments are available for classroom use today. These have a variety of timbres and ranges. Within this group are:

xylophones - wooden bars (bass, alto, soprano range)
metallophones - thick metal bars (bass, alto, soprano range)
glockenspiels - small thick metal bars (alto, soprano range)

These instruments may be used singly, a few at a time, or in a large ensemble. Their use can provide a more extensive exploration of sound, because of their wider ranges and contrasting timbres.

The instruments may be obtained with bars arranged either in a diatonic or chromatic scale. The bars on each instru-

ment are removable, again making it possible to deal with specific pitches.

Numerous accompaniment parts and ideas for improvisations for these instruments are included in this book. The teacher may substitute other sounds such as resonator bells when xylophone-type instruments are not available.

The **autoharp** provides an opportunity for children to hear and play harmonic accompaniments with little technical skill required. Although the teacher may often play the autoharp for the class, young children may learn to play the instrument in pairs. One child is assigned the responsibility of pushing the appropriate buttons while the other child strums rhythmically.

The **piano** should be available to the children as well as to the teacher. Simple melodies can be produced using only the black keys of the piano. Pentatonic songs such as "Trot, Pony, Trot" may be accompanied by playing on combinations of the black keys.

The **guitar** has become a favorite instrument for children. Even if the children themselves are unable to play it, the teacher's use of this instrument is very exciting to them. The teacher may accompany many of the children's songs with only two or three chords.

Little children may play the guitar if it is re-tuned to a C major chord in the following manner:

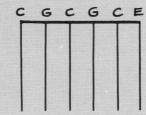

The teacher should make children aware that the guitar they are using is specially tuned so that they will not expect the same success on every guitar they happen to find.

Children may strum this chord as an accompaniment to rounds such as "Are You Sleeping" and "Row, Row, Row Your Boat." Songs using the "C pentatonic" scale (C D F G A) may also be accompanied in this manner.

Children may strum and pluck the guitar to express extra-musical sounds and ideas, such as the wind or rain, with the instrument.

Provide many opportunities for children to play classroom instruments individually. During most class sessions, time limitations will allow only a few children to participate.

Instruments Appropriate for the Classroom

The following percussion instruments are appropriate for use in a primary music classroom. The illustrations indicate playing positions appropriate for producing acceptable timbral quality. In addition to helping children develop skill in playing these instruments correctly in the traditional ways, teachers will want to give them many opportunities to experiment with other ways of producing sounds on each instrument. Suggestions for such sound exploration are found throughout the book.

When appropriate, follow up these presentations by placing the instruments in the Music Learning Center. Provide simple instructions and allow children to pursue exploration of the instruments on their own.

The Young Musician Uses His Body as a Musical Instrument

The young child first learns through large, sensory-motor activities, later refines these movements to smaller gestures, and eventually internalizes them into abstract understandings. Thus, movement becomes a vital route to the development of specific musical concepts. Children will use movement not only to respond to the duration and pitch of music, but also to indicate their awareness of timbre, musical controls, and structure.

Encourage the child to explore ways of using his body as a musical instrument.

Experiment with different ways of using one's two hands: clap with palms cupped, palms flat, fingertips only, "heel" of hand only; snap fingers, "swish" palms.

Explore differences in sound quality and pitch when hands are used as "beaters" against knees, thighs, upper chest, and arms.

Explore sounds that feet can make: stamping, sliding, and tapping.

Experiment with "mouth sounds" such as clicking tongues, blowing, hissing.

As the child uses his body as a musical instrument, he will acquire the ability to respond with accuracy to the basic beat and to rhythmic patterns. The child may hear a rhythmic pulse but lack the coordination to respond accurately. By using his body as a musical instrument in a variety of repeated activities, he will develop the motor skills necessary for a more successful response.

Combining speech with such movements challenges a child to do more than one thing at a time and to become aware of the possibilities of multiple sounds. Some possible activities:

. . . Clap and chant rhythmic patterns of songs or poems.
. . . Produce the basic beat with body sounds while chanting or singing a rhythmic pattern.
. . . Experiment with different sound qualities to accompany chants which contain expressive ideas.
. . . Plan contrasting body sounds to be used with different sections of a chant or song to reflect its design.

Only after the children have had many experiences in responding through movement will they be ready to grasp the visual representation of musical ideas. Because of the importance of maintaining the developmental sequence from sensory-motor activity to visual imagery, some physical activity should be used frequently in the music class. The child who explores music through more than one sense simultaneously is truly the involved learner.

The Young Musician Describes

The young child grows in his understanding as he describes music with movement, words, and "pictures." His ability to describe may range from non-verbal responses to the use of specific musical terminology. If the child does not verbalize, the teacher must become a skillful observer and interpreter of the child's movement in order to determine his current level of understanding. As the child grows in his translative skills, he will begin to communicate verbally and use visual representation. The following information may be helpful as the teacher guides the child in developing the appropriate Musical Behaviors, pages iv-vi, for young children.

The Young Musician Moves

The young child is very sensitive to the beauty he sees and hears. He may want to talk about it, but his limited vocabulary and concepts make it difficult for him to describe an abstract experience. However, the child usually has few inhibitions about moving to music. Through movement, the child can provide many clues to the observer about what he is hearing, understanding, and feeling. As the child moves he is involved in the sensory experience through which all understanding of musical concepts takes place.

Expressive Movement

The teacher should provide many opportunities for young children to respond to music through expressive movement. Too often, the teacher falls into a trap of playing a recording and asking children to move "however the music makes you feel." The child has an overabundance of ideas, usually disorganized, and often becomes overwhelmed and frustrated. What might have been a beautiful experience results in chaos. After several unsuccessful experiences, children may become self-conscious and reluctant about participating in other such activities.

Just as children cannot compose music without first developing concepts about music, they cannot respond through movement without first developing some basic understandings of how the body moves in space. Children need to develop a repertoire of movement through which they can express musical ideas. At first, these movements will be used to express isolated sound ideas such as pitch level, tempo, and volume. Later, movements will be combined to reflect musical structure.

Included in this book are ideas for ways to encourage children to explore a variety of motions: swinging, sustained, and sharp (percussive) movements. The child may use these movements in response to a variety of composed pieces, or to specific sound ideas. These motor responses give the child another means of communicating and reinforcing concepts concerning duration, melodic contour, change of volume, and musical structure, as they affect the musical totality.

Sustained Movement

The young child has experiences in sustaining movement when reponding to a smooth melodic line or to specific sounds which have extended duration, such as those produced by finger cymbals, larger cymbals, gongs, metallophones, or resonator bells. He may use small or larger body movements as he responds to contrasting volume and duration of sound. Ultimately, he will combine these movement ideas with others when responding to a variety of musical selections.

Sharp, Percussive Movement

Percussive sounds may be reflected with brisk, angular movements. The use of imagery, such as "make a straight stick with your arm," with movement initiated by a sharp, accented sound on a drum or claves, provides experience with this type of movement. Small or large movements of this type may later be incorporated when planning a sequence combining music and dance.

Swinging or Swaying Movements

These types of movement reflect an understanding of and feeling for meter and articulation. The child should have many opportunities to select this type of movement when responding to music.

These basic ideas are explored when the child responds to repeated accent such as "1 2 3 - 1 2 3" or "1 2 - 1 2." The child may open and close, move in and out, and turn. The teacher might suggest that children work in small groups to develop movements which sway or swing as appropriate music is played.

SIT FACING INSIDE THE CIRCLE. SWAY IN WITH ARMS; SWAY OUT. WHAT OTHER MOVEMENT CAN YOUR GROUP DO THAT SWAYS OR SWINGS?

Body movement may be used to reflect the characteristic sounds of an instrument. Shake a maraca. LET YOUR FINGERS . . . YOUR FEET . . . YOUR TOES TELL ME ABOUT THIS SOUND. Strum the autoharp. LET YOUR FINGERS TELL ME ABOUT THIS SOUND.

Through repeated expression, the child becomes aware of his body and how it can move in space. He learns that it takes time to move from one place to another and that there are many different ways the body may move. He learns to discipline his body, to stop and start at appropriate times and in appropriate ways and to use only the space his "neighbor is not in." He may move to imagery suggested by single words, poems, or stories. Single sounds as well as complete musical compositions may suggest images that motivate movement.

Though initial ideas may include responses to specific sounds or extra-musical ideas, the goal of such movement should be to combine movement ideas into responses which reflect the expressive totality of musical compositions. As the movement becomes dance, the children may serve as models for one another. Someone may notice that Sandy may have just the right idea for the first part of the piece; others will eagerly adopt the idea. Careful listening and planning is soon taking place.

Thus when we say to a child "dance your own dance" in response to music, he will have many movement experiences from which to draw, in addition to others he will invent. He will be able to make appropriate movement choices that reflect a sensitivity to what is happening in the music itself.

The following suggestions may be of help when guiding children in dance experiences.

- Adequate space is essential. If necessary, divide the class into groups so that not too many are on the floor at one time.

- Provide "warm-up" time for children to dance freely and find new ways to move.

- Let the movements be as natural and spontaneous as possible.

- Remind children often that dancing will be more fun if they think of the music and not of themselves.

- Children will move more freely if they dance in bare feet. Slippery soles and heavy shoes inhibit movement.

Patterned Movement

In addition to improvised movement, young children should have experiences with patterned movement, as in singing games and folk dances. A number of songs and other compositions in the text are suitable for dancing. While some dances are learned through specific instructions, the figures can be varied by children as they improvise original dances and singing games.

- Make sure that children hear the beat and the accent of the music, since folk-dance figures are usually based on the rhythmic movement of the music.

- Guide children to dance with the style and vitality characteristic of folk dance.

The Classified Index of this book lists specific lessons which involve the child in expressive movement and dance.

The Young Musician Visualizes

An important long-range goal for the musically educated person is the ability to come in contact with an unknown piece of music and independently read, sing, or play the piece. Hence, understanding of the visual representation of music and how it communicates musical ideas, is most important.

As the teacher works toward this long-range goal of reading notation, the true goal of the activity must be kept in mind. A teacher might feel that a great deal has been achieved when students parrot back the correct name or definition of a notational symbol. However, the child's learning can only be evaluated by his ability to translate these symbols into sound, within the context of an existing piece of music. He may also demonstrate his understanding by using traditional musical symbols to notate his own compositions.

As the child moves through the enactive and ikonic stages to the stage of symbolic thinking, it is important to remember that the musical symbol is merely the label for a given musical sound, or sound pattern. Understanding of the musical concept must come first; the symbol may then be learned easily.

Prior to the introduction of traditional notation, the child must have developed musical concepts at the enactive level—through physical movement. He will communicate his understanding of concepts related to pitch and duration through singing, playing, and moving in response to music he hears. He will also demonstrate his conceptualization through his own improvisations. Involve the child in such activities as the following:

- Use large movements to show melodic contour: high and low relationships; walk, run, or skip to demonstrate understanding of overall rhythmic organization; demonstrate awareness of same and different patterns by moving in appropriate ways.

- Use hand movements to demonstrate more specific pitch directions and relationships.

- Echo-sing and echo-clap to reproduce melody and rhythm patterns.

- Use terms descriptive of movement to discuss the sound patterns to which he has physically responded.

When the child can move to what he hears, echo what he hears by playing or singing, and improvise his own patterns, he is ready to begin to associate visual images with sounds. By associating "pictures of sound" (ikons) with musical sound, he will develop a more precise understanding of musical organization. Possible "pictures of sound" include:

- Rhythm patterns represented by "line notation"; lines representing varying durations relative to one another in a given piece of music:

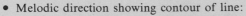

- Metric groupings showing heavy and light beats:

- Melodic direction showing contour of line:

- Melodic movement showing stepwise or skipping movement:

- Form, shown by same and different shapes:

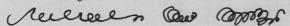

The child should be encouraged to devise his own visual images when communicating his ideas for his own improvisations.
He may use pictures:

or abstract designs:

At this level, the visual image or "ikon" will look like the music sounds. As children explore ways of representing pictorially what they hear, they will develop the ability to conserve the musical sound image and to build a "memory bank" of musical ideas. When children can associate pictorial images with patterns of sound, they are ready to move to the symbolic level.

At the symbolic level the child learns to associate traditional notational symbols with the musical sounds they represent. Young children will begin to transfer their understanding of pictorial representations to traditional notation. Rhythm patterns made up of longer and shorter sounds may be represented by notes.

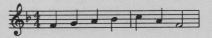

Melodic shapes which move up and down by steps or skips may be shown on a staff.

This book guides the child through a sequential development of basic musical understandings based on representation of those understandings at each of the three levels.

1. Enactive level: moving, singing and playing in response to the sound of music; **2. Ikonic level:** retaining a mental image which can be represented with pictures of sound **3. Symbolic level:** associating the traditional symbols with the musical sound. Only a few of the traditional symbols will be introduced: emphasis at this level should be on building the concepts that the child may later associate with the symbol.

The book should be used in sequence, beginning with the first page and moving through to the end. Detailed suggestions for introducing musical concepts at various levels of learning are presented on each page of the teacher's book. As new ideas about musical notation are introduced, return to familiar songs and associate what the children can already hear and sing with the appropriate "sound pictures" or symbols.

As children increase in their ability to use visual imagery and musical notation, they will become aware that they no longer have to depend upon listening in order to learn new music, but can *learn new melodies all by themselves.*

The Young Musician Verbalizes

The child should begin to acquire a vocabulary to help him describe what he hears. The acquisition of verbal skills should not be seen as the primary goal of the music lesson, but simply as one more way in which the child can express his ideas about music.

It is important, however, that attention be given to vocabulary because many commonplace words have different meanings used in a musical context. Young children often confuse a word such as "high" with "loud" (as in "turn the T.V. up higher"). A "tall" instrument may be thought of as being "higher," because, spatially, it is. The young child will not necessarily associate "low," with "big"; the fact that larger instruments usually make a lower sound must be taught. Because of these multiple connotations of words, the teacher must make a point of helping the children sort out and identify the word meanings as they apply to music.

The teacher should discuss music or label a particular sound pattern only as a consequence of the child's interaction with music or sound. The child should be initially encouraged to devise many of his own descriptive words. In this way, the teacher may discern and help to clarify confusions. Gradually, the teacher will introduce traditional terminology and the child will begin to use the terms by imitating the model set by the teacher, just as he acquires other new vocabulary.

Typical descriptive words which a young child may use when describing music are included in the Musical Behavior Charts (pages iv-vi).

The Young Musician Organizes

The young child organizes when he solves musical problems by improvising his own responses. He makes judgments based upon his acquired musical understandings. When the child uses his knowledge about music in this manner, he is operating at the highest level of learning. Ideas for setting the environment so that the child can develop appropriate Musical Behavior (page vii) through the creative process are included in the discussion below.

The Young Musician Improvises

A child makes music during his pre-school years in a variety of ways. One of the most creative of those activities is singing his own made-up songs. Such songs are, more often than not, rambling lines which lack traditional rhythmic or melodic organization. The child sings to himself about play, playmates, and pets. He sings for his own pleasure, for the joy of the words and melody. He is not performing in any sense of the word but is using melody as a natural extension of language development.

When the child enters school, we are anxious for him to match tones and learn to perform within a group. This is certainly a valid goal, but many times we become so concerned with his group response that we stifle his individual creative development. The natural improvisational ability he brings with him should continue to be a very exciting part of the child's experiences in the classroom. The child now has the opportunity to improvise not only song, but also to explore instrumental sounds and to use movement as a means of musical expression. Setting the learning environment that will promote this kind of growth becomes a challenge for the teacher in order to allow for individual creativity within all sizes of groups.

Improvise with Voices

• Help the child make up introductions and codas to songs. For example, a simple introduction to a song about cats might be to sing "me-ow" on the beginning pitch of the song (or two tones which will lead to beginning pitch).

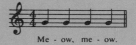

Me - ow, me - ow.

If appropriate to the song text, the coda might be the "Phist!" of the hissing cat.

• Ask the class to sing a two-tone chant which ends with a question.

TEACHER: Look in my hand. What do you see? CHILDREN: (I see . . .)

Ask one child to sing an answer using his own words and melody. Help him to make the second pattern different from the first. (The teacher may need help by singing part of the answer. As the child gains confidence, the teacher drops out.)

• Make up an introduction, accompaniment, and coda for a chant by extracting one or two words from the chant and repeating these rhythmically as others perform the complete chant.
• Make up original lyrics for songs through rhyming games: Ask the class to think of rhyming words.

1. Write rhyming words on chalkboard (red, bed, said, lead, Fred).
2. Chant the words, adding clicking sounds (pencil tap, tongue click).

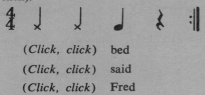

(*Click, click*)   bed

(*Click, click*)   said

(*Click, click*)   Fred

3. Use words to make sentences the same length. Some make sense, others nonsense.

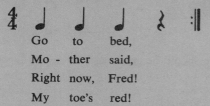

Go   to   bed,

Mo - ther   said,

Right   now,   Fred!

My   toe's   red!

Make up other words. "What rhymes with blue"?

• Make up an original melody using children's lyrics:
1. One child is the leader and sings his melody for each line of the song. The class echoes what the leader sang.

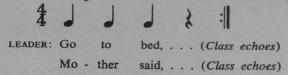

LEADER: Go   to   bed, . . . (*Class echoes*)

Mo - ther   said, . . . (*Class echoes*)

2. Choose a new leader and make up new melodies.
• Add new verses to familiar songs.

Agree on a basic idea to be stated in the new verse. Put key words or pictures on the chalkboard as children make suggestions, so that the ideas can be easily recalled as the poem is developed. The teacher should try to work with simple words and help the children get the sounds and patterns of language "in their ears" and "under their tongues."

Decide whether there are any phrases in the existing stanzas or verses which should be repeated in the new words to be added to the song.

Before trying to compose new words, have the rhythm of the melody well in mind by tapping and chanting existing verses.

Improvise Using Instruments

1. Make available many different instruments with which children can explore sounds. Provide problem-solving experiences through which the child can make decisions regarding the appropriate use of sounds.

Allow two or three children to work with "an event" to develop improvisations or engage in sound exploration while other children are engaged in different activities. (Several such strategies are included in their book.)

2. Use instruments to express the child's ideas about sounds of nature, poems, feelings, and moods. Make up sound stories in which the sounds of instruments, rather than words, are used to tell the story.

• Make up rhythm patterns. Select two or three contrasting patterns and repeat them throughout the song.

DOES YOUR RHYTHM PATTERN HAVE BOTH SHORT AND LONG SOUNDS?
(Children may tend to play a steady beat rather than a more complex pattern.)

• Use percussion instruments which have contrasting tone qualities and are appropriate to the mood of a song.

• Find interesting word patterns within a song. Play the rhythm of these word patterns on percussion instruments as an accompaniment to the song.

• Improvise on pitched instruments such as resonator bells, xylophones, or black keys of the piano. Use songs based on a pentatonic scale. A pentatonic scale that contains no half steps occurs when the black keys of the piano are played in sequence. Because of the structure of this scale, any two tones sounded together will produce acceptable harmony. A child may freely choose tones to make up an accompaniment for songs such as "Go to Sleep," page 138.

2. Use tones freely, but work within a repeated rhythm pattern.

3. Make up a melody for a given poem or children's original words.

4. Make up a melodic interlude between the verses of a pentatonic song.

5. Make up a two-part instrumental piece by using two tones of the scale to play the basic beat, while a second performer improvises a melody.

Improvise a Dramatic Play

Almost any song that tells a story can be a point of departure for creative dramatics. Encourage children to extend the story, bring in new characters, and weave related poetry, music or sound effects into their production.

Improvise Using Expressive Movements

Specific instructions are given for a few patterned dances to accompany some of the songs in this book. In addition, many songs and listening lessons will provide opportunity for original creative movement. For additional information and ideas, see "The Young Musician Moves" on page xiii.

Events

The teacher sometimes may set the environment for creative experiences in which the entire group is involved. Each child also needs times when he can interact with music as an individual or as part of a small group. When he improvises his own piece or makes a discovery about a specific sound on his own, it is a truly exciting time for him—it becomes an event.

Events can involve one or a few while the remainder of the class is busy with another project. Later, the Event can be shared with the class in a performance. Events may be nicely accommodated in the classroom by setting aside a special area as Music Learning Center.

The teacher provides limited directions and materials for children; the resulting discoveries and improvisations comprise the Event.

Included in this text are several ideas for Events. These are designed as models to trigger the imaginative teacher into designing many of her own settings for Events. A classroom in which children improvise and solve problems by making judgments and choices is one in which valuable learning is taking place.

The Young Child Composes

Most of the child's early organizational efforts will be at the improvisational level: he will develop his musical ideas as he experiments with sounds. The planning and organization of patterns into a coherent whole occurs simultaneously with the production of the sound.

Gradually, the teacher may wish to extend the children's improvisational activities by suggesting that they make a "sound picture" of their music so that they can remember it. Their experiments then become, in a sense, "compositions."

Such sound pictures may be very simple, showing only the sequence of timbres to be played. This can be done with pictures:

or with shapes, one for each instrument.

Gradually, children may wish to add other dimensions to their "scores."

changes in volume: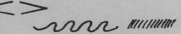
changes in tempo:

More specific "scores" might show relative duration of sounds or the melodic shape of the patterns improvised.

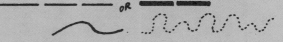

Some children may begin to plan their composition in advance by first preparing a "score" as they decide which musical ideas they wish to use, and then turning the score into sound. However, this activity requires an ability to internalize musical ideas and to synthesize prior experiences. Some young children may continue to confine their organizational activities to improvisation, leaving the more sophisticated activity of composing for later in their musical careers.

MUSICAL CONCEPTS FOR THE YOUNG CHILD

As children grow in their understanding of musical concepts, they will acquire skills for manipulating their own musical environment. The following chart lists some musical concepts with which the teacher should be thoroughly familiar. It is on these concepts that the Musical Behaviors Chart is based. Some will be explored in depth through the activities suggested in this book. Others will only be introduced, leaving more complete investigation for later in the child's musical development. The chart below indicates some visual representations (ikons) that might be appropriate (see "The Young Musician Visualizes," page xiv), the verbal symbol that is attached to the concept (see "The Young Musician Verbalizes," page xv), and the musical symbol (see "The Young Musician Visualizes," page xiv).

Concept Area	Statement	Ikon	Verbal Symbol	Musical Symbol
TIMBRE	**1.** Sounds produced by different sources have distinctive characteristics.	pictures of instruments	instrument name	
	2. Sounds have distinctive qualities which may suggest ideas or feelings.	abstract designs	descriptive words	
	3. Distinctive sound characteristics are the result of the material and construction of the sound source and method of sound production.		descriptive words · instrument families	
DURATION	**1.** Music may move in relation to an underlying, steady pulse.		beat	
	2. Beats may be grouped by stresses.		accent · meter	
	3. A sound or silence may be longer, shorter, or the same as another.		notes · rests	
	4. Longer, shorter, and the same sounds and silences may occur in a sequence.		rhythm of the beat · rhythm of the melody	
	5. Longer and shorter sounds may move in relation to an underlying pulse.	(see above)	rhythm pattern	(see above)
PITCH	**1.** Pitches may be sounded in a sequence.		melody	
	2. Pitches within a melody may move up, down, or remain the same.		ascending · descending · repeated	
	3. Pitches within a melody may move by step or skip.		step · skip · interval	
	4. Tones within a series of pitches may be related to each other and form a pitch group.		scales (major, minor, pentatonic)	
	5. Pitches within a melody may "belong together," or come from a common group of tones.		key, tonality · scale numbers	
	6. Individual pitches, when compared to each other, may be higher, lower, or stay the same.		interval · moves up · moves down	
	7. A melody may have an overall characteristic of highness or lowness, or be "in the middle."		treble · bass · ranges	
	8. Two or more pitches can be sounded simultaneously.		harmonic interval · chord · tone cluster	
	9. A sequence of simultaneous sounds may create feelings of rest or unrest.		consonance · dissonance · chord names	
	10. Two or more melodies can occur simultaneously.		round · canon · polyphony	
	11. Chords may be sounded simultaneously with a melody.		accompaniment · homophony	the musical score

Concept Area	Statement	Ikon	Verbal Symbol	Musical Symbol
MUSICAL CONTROLS	**1.** A sound may be comparatively loud or soft.		dynamics · volume	*p* *mp* *mf* *f*
	2. A sequence of sounds may grow louder or softer.		crescendo · diminuendo	
	3. Sounds may be sustained and smoothly connected or short and detached.		legato · staccato	
	4. A sequence of sounds can be fast or slow, depending on frequency of beat recurrence.		Allegro · Largo · Slowly	♩. = 72
	5. A sequence of sounds can become faster or slower.		accelerando · ritardando	
	6. Dynamic, articulation, and tempo controls may be changed, or contrasted, to help express both musical and extra-musical ideas.		descriptive language	
STRUCTURE	**1.** A pattern may be formed by combining tones into a coherent series.		motive	
	2. A series of sounds may be grouped into a single musical idea.		phrase	
	3. A phrase ends when it comes to rest.		cadence	
	4. Phrases and motives can be combined to form larger musical events.		sections	
	5. A musical segment (motive, phrase, or section) may be repeated or altered, or a different segment may be stated.		repetition · contrast	D.C. D.S. al Fine 𝄌
	6. A musical whole results from the combination of smaller segments into a coherent totality. The totality may be made up of same, varied, or contrasting segments.	(see above)	ABA · Rondo · theme and variations	
	7. A musical totality may include introductory and concluding segments.		introduction · coda	
	8. Two or more strands of sound may be combined vertically.		texture	
	9. The combination of vertical and horizontal elements creates a form which embodies musical meaning, resulting in a complete musical structure.	abstract designs	unity · variety	the complete musical score
EXPRESSIVE TOTALITY	The unique organization of all elements into a totality results in the expression of a musical idea or an extra-musical feeling.	abstract designs	descriptive language	the musical score
CONCEPTS OF TIME AND PLACE	The elements of music are combined in distinctive ways which reflect the time or place of origin of a piece of music.	pictures	descriptive language	the musical score

Exploring Music: A Minimum Program

For classrooms where the teacher cannot plan to have music daily, the following suggested minimum program may be of assistance in selecting materials to be used during the year. Minimum teaching suggestions for each lesson are enclosed by a thin black rule.

(PB = Pupil's Book)

Exploring Music: Page by Page

Exploring Music: A Guide for the Teacher

The lessons in this book are presented in outline form. The **Concept** to be explored is identified first. The activities which will lead the children towards understanding the concept are explained under **Discover**. The material found under **Extend** provides reinforcement of the concept and should be an integral part of the lesson. When a particular piece of music offers opportunity for exploration of more than one concept, additional concepts are presented under the heading **Other Concept(s)**, and the procedures of the minimum program are outlined by a thin black rule. The illustrations throughout the book will help to "set the stage" for creative activities and Events.

The remainder of the book contains a sequential development of songs, teaching suggestions, and listening lessons for each quarter of the school year.

Using the Recordings

All listening lessons and songs in the teacher's and pupil's books are recorded. The record number, side, band, and information about performance are given.

For teaching convenience, the recordings are banded. The songs are simply separated by locked grooves. The appreciation records, however, have three types of bands: (1) locked grooves to separate major compositions or complete listening lessons; (2) standard five-second bands to separate movements of a larger work; and (3) bands of a continuous sound to isolate particular sections of a composition for concentrated study. The recordings come in a boxed set of ten 12-inch long-playing records and are available from Holt, Rinehart and Winston, Inc., 383 Madison Avenue, New York, N.Y., 10017.

Exploring Music Individualized Program

A supplementary cassette program provides further reinforcement of the concepts presented in this book. The kit contains 24 lessons on 12 cassettes, along with ditto-master—activity sheets for the pupil, 24 posters for music centers, and a teacher's guide. The cassette lessons correlate with material found in this book, and are designed to be used for individualized learning. This program is available from the publisher at the address given above.

Exploring Music through the Year

Exploring Music: the First Quarter

DT/ Record 1   Side A   Band 1   VOICES: children's choir.
ACCOMPANIMENT: percussion.
FORM: Instrumental; Vocal; Instrumental; Vocal; Instrumental.

Toodala

Play-Party Game
Version by Helen Gates

Tonality: Pentatonic   Starting Tone: C

Meter: $\frac{2}{4}$ $\left(\frac{2}{\downarrow}\right)$

Concept   DURATION: Music moves with a steady beat.

Discover   CAN YOU MAKE A PRETTY MOTION AS YOU LISTEN TO THIS MUSIC? Invite children to experiment as they listen to the recording. They might swing their arms, nod their heads, twist, or bend and stretch.

beat 1: Swing arms left.	beat 1: Stretch up.
beat 2: Swing arms right.	beat 2: Stretch down.

At first, children may do the motions as they listen. A leader chooses a motion to do while the class sings the verse; the rest imitate him during the instrumental. Later, children may sing and move without the recording.

Extend   Guide children to sense a steady beat in other music. SUZY HAD A FINE MOTION. CAN WE MOVE THE SAME WAY TO THIS MUSIC? Play "Soldier's March," page 5.

Other Concept   DURATION: Music contains rhythm patterns.

Discover   Suggest that children make up verses to "Toodala" about their classroom instruments. "Listen to my wood block" (drum, cymbals, etc.). One child could play the "toodala" rhythm ♩. ♪ ♪ 𝄽 on the appropriate instrument each time that pattern is sung.

Jauntily

Might-y pret-ty mo-tion, too-da-la,   too-da-la,   too-da-la;

Might-y pret-ty mo-tion, too-da-la,   too-da-la, my la-dy.

Hey Lidee

Calypso Folk Song
Words by James Leisy

Key: D Starting Tone: A(5)
Autoharp Key: C Starting Tone: G(5)

Meter: $\frac{2}{2}$ ($\frac{2}{\text{♩}}$)

DT/ Record 1 Side A Band 2 VOICES: children's choir.
ACCOMPANIMENT: electric guitar, acoustic guitar, tack piano, electric bass, drums, percussion.
FORM: Introduction; Refrain; v. 1; Refrain; v. 2; Refrain; v. 3; Refrain; v. 4; Refrain; Coda.

Concept DURATION: Music moves with a steady beat.

Discover Introduce the song by playing the recording. Have children tap lightly with the music and invite them to imitate your motions.

> beat 1: Clap hands together.
> beat 2: Rest, hands apart.

Extend After children show that they sense the pulse as they clap, suggest that they invent other ways to move to the steady beat.

> beat 1: Tap knee with right hand.
> beat 2: Tap left shoulder with right hand.

> beat 1: Clap hands together.
> beat 2: Clap right thigh with right hand.

Refrain

Hey Li - dee, Li - dee, Li - dee,___ Hey Li - dee, Li - dee-lo.___

Hey Li - dee, Li - dee, Li - dee,___ Hey Li - dee, Li - dee-lo.___ *Fine*

Verse

1. This is a cra - zy kind of song,___ You
2. First you___ sing a sim - ple line,___ Then
3. What do we do when sum - mer ends?___ We
4. What can we do when mu - sic comes?___ We'll

Hey Li - dee, Li - dee-lo.___

make it up as you go a - long,___
___ you try___ to make it rhyme,___
go to school___ and make new friends,___
play the drums___ and sing our songs,___

Hey Li - dee, Li - dee-lo.___

D.C. al Fine

2

Record 1 Side A Band 3 VOICE: woman.
ACCOMPANIMENT: string quartet.
FORM: Introduction; Vocal, *v. 1;*
Interlude; Vocal, *v. 2;* Interlude; Vocal, *v.*
3; Interlude; Vocal, *v. 4;* Interlude:
Vocal, *v. 5.*

Stretching Song

Words and Music by Eunice Boardman

Key: C   Starting Tone: E(3)

Meter: $\frac{2}{4}$ $\left(\frac{2}{\downarrow}\right)$

Concept PITCH: Melodies move up, down, or stay the same.

Discover Play the recording or sing the song at times when children need to relax and stretch. Invite the class to do the motions suggested by the words. After they have enjoyed moving to the song, invite them to sing it alone.

Sing the melody on "loo." CAN YOU TELL HOW TO MOVE? WHAT HELPS YOU KNOW? Guide children to discover that the melody moves **up** and **down,** as the words suggest.

Play the song on step bells as children watch. This will help them associate the sound of tones moving "up" with the spatial concept "up."

Extend Give children time to experiment on the step bells until they find the pattern for "Now tall! Now small!" DID YOU HAVE TO SKIP BELLS TO PLAY THAT PATTERN, OR DID YOU GO UP AND DOWN BY STEPS? (Skip.) Play the pattern for "I'm a tiny ball" on the step bells. WATCH CAREFULLY. DID MY PATTERN MOVE BY STEPS OR BY SKIPS? (Steps.)

1. I'm stretch-ing ver-y tall, And now I'm ver-y small. Now tall!
2. My hands I stretch out wide, Be-hind me they will hide. Now wide!
3. My hands I stretch up high, Now on the floor they lie. Now high!
4. Now with my head I shake, Now not a move I make. Now shake!
5. Now all the girls and boys Don't make a sin-gle noise! Sit down!

Now small! Now I'm a ti-ny ball.
Now hide! I put them at my side.
Now lie! Now   way up to the sky.
No move make! Now my whole bod-y I shake.
No sound! And dream of man-y toys.

Response to Duration and Timbre, No. 1

Concepts   DURATION: Sounds may be long or short.

    TIMBRE: Different sound sources have distinctive qualities.

Discover   Help children respond to long and short sounds through body movement by reading the following statements. When indicated, play the appropriate sound (drum or triangle) to initiate the movement.

USE YOUR FINGER TO DRAW A STRAIGHT STICK IN THE SKY

DRAW ANOTHER STRAIGHT STICK . . . AND ANOTHER . . .

USE YOUR FINGER AND DRAW A BENT LINE IN THE SKY . . . ANOTHER . . . AND ANOTHER!

MAKE A BENT LINE WITH YOUR ARM WITH BOTH ARMS WITH AN ARM AND A LEG!

MAKE A STRAIGHT STICK WITH ONE ARM   drum:

WITH TWO ARMS

WITH AN ARM AND A LEG!

The following chant will help to reinforce the idea that a sharp, quick sound can be expressed through sudden, straight movements. Ask children to speak the chant and move appropriately. You may wish to accompany the chant with a drum pattern.

drum:

Sharp! Sharp!
Up and down!
Jabbing, jabbing
Through the town.

Contrast short, thumping sounds with long, ringing sounds. Ask children to respond with movements as you read the next set of statements. Most children will respond with curved, sustained movements.

USE YOUR FINGER AND DRAW A CIRCLE IN THE SKY . . .
ANOTHER . . . AND ANOTHER!   triangle:

MAKE A CIRCLE WITH TWO ARMS
WITH YOUR WHOLE BODY!

Ask children to move to the words of the following chant. Suggest that they use "small parts" of their bodies to show the movement suggested by the words. (Use eyes, nose, head, elbow, tongue, finger.) You might accompany their movement with triangle sounds.

triangle:

Round and round
Up and down!
Circling, circling
Through the town.

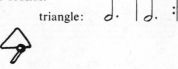

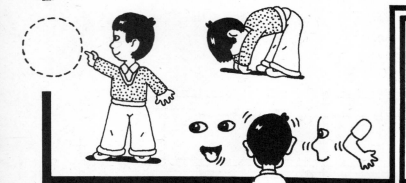

Extend   Play "Catch Me" from *Scenes from Childhood* by Schumann, page 156. LISTEN TO THIS MUSIC. HOW WILL YOU MOVE TO THIS MUSIC? WILL YOU USE SHORT MOVEMENTS OR LONG MOVEMENTS? WILL THEY BE CIRCLING MOVEMENTS OR STRAIGHT MOVEMENTS? (Short, straight movements.)

Music for Fundamental Movements

Return to the following short piano selections often throughout the year as children develop skill in using fundamental movements such as stepping, leaping, sliding, hopping, and combinations of these in musical response.

Remember that body movements should be used to help children sense all aspects of music, not only rhythm. Different aspects of the music may be stressed as children grow in their perception of various musical elements.

Compare the different compositions. Help the children to develop a vocabulary with which to verbalize the differences they hear and feel in relation to rhythmic movement **(even-uneven, long-short)**, melodic movement **(direction, step-skip)**, form **(number of phrases, same-different)**, musical controls **(fast, slow, loud, soft, smooth, detached)**, and harmony **(many sounds, few sounds, unrest-rest)**. The following outlines suggest appropriate activities.

Gavotte $\left(\frac{4}{4}\right)$

by George Frideric Handel (hand'l)
BORN 1685   DIED 1759

RHYTHM: Step with the steady beat, perhaps on tiptoe. The rhythm of the melody is **even** most of the time.

MELODY: Show melodic contour with arms and body while feet step with the rhythm of the beat. The melody moves primarily by **steps.**

FORM: The music is divided into two phrases. The end of the first phrase is marked by a downward leap.

MUSICAL CONTROLS: Notice the short, crisp quality of each sound.

Bagatelle, Opus 33, No. 3 $\left(\frac{6}{8}\right)$

by Ludwig van Beethoven (bay'-toh-vun)
BORN 1770   DIED 1827

RHYTHM: Although this music is in $\frac{6}{8}$ children will sense a movement in threes. Use sustained movements such as sliding, skating, swaying, pushing.

MELODY: The contour suggests "rocking." The melody skips up, then down at the beginning of each phrase.

MUSICAL CONTROLS: Smooth, legato sounds.

Hunting Song $\left(\frac{6}{8}\right)$

by Cornelius Gurlitt
BORN 1820   DIED 1901

RHYTHM: The **uneven** rhythm of the melody may be reflected in a gallop. The same foot should always lead.

HARMONY: Show the difference between a single melody line (first phrase) and simultaneous sounds (second phrase).

For Children
Volume 1, No. XI $\left(\frac{2}{4}\right)$

by Béla Bartók (bahr'tock)
BORN 1881   DIED 1945

RHYTHM: Combinations of movements may be used to show the interesting rhythm. **Long** steps will reflect the rhythm of the upper voice. **Smaller** steps will reflect the rhythm of the lower voice. Some children may move to reflect the combined rhythms.

PITCH: The range is **low.** Children might bend over as they step.

MUSICAL CONTROLS: The tempo is **slow;** the volume is **soft,** compared to the **louder** sound of "Soldiers' March."

Soldiers' March $\left(\frac{2}{4}\right)$

by Robert Schumann
BORN 1810   DIED 1856

RHYTHM: The steady rhythm of the beat suggests a march. Each new phrase begins with an uneven pattern ♩. ♪ ♪ ♪ Compare the **heavy** light **heavy** light grouping of beats with **heavy** light light of the "Waltzes."

FORM: Each phrase begins with the **uneven** rhythm pattern. Turn each time a new phrase begins.

Waltzes, Opus 9b $\left(\frac{3}{4}\right)$

by Franz Schubert
BORN 1797   DIED 1828

RHYTHM: The movement in threes (**heavy** light light, **heavy** light light) suggests a sliding or swaying motion.

MELODY: The melody contains big skips and many changes of direction. This reinforces the impression of swaying.

Record 8   Side B   Bands 1-6
Paul Sheftel, pianist.

Who Will Come with Me?

American Folk Song

Key: E♭
Autoharp Key: F Starting Tone: A(3)

Meter: 6/8 (𝅗𝅥.)

DT/ **Record 1 Side A Band 4** VOICE: man.
ACCOMPANIMENT: flute, bassoon, violin, cello, percussion, trumpet, trombone.
FORM: Introduction; *v. 1;* Interlude; *v. 2;* Instrumental; *v. 3;* Instrumental.

Concept DURATION: The rhythm of a melody may move evenly or unevenly.

Discover Play the first verse and the instrumental. HOW WILL YOU MOVE WHEN YOU GO WITH THE JOLLY ROVER? Observe children as they move.

Some may step to the underlying **even** beat:

Others may move to the **uneven** rhythm of the melody:

Both responses are appropriate. Encourage each child to practice moving both ways. To help the children sense the differences, isolate the two patterns. Play a steady beat on the drum; then play the uneven rhythm of the melody on the wood block.

Play verse two. DID YOU MOVE AS THE JOLLY ROVER SUGGESTED? Play the instrumental between verses two and three. WILL YOU MOVE THE SAME WAY NOW? Children should sense that the rhythm of the melody is now **even.**

Extend Show the pictures of the two rhythms.

Even:

Uneven:

Ask children to describe in their own words the differences they see. Match the pictures with the music as they listen to the recording again.

Play the complete recording. CAN YOU CHANGE THE WAY YOU MOVE EACH TIME THE RHYTHM OF THE MELODY CHANGES?

Other Concept STRUCTURE: Music is made up of small sections.

Discover Have children move to the music. Ask them to decide when they need to "turn a corner" as they do with the Jolly Rover. Help them decide that there is time to turn when they hear the long tones on the word "rover" at the end of each **phrase.**

1. Who will come with me, the jol - ly, jol - ly ro - ver?
2. Who will skip with me, the jol - ly, jol - ly ro - ver?

Who will come with me, the jol - ly, jol - ly ro - ver,⎫
Who will skip with me, the jol - ly, jol - ly ro - ver,⎬ And

see, _____ and see, _____ and see what we can see?

Record 1 Side A Band 5 VOICE: man.
ACCOMPANIMENT: clarinet, piano, guitar,
double bass, percussion.
FORM: Instrumental; Vocal, *vv. 1–2;*
Instrumental.

Hey, Betty Martin

Early American Song

Key: G   Starting Tone: B(3)

Meter: $\frac{4}{4}$ $\left(\frac{4}{\text{♩}}\right)$

Concept STRUCTURE: A phrase is a complete musical idea; it may end with a long tone.

Discover Play the recording; invite children to tiptoe in a circle. CAN YOU HEAR A PLACE WHERE BETTY "RESTS" FOR A MOMENT BEFORE SHE GOES ON? Help children hear the long tones on the words "fine" and "mine." Suggest that they bow at these places, then continue to tiptoe.

Extend Make up a dance based on the phrases of the music. Everyone forms a circle. Choose a "Betty."

Verse 1 phrase one: Betty tiptoes around the circle.
       phrase two: Betty reverses direction.

Verse 2 phrase one: Betty chooses a partner.
       phrase two: Betty and partner tiptoe together.

Repeat song, substituting "Billy" for "Betty." This time the boy does the actions.

Other Concepts: TIMBRE: Instruments have distinctive tone qualities.

Discover After children have become acquainted with their classroom instruments, have them look at pages 6–7 of their books. Play the recording again. CAN YOU HEAR THE INSTRUMENT THAT PLAYS THE RHYTHM PATTERN FOR "HEY, BETTY MARTIN"? (Wood block.) WHAT INSTRUMENT PLAYS "TIPTOE, TIPTOE"? (Triangle.)

Children may add their own accompaniment using these two instruments. They might choose a third one with appropriate timbre for "tiptoe fine."

   DURATION: Rhythm patterns include long and short values.

Discover As children listen to the patterns they are playing, discuss the differences in terms of long and short.

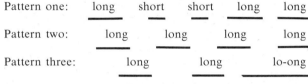

Pattern one: long   short   short   long   long
Pattern two: long   long   long   long
Pattern three: long   long   lo-ong

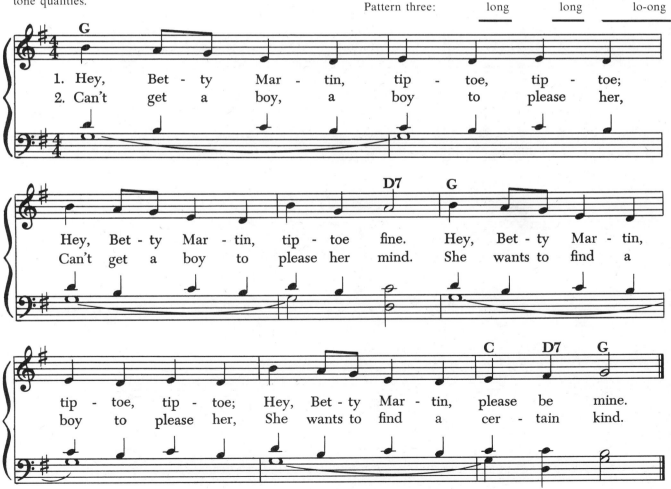

Sleep, Baby, Sleep

German Folk Song

Key: F   Starting Tone: A(3)

Meter: $\frac{2}{4}$ $\left(\frac{2}{\downarrow}\right)$

DT/ Record 1   Side A   Band 6   VOICE: woman.
ACCOMPANIMENT: string quartet
FORM: Introduction; *v. 1;* Interlude; *v. 2;* Coda.

Concept   PITCH: Melodies move up and down by steps or skips.

Discover   Play the recording for children during rest time for several days before beginning this activity. When children have become familiar with the melody, sing the pattern for "Sleep, baby, sleep" on "loo."

WHAT WORDS ARE SUNG TO THIS MELODY? HOW MANY TIMES DO YOU HEAR IT? (It is repeated three times; in addition, the melody for "Father guards the sheep" is almost the same.)

Place the F G A bells on the stairsteps. WHO CAN PLAY THIS MELODY? WHERE WILL WE BEGIN? One child may experiment as the class helps him decide that he should begin with the **highest** bell, then move down by steps: A G G F. CAN YOU PLAY THIS PATTERN AS WE SING?

Extend   HOW MANY BELLS DO WE USE TO PLAY THIS PATTERN? (Three.) WE CAN GIVE EACH BELL A NUMBER NAME. THE LOWEST BELL WILL BE "1." WHICH BELL WILL WE START ON? (Three.) Show the children how their pattern will look when written with numbers

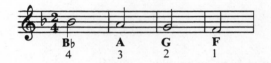

Some children may also be able to play the following pattern during phrase two. Add the B♭ bell; its number name will be "4."

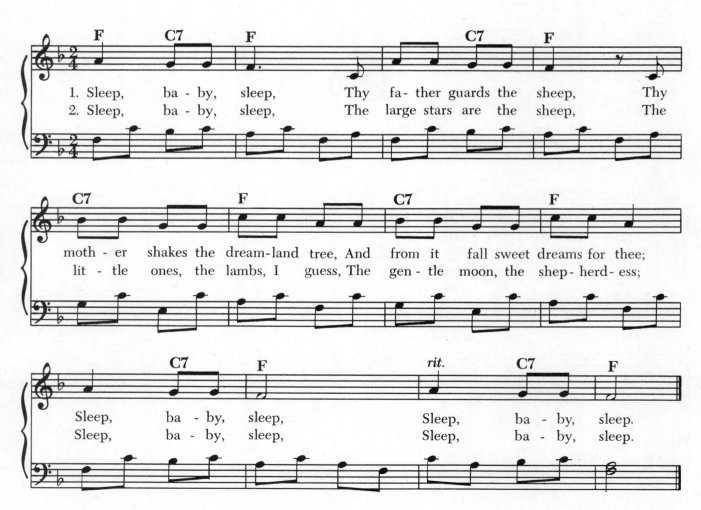

8

Let's Explore Music

Here are some ways we can make music.

1

Let's Explore Music (1)

This will be most children's first experience with their own music books. Plan to introduce the book during one of the first music sessions and return to it regularly.

The first time the books are used, invite children to look through them and to discover how this book is different from other books they have used. (It has "pictures" of music.)

Draw attention to the illustrations on the first page. Discuss ways that we can enjoy music: by singing, moving, and playing instruments. As each picture is discussed, you may wish to involve the class in the activity indicated. Use music with which the children are already familiar.

Find New Sounds (2–3)

Concept TIMBRE: Sounds have distinctive characteristics.

Discover Help children explore sounds of their bodies. HOW MANY DIFFERENT SOUNDS CAN YOU MAKE, USING YOUR HANDS? YOUR FEET? YOUR MOUTH?

Help children explore different ways of making sounds on the drum. Use different beaters.

1. Explore the middle of the drum, the outer circle, the rim, and drums of different sizes.

2. Try sliding the beater on the drum head.

3. Try striking with beaters made of different materials. What happens to the sound?

4. Place a cloth on the drum before striking. What happens to the sound?

Extend Use the sounds children have discussed. Ask one child to make a group of sounds. They could be either body or drum sounds. Ask the child to repeat his group of sounds as the class moves "like the sound." The pattern then is:

Child: make up a "sound idea"   Class: listen

Child: repeat the idea   Class: move

Find new sounds with your hands and feet.

2

10

Find new sounds with drums.

3

Music for Quiet Listening

In addition to structured music activities, children should have many opportunities to enjoy music in a relaxed atmosphere, when they are resting or working quietly. In such situations, longer and more complex music which might be impractical for structured listening may be used. Through hearing music in a relaxed atmosphere, children may come to find personal satisfaction in listening as a mode of musical involvement.

The compositions described here are included primarily to be used in this fashion. After the children have become familiar with the music through informal listening, you may wish to use these works in a more structured way.

Scherzo
from *String Quartet in G Minor,*
Opus 10, No. 1

by Claude Debussy (deh'byoo-see)
BORN 1862   DIED 1918

INSTRUMENTATION: String quartet (two violins, viola, cello).

One of the ways this music is given interest is through the contrast of sounds resulting from bowing and plucking.

The main melody is usually bowed, while the accompaniment is often plucked.

The composition is in three sections. The second section begins with a sustained melody. The third section is marked by the return of the plucking sounds.

Divertimento in B Flat (K. 186)
"Adagio" and "Allegro"

by Wolfgang Amadeus Mozart (moh'tsart)
BORN 1756   DIED 1791

INSTRUMENTATION: Woodwinds and brass.

Two contrasting movements are included on the recording. The "Adagio" moves in a slow tempo, in threes, while the "Allegro" moves quickly, in twos.

Compositions such as the following might be introduced as quiet listening, and later used as part of a structured music activity.

Nocturne, from *Divertissement,* page 53
Dream March, from *The Red Pony,* page 87
Dreaming, from *Scenes from Childhood,* page 156
Dance of the Swans, from *Swan Lake,* page 185

Record 8   Side B   Band 7
The Budapest String Quartet.
TIME: 3:13

Record 8   Side B   Band 8
Vienna Philharmonic Wind Group.
TIME: 4:54

Use New Sounds (4–5)

Concept   TIMBRE: Sounds may be used expressively because of their distinctive qualities.

Discover   Give children time to look at the pictures in their books. WHAT IS THE LITTLE CHICKEN DOING? Point to the Mother Chicken and read the stanza beside the pictures aloud. After children have talked about the pictures, read the following poem. Invite children to join you in speaking the stanzas that appear in their books.

The Tiny Chicken lived in an egg
That was as warm as a little bed.
Mother Chicken kept the egg warm
With her feathers so pretty and red.

The Tiny Chicken would sleep in his egg
And sometimes he would move around.
But when the Mother Chicken listened
. . . she couldn't hear a sound!

Children join:
So, she rustled her feathers
And looked all around,
Then gently, so gently
On the egg she sat down.

The Tiny Chicken would sleep in his egg
And sometimes he would BUMP up and down!
But when the Mother Chicken listened,
. . . she couldn't hear a sound!

Children: So, she . . .

The Tiny Chicken would sleep in his egg
And sometimes he would PECK up and down
And when the Mother Chicken listened,
. . . she thought she could hear a sound.

Children: But, she . . .

The Tiny Chicken broke his egg,
Wiggled up and looked around,
And when the Mother Chicken listened,
. . . she KNEW she heard a sound!

Children: So, she . . .

After reading the poem, provide drums and finger cymbals. Ask children to describe the pictures using these instrumental sounds.

chicken moves in egg—rubbing sound (drum)

chicken bumps—thumping sound (drum)

chicken pecking—sharp sound (drum rim)

chicken peep—ringing sound (finger cymbal)

Mother Chicken moving—rustling sound (drum)

Make a sound story out of the poem by pointing to the pictures in the pupil's book as assigned children perform the descriptive sounds.

USE NEW SOUNDS

So, she rustled her feathers
And looked all around,
Then gently, so gently
On the egg she sat down.

4

So, she rustled her feathers
And looked all around,
Then gently, so gently
On the egg she sat down.

But, she rustled her feathers
And looked all around,
Then gently, so gently
On the egg she sat down.

So, she rustled her feathers
And looked at the sound,
And the little tiny chicken
Was what she found!

5

Extend Guide children to move as you play the drum sounds indicated and tell the following story.

YOU ARE A LITTLE CHICKEN INSIDE AN EGG. FIND A PLACE FOR YOUR EGG . . . A PLACE WHERE THERE ARE NO OTHER EGGS! (Help children find an area in which to move.)

YOU ARE VERY TINY. MOVE IN YOUR EGG. WILL YOU MOVE QUICKLY OR SLOWLY? (Slowly.) FEEL THE SIDES OF THE EGG WITH YOUR WINGS . . . WITH A FOOT . . . (rubbing sound on head of drum) . . . WITH THE OTHER FOOT!

BUMP! THE SIDES OF YOUR EGG WITH YOUR TINY TAIL. (Strike drum head.)
PECK THE SHELL TO BREAK OUT. (Wood rim sound of drum.)

BREAK THE EGG! (Wood rim sound of drum.)
STEP OUT AND DISCOVER YOUR NEW WORLD. (Finger cymbal.)

13

Early in the Morning

American Chantey

Key: D Minor Starting Tone: A(5)

Meter: $\frac{4}{4}$ ($\frac{4}{\quarternote}$)

Record 1 Side A Band 7 VOICES: 3 men.
ACCOMPANIMENT: accordion.
FORM: Instrumental; Vocal, *v. 1;*
Instrumental; Vocal, *v. 2;* Instrumental.

Concept DURATION: Music moves in relation to underlying beats, some of which are accented.

Discover Draw attention to the men's voices as the children listen to this sea chantey. Talk about the work of the sailor. As children listen, invite them to pretend they are pulling the anchor. CAN YOU PULL IN THE ANCHOR WITH LONG, STEADY PULLS? BEGIN TO PULL AGAIN EACH TIME YOU HEAR A STRONG BEAT. (On "Hear" and "early.")

Help children sense **strong** and **weak beats.** Play the drum on every beat; strongly accent the first of each group of four:

drum:

WHAT OTHER WORK DO SAILORS DO? CAN YOU MAKE UP A VERSE TO MATCH THE RHYTHM OF THE SONG? CAN YOU SHOW THE SAILORS' WORK IN YOUR MOVEMENTS?

"Heave ho, and raise the sails . . ."

"Heave ho, and clean the decks . . ."

Extend Return to this song later in the year. Show a picture of the strong and weak beats:

CAN WE THINK OF OTHER WAYS TO GROUP STRONG AND WEAK BEATS? Cut strips of construction paper in two shades of the same hue. Allow children to group them, using the darker shade for the **strong beats,** the lighter shade for the **weak beats.** Group them with the strong beat

on every other beat:

or on every third beat:

Match the picture with music that moves in twos such as "An Amer'I'can," p. 20 and threes, such as "Autumn Leaves," p. 40.

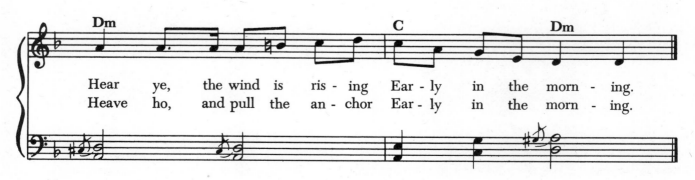

Vigorously

1. Hear ye, the wind is ris - ing, Hear ye, the wind is ris - ing,
2. Heave ho, and pull the an - chor, Heave ho, and pull the an - chor,

Hear ye, the wind is ris - ing Ear - ly in the morn - ing.
Heave ho, and pull the an - chor Ear - ly in the morn - ing.

Les Aventures de Mercure
The Adventures of Mercury

Excerpts

by Erik Satie
BORN 1866   DIED 1925

These three brief movements from the ballet should be played often during the year. Each time a different aspect of the music may be enjoyed. A fourth movement may be found on page 134. Give children ample opportunity to listen quietly, then to move freely, before asking them to talk about what they hear.

Signs of the Zodiac

Concept   STRUCTURE: Music is made up of sections.

Discover   CLOSE YOUR EYES AS YOU LISTEN! PRETEND YOU ARE DANCING! Play the complete composition. DID YOU DANCE THE SAME WAY ALL OF THE TIME, OR DID YOU WANT TO DANCE A DIFFERENT WAY?

Repeat the music, this time inviting children to move freely. Note when children make changes in their movements in response to musical changes.

Ask ten or twelve children to stand in a row. As they listen, indicate that one child should step forward each time a new section begins! HOW MANY PEOPLE HAD TO MOVE? (Eight.) THERE ARE EIGHT PARTS IN THIS MUSIC!

Other Concepts   STRUCTURE: Sections within a composition may be the same or different.

Discover   DO YOU REMEMBER HOW MANY PARTS THIS MUSIC HAD? WE FOUND THAT THE MUSIC HAD EIGHT PARTS. DID YOU HEAR ANY PARTS THAT SOUNDED THE SAME? WERE SOME DIFFERENT? CAN YOU SHOW THE SAME AND DIFFERENT PARTS WHEN YOU MOVE?

Some children may respond to differences in timbre or over-all "highness-lowness." Others may respond to contrasts in melody or rhythm.

Response to timbre (tuba, trumpet, tuba, trumpet, tuba, trumpet, strings, tuba)

Tuba (low)   Trumpet (high)   Strings ("middle")

Response to contrasts in melody (AABC, AABC)

A Theme   B Theme   C Theme

Response to contrasts in rhythm (AABA, AABA)

run (even)   skip (uneven)

Entry and Dance of Mercury

Concept   MUSICAL CONTROLS: Sounds may move smoothly from one to the next, or they may be detached.

Discover   This movement might be introduced after children have experienced the "Response to Duration and Timbre No. 1," page 4. LISTEN TO THIS MUSIC. WILL YOU BE A STICK OR A BALL? WILL YOU MAKE STRAIGHT, STIFF MOVEMENTS, OR SMOOTH, CIRCLING MOVEMENTS?

Play as children listen; repeat the first section while children move. Draw attention to those who become "sticks" in response to the detached sound of the first pattern.

Repeat this section and continue to the middle section, noticing those children who change to smoother gestures in response to the smoother sound of the strings. DID YOU HEAR SOMETHING THAT MADE YOU WANT TO REPEAT YOUR STRAIGHT MOVEMENTS? (Yes, when the original musical idea is restated by the strings.)

The Music

First Section: Melody introduced by brasses, repeated with additional instruments.

Second Section: Strings and woodwinds predominate. The theme is more sustained and the end of this section is signalled by the return of ideas similar to the opening section.

Third Section: Same melody as in first section. The theme is first stated by the strings; later, the strings are joined by other instruments.

Bath of Graces (See page 134.)

Anger of Cerberus

Concept   TIMBRE: Instruments have distinctive qualities.

Discover   Prepare two pictures. One should be made up of circles of several colors with one color, perhaps red, predominating. The other picture should be made up of circles that are all the same color.

Listen to this music. WHICH PICTURE SEEMS TO BEST DESCRIBE WHAT YOU HEAR? Decide that the picture which uses several colors is best because there are several different kinds of sounds heard.

Give some children shapes cut from red construction paper. These represent the sound of the trumpet. Give others shapes cut from paper of other colors. These represent other instruments. Ask children to hold up their colored shapes when they hear "their sounds." (The sequence "trumpet—others" occurs four times.)

Record 8   Side B   Band 9
The Utah Symphony Orchestra.
Maurice Abravanel, conductor.
TIME: 3:25

The Monkey (Hakof)

Hebrew Folk Song
Words by Judith Eisenstein

Key: D Minor   Starting Tone: A(5)

Meter: $\frac{6}{8}$ $\left(\begin{smallmatrix}2\\ \end{smallmatrix}\right)$

DT/ **Record 1   Side B   Band 1**   VOICES: children's choir.
ACCOMPANIMENT: flute, bassoon, violin, cello, percussion, trumpet, trombone.
FORM: Introduction; Vocal—English; Interlude; Vocal—Hebrew; Coda.

Concept   PITCH: Melodies move up, down, or stay the same.

Discover   Play the recording. WHAT DO YOU THINK HAKOF IS? After children make suggestions, identify Hakof as a monkey.

CAN YOU SHOW HOW HAKOF MOVES IN HIS TREE? THE MUSIC WILL HELP YOU KNOW! Children may stretch up, crouch down, and stand "at ease" as they respond to words and melodic contour.

"Hakof goes up" (stretch hands above head)
"Hakof goes down" (crouch down)
"Oh, he is so gay" (stand at ease)

CAN YOU MAKE HAKOF GO UP AND DOWN THE TREE WITHOUT HEARING THE WORDS? Play the instrumental. Guide children to listen carefully for the "up-down-same" movement of the melody.

Extend   Place the D, A, and high D bells on a table.

Give five individual children time to work with the bells until they can play the first phrase. You may wish to put the pictures of the melody on a chart to guide them:

Other Concepts   DURATION: The rhythms of the melody may be even or uneven.

Discover   HOW DOES HAKOF MOVE AS HE SCAMPERS FROM ONE TREE TO THE NEXT? THE MUSIC SHOULD HELP YOU DECIDE! Invite children to demonstrate; draw attention to those who respond to the uneven rhythm of the melody by skipping or galloping.

STRUCTURE: Music is made up of phrases.

Discover   WHEN DOES HAKOF STOP FOR A MOMENT? THE MUSIC HELPS YOU KNOW! Remind children to listen for the long tones which mark the end of the phrase (gay, play).

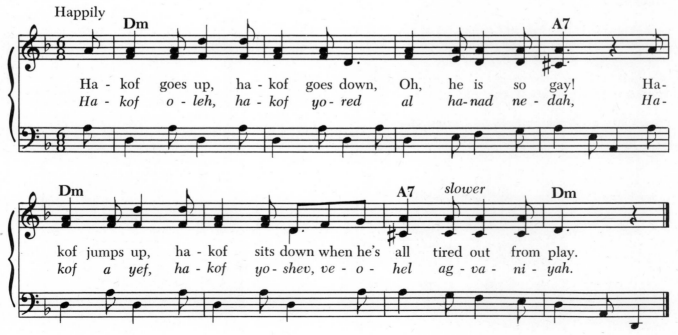

Happily

Dm ... A7

Ha - kof goes up, ha - kof goes down, Oh, he is so gay! Ha-
Ha - kof o - leh, ha - kof yo - red al ha-nad ne - dah, Ha-

Dm ... A7 *slower* Dm

kof jumps up, ha - kof sits down when he's all tired out from play.
kof a yef, ha - kof yo - shev, ve - o - hel ag - va - ni - yah.

Response to Duration and Timbre, No. 2

Concepts DURATION: Sounds may be long or short.

TIMBRE: Different sound sources have distinctive qualities.

Movement Idea No. 1

Ask the child to become as "closed" as he can be. (He should crouch or curl up.) Play the finger cymbals; the child may slowly open one part of himself (fingers, hand, eyes, mouth, neck). He "opens" for as long as he hears the sound, then he must freeze.

When the finger cymbal sound is gone, play a hand cymbal. The child now opens any part of himself from the knees up, continuing the movement for as long as he hears the sound.

Finally, play a gong or larger cymbal; the child now becomes as "open" as he can be. BE SURE YOU CONTINUE TO "OPEN UP" FOR AS LONG AS YOU HEAR THE SOUND! You may wish to reverse the sequence of sounds and let the child "close up" again.

Movement Idea No. 2

Begin with child in "closed" position. Play a finger cymbal; ask the child to open with a curved feeling. Play a wood block and ask the child to close with a short straight feeling.

Movement Idea No. 3

The child begins in "closed" position. Play appropriate sounds and ask him to show whether he should open with short straight feelings or curved feelings.

Goodnight

Music by Edna G. Buttolph
Words by Lucy Sprague Mitchell

Key: D   Starting Tone: A(5)
Autoharp Key: C   Starting Tone: G(5)

Meter: $\frac{4}{4}$ ($\frac{4}{\quarternote}$)

Record 1   Side B   Band 2 VOICE: woman.
ACCOMPANIMENT: string quartet.
FORM: Introduction; Vocal; Instrumental; Vocal.

Concept   STRUCTURE: Sections of music may be made up of short patterns.

Discover   Introduce the song by playing the recording during quiet times in the day. Later, help children sense the eight patterns which make up the song. Put pictures which illustrate the words of the song on individual cards.

Give one card to each child; he must hold up his picture as his pattern begins. Later suggest that children sing the song on a neutral syllable. CAN YOU HOLD UP YOUR CARD AT THE RIGHT TIME?

Extend   Invite children to make their own pictures of the individual patterns of a song. HOW MANY DIFFERENT PICTURES WILL YOU NEED TO MAKE TO SHOW ALL THE PATTERNS IN "HAKOF"? (page 16) (Six.)

Other Concepts   EXPRESSIVE TOTALITY: Tone qualities, volume, and melodic shape help to express musical ideas.

Discover   Invite children to comment on the feelings that this music suggests. (Laziness, sleepiness, quietness.) WHAT HELPS TO MAKE THESE FEELINGS? The sound of string instruments, the soft sound of the instruments and voice, the up-down "rocking" motion of the melody.)

PITCH: Melody patterns move up, down, or stay the same.

Discover   Later in the year, put the melodic contour for each pattern on an individual card:

Scramble the cards and challenge the children to put them in correct order. Notice that all the patterns have a similar contour except the fourth and eighth.

Quietly

Good-night, room; good-night, light; Good-night, win-dow; trees, good-night.

Good-night, stock-ings; good-night, chair; Good-night, peo-ple, ev-ery-where.

From Music Is Motion by Edna G. Buttolph. Used by permission of The Willis Music Company, Cincinnati.

DT/ Record 1   Side B   Band 3   VOICES: children's choir.
ACCOMPANIMENT: electric guitar, electric piano, electric bass, bell.
FORM: Introduction; Vocal; Interlude; Vocal; Coda.

The Birthday Child

Melody by Barbara Andress
Words traditional

Key: C   Starting Tone: C(1)

Meter: $\frac{4}{4}$ ($\frac{4}{\quarternote}$)

Concept   DURATION: Rhythm patterns move in relation to an underlying beat.

Discover   Learn the song. Sing it on special occasions to honor the one who is the "Birthday Child." Use the chant given below to help children respond to a feeling of basic beat. Chant the poem, using the name of the child.

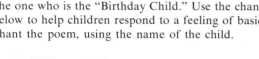

Tell me John-ny, Tell me quick!

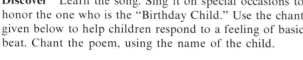

How man-y spank-ings do you get?

one (clap) two (clap) three (clap) four (clap)

five (clap) six (clap) or sev-en?

Make sure that the child's name is set within the rhythm of the chant.

When counting the spankings, chant the number and clap without losing the basic beat.

When the children are familiar with both chant and song, invite them to combine the two in the following way: song —chant—song.

Birthday Candles

by Barbara Andress

Count all the candles on the cake,
How many candles does it take?
One for the baby, on a cake so brown,
Fifty for Grandpa, see the cake squish down!

Light all the candles on the cake,
How many candles does it take?
One for the baby, a tiny little light,
Lots for Grandpa, see them burning bright!

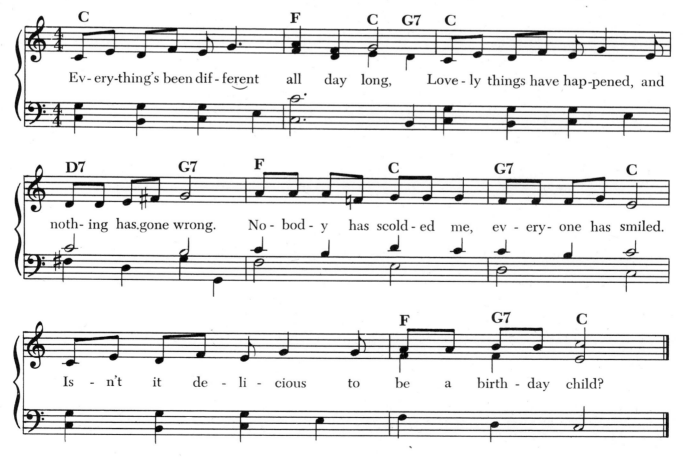

Ev-ery-thing's been dif-ferent all day long, Love-ly things have hap-pened, and noth-ing has gone wrong. No-bod-y has scold-ed me, ev-ery-one has smiled. Is-n't it de-li-cious to be a birth-day child?

An Amer"I"can

Words and Music by Barbara Andress

Key: F   Starting Tone: C(5)

Meter: $\frac{2}{2}$ ($\frac{2}{\downarrow}$)

DT/ Record 1   Side B   Band 4   VOICES: children's choir.
ACCOMPANIMENT: drums, guitar, bass, piano, percussion, trombone, French horn, trumpet, piccolo.
FORM: Introduction; *v. 1*; Interlude; *v. 2*; Interlude; *v. 3*.

Introduce the song by playing the recording. Discuss pride in one's country and our custom of honoring the flag.

Add movement to the song with a crisp salute on the words, "Yes, Ma'am" and "Yes, Sir." Encourage children to say the words "shout high" with a feeling of firm conviction rather than as an actual shout.

Concept   DURATION: Music moves in relation to an underlying steady beat.

Discover   Ask children to march to the **basic beat** as they sing.

Children may want to plan a formation for their march.

Extend   Ask some children to improvise a drum pattern which they may use to accompany the song. They may play **on the beat** or play a **pattern** such as:

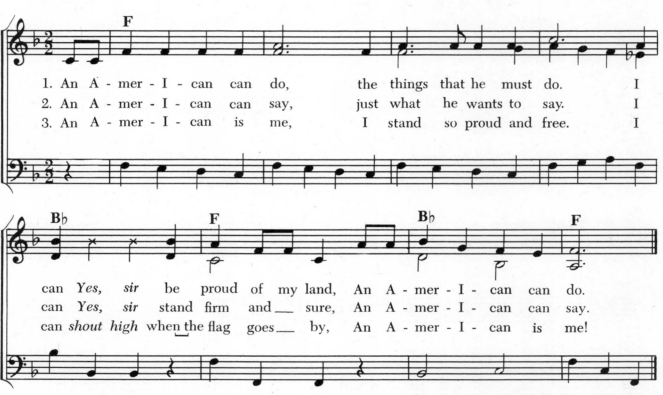

Fanfare for Two Trumpets

by Igor Stravinsky
BORN 1882   DIED 1971

Record 8   Side B   Band 10
Robert Heinrich and Robert E. Nagel, trumpets.
TIME: :33

Concept   EXPRESSIVE TOTALITY: Timbres, dynamics, patterns of rhythm, and melody may be used to communicate an idea.

Discover   LISTEN WHILE TRUMPETS PLAY A FANFARE! CAN YOU DECIDE WHAT A FANFARE IS? (An announcement that something special is about to happen.) WHAT HELPED YOU DECIDE THAT IT WAS EXCITING? (The sounds of the trumpets, the loud sounds, the skips in the melody that sound like a bugle call, and the short detached sounds.)

Extend   Put out the bells in the following "tone row": A♯ A B C E D C D♯ F E F♯ G♯ G. Play the bells, using the same rhythm pattern as first stated in Stravinsky's fanfare.

The child may decide to play one bell or several simultaneously as he repeats his rhythm pattern.

20

Napoleon

French Folk Song

Key: G   Starting Tone: G(1)

Meter: $\frac{2}{4}$ $\left(\begin{smallmatrix} 2 \\ \downarrow \end{smallmatrix}\right)$

DT/ Record 1   Side B   Band 5   VOICES: children's choir.
ACCOMPANIMENT: trumpet, clarinet, viola, trombone, percussion.
FORM: Introduction; English verse; Interlude; French verse; Coda.

Concept   DURATION: Rhythm patterns move in relation to an underlying beat.

Discover   Begin the lesson by reviewing "Fanfare," page 20. SOMETHING SPECIAL IS GOING TO HAPPEN! LISTEN! WHAT MIGHT IT BE? Play the introduction for "Napoleon." Guide children to conclude that a parade might be coming because the music sounds like a march.

Invite children to plan their own parade. One child may be "Napoleon" and be the leader as the others follow him, in pairs, around the room.

Choose one child to play the **beat** on the drum.

drum:

(*Continued on page 22*)

Na - po - le - on, he had five hun - dred men,
Na - po - lé - on a - vait cinq cents sol - dats,

Na - po - le - on, he had five hun - dred men,
Na - po - lé - on a - vait cinq cents sol - dats,

Na - po - le - on, he had five hun - dred men, All
Na - po - lé - on a - vait cinq cents sol - dats, Mar -

march - ing side by side. _____
chant du mê - me pas. _____

("Napoleon," continued)

Add word patterns for other instruments that describe the parade.

Down the street, down the street,

step to - geth - er, step to - geth - er.

Make up a fanfare introduction on the bells: D G B D.

Pronunciation for the French follows.

> naa-poh-leh-o[n] ah-veh saa[n]k sah[n] sohl-dah
> (three times)
> maar-shah[n] du meh-muh pah

Find Other New Sounds (6–7)

Concept TIMBRE: The same sound source may produce different sound qualities.

Discover Invite children to experiment with the ways of making sound which are pictured in their book. Use the triangle first.

Suspend the triangle
  on a cord,
  on one child's finger while another plays it,
  by holding it with a clothespin.

While the triangle is suspended, strike it with different types of "beaters" such as a nail or a wire brush. Strike the triangle and submerge it in water. WHAT HAPPENS TO THE SOUND?

Make similar experiments with other instruments. Strike the cymbal and wave it slowly in the air. WHAT HAPPENS TO THE SOUND?

Hold one maraca and tap it in the palm of the opposite hand. Compare that sound with the one produced by shaking two maracas in the air.

Cover the ball of a maraca with both hands before shaking it. WHAT HAPPENS TO THE SOUND?

How many ways can you play the triangle?

Experiment with the tambourine. Strike it
  in the middle of the head,
  on the rim,
  on the metal jingles.
Tap it against your knee, thigh, a desk top.
Shake it in the air.

CAN YOU MAKE SOUNDS THAT:

ring	bang	click	crack	buzz
rattle	swish	ching	thump	

Encourage children to think of words which describe the sounds they make.

CAN YOU FIND WAYS TO MAKE NEW SOUNDS THAT WERE NOT ILLUSTRATED IN YOUR BOOK?

Extend Invite children to plan a parade with their sounds. PLAN A PARADE, BUT DO NOT MOVE. HOW CAN YOUR SOUNDS SEEM FAR AWAY? VERY CLOSE? WILL ALL THE SOUNDS BEGIN AT THE SAME TIME? END AT THE SAME TIME?

The lesson on Colgrass' *Percussion Music*, which follows, provides further extension of this lesson.

How many ways can you play other instruments?

7

Record 9   Side A   Band 1
Paul Price, percussionist.
TIME: 1:27

Allegro
from *Percussion Music*

by Michael Colgrass
BORN 1932

Concept   TIMBRE: Different sound sources create distinctive qualities of sound. The same sound source can produce different kinds of sounds.

WE'VE EXPLORED DIFFERENT WAYS TO MAKE SOUNDS ON INSTRUMENTS. LISTEN TO THIS MUSIC! HOW MANY DIFFERENT KINDS OF INSTRUMENTS DO YOU HEAR? (Two: temple blocks and drums.)

LISTEN AGAIN! DO THE DRUMS ALWAYS SOUND EXACTLY THE SAME? WHAT ABOUT THE TEMPLE BLOCKS? DO THEY SOUND THE SAME, OR DO THEIR SOUNDS CHANGE IN SOME WAY? (Both the drums and the temple blocks play high and low sounds; they also play soft and loud sounds.)

Extend   Invite children to experiment with their own instruments to find sounds similar to those heard on the recording. (Tone blocks may be substituted for temple blocks, if the latter are not available.) Discover that drums have different sounds by selecting two or more drums of different sizes and applying tension to the surface of each drum. (Play with one hand, while pressing firmly on drum head with the other.)

lower   higher

Other Concept   TEXTURE: Sounds may be heard alone or in groups.

Discover   Help children listen for the grouping of sound patterns. WHEN DO YOU HEAR ONLY ONE KIND OF INSTRUMENT PLAYING? WHEN DO YOU HEAR BOTH AT THE SAME TIME?

To help children hear the differences in texture, you might diagram the contrasts.

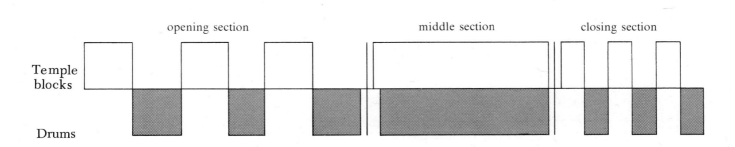

The Poi Man

Words and Music by Latitia M. Walker

Key: E♭ Starting Tone: G(3)
Autoharp Key: F Starting Tone: A(3)

Meter: $\frac{2}{4}$ ($\begin{smallmatrix}2\\♩\end{smallmatrix}$)

DT/ Record 1 Side B Band 6 VOICES: children's choir.
ACCOMPANIMENT: percussion.
FORM: Introduction; Vocal; Interlude; Vocal.

Concept DURATION: Rhythm patterns are made up of long and short sounds.

Discover Listen to the recording. Poi is a Hawaiian food made from *taro*, a root.

LISTEN! WHAT WORDS SOUND IN THIS PATTERN? ("pound-ing, pound-ing")

CAN YOU HEAR A PATTERN THAT SOUNDS LIKE THIS? ("pound-ing poi")

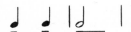

Invite children to accompany the song by pounding their fists together lightly in the even rhythm of the words, "pound-ing, pound-ing."

Extend Children may enjoy adding a pattern with rhythm sticks or *puili* sticks, if they are available. Use the "short, short, long" pattern.

tap floor with both sticks   tap sticks together

Children may wish to add their own patterns.

Other Concept PITCH: Tones may be sounded simultaneously to support a melody.

Discover LISTEN TO MY AUTOHARP! CAN YOU TELL WHEN IT PLAYS A DIFFERENT SOUND? RAISE YOUR HAND EACH TIME I PLAY A NEW SOUND! Strum the autoharp on the first beat of each measure. Play the autoharp chords indicated in the music as you sing the melody. Help children hear the difference between the repetition of the same sound, as in measures one and two, and a change of sound, as between measures two and three.

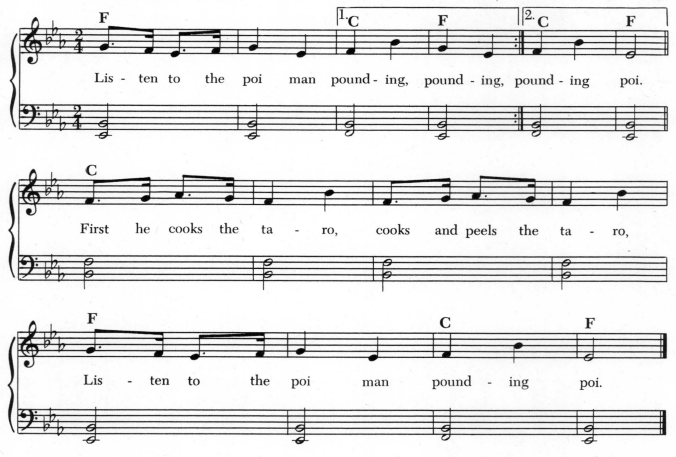

A Small Group Event, No. 1

Concept   TIMBRE: The distinctive quality of a sound is a result of the material used in the sound source and the way the sound is produced.

Discover   All the children need not be involved in this activity at the same time. Provide time when small groups may explore, then let them share their findings with others.

Provide children with the following sound sources:

10 paper cups
8 lids for cups (optional, but helpful)
small amount of raw popcorn or dry beans
small amount of dry rice

Ask children to work in groups of three or four to find sounds that rattle, swish, click, and thump.

Place a small amount of rice or corn in cup to make a rattling sound (place hand over top if lid is not available). Place only one piece of corn in the cup.

Allow the groups to experiment on their own. They may discover the sounds in the following ways:

thumping cups upside down on table

(clip-clop sound)

rubbing cup on table top

thumping cups together

Extend   Invite children to make up their own music using the sounds they have discovered. Encourage them to include long and short sounds, loud and soft sounds in their music. CHOOSE A LEADER TO TELL YOU WHEN TO PLAY. PERFORM YOUR COMPOSITION FOR THE CLASS.

Jimmy Crack Corn

American Folk Song

Key: F   Starting Tone: C(5)

Meter: $\frac{2}{2}$ $\left(\frac{2}{\downarrow}\right)$

DT/ Record 1   Side B   Band 7 VOICES: children's choir.
ACCOMPANIMENT: guitar, fiddle, banjo, bass, percussion.
FORM: Introduction; *vv. 1-5;* Instrumental.

Concept   STRUCTURE: Music is made up of short sections called phrases.

Discover   Play the recording. As children listen to the words and melody, guide them to clap lightly at the beginning of each new **phrase**. ON WHICH WORDS WILL YOU CLAP? ("Jimmy" and "master's.")

Show the design of the melody with shapes. Use three shapes of the same color to show the similarity of the first three phrases. They can be placed on a magnetic or flannel board at different heights to show the pitch difference. The fourth shape should be different.

Extend   Invite children to dance as people might have danced long ago. Have them form two lines. Partners face each other.

Verse 1: phrase one: First child steps forward four steps.

    phrase two: First child steps backward four steps to place.

    phrase three: Second child steps forward.

    phrase four: Second child steps back to place.

Verse 2: phrase one: Each child steps forward with right hand raised.

    phrase two: Partners clasp right hands; circle around each other.

    phrase three: Continue to circle.

    phrase four: Drop hands, step back to place.

Verse 3: Same as verse two, but clasp left hands.

Verse 4: Same as verse two, but clasp both hands.

Verse 5: Same as verse one.

Other Concept   PITCH: Melodies may move up and down.

Place these bells in a row.

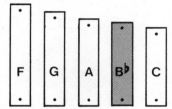

To help children sense the rising contour of the melody, guide one child to play the following pattern.

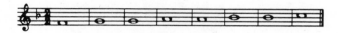

To help the bell player, you may wish to write the letter names of the bells on a chart:

F   G G   A A   Bb Bb   C

Ask the class to sing softly as he plays. Help them realize that the bell pattern keeps rising as their melody does (except at the end).

Record 2 Side A Band 1 VOICE: man.
ACCOMPANIMENT: bassoon, bass clarinet,
French horn, tuba, percussion.
FORM: Introduction: Vocal; Instrumental;
Vocal; Coda.

The Elephant

American Folk Song

Key: C   Starting Tone: E(3)

Meter: $\frac{4}{4}$ $\left(\frac{4}{}\right)$

Concept DURATION: Rhythm may move with steady beats, some of which may be accented.

Discover As children listen to the recording, invite a few to show how an elephant might move. Draw attention to different ways the children move.

Some may step with the **beat**:

Others may step only on **accents**:

When children can sing the song without assistance, choose one child to be the "elephant." He moves around the room as all sing. During the last phrase, he chooses a second elephant to join him. They may "hook their trunks" as elephants in the circus do. Sing "Two elephants went out to play" and continue indefinitely. End the song by changing the words of the last phrase to "They had such enormous fun, They played and they played until the day was done."

Extend Play "For Children," page 5, for the class. WILL YOU MOVE IN THE SAME WAY THAT YOU DID FOR "THE ELEPHANT"? IN WHAT WAYS MIGHT YOUR MOVEMENT BE DIFFERENT? Give individual children time to demonstrate.

Other Concept PITCH: Melodies move up, down or stay the same; they move by skips or steps.

Discover When children have been introduced to the idea that melody patterns can be shown with lines, show the melody pattern for measures one and two:

WHO KNOWS A SONG THAT MOVES LIKE THIS? As children suggest titles, sing each song they mention until they discover the correct title.

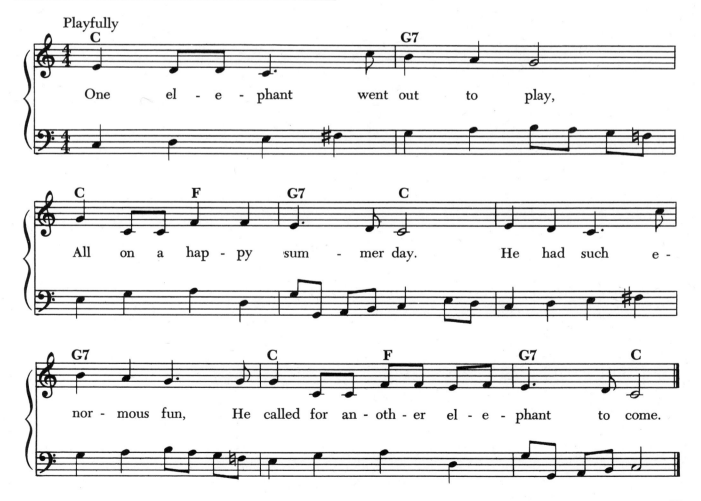

27

Goin' to the Zoo

Words and Music by Tom Paxton

Key: E   Starting Tone: E(1)
Autoharp Key: F   Starting Tone: F(1)

Meter: $\frac{4}{4}$ $\left(\frac{4}{\quad}\right)$

Record 2   Side A   Band 2   VOICES: children's choir.
ACCOMPANIMENT: woodwind quartet, percussion.
FORM: Introduction; Vocal, v. 1; Interlude; Vocal, v. 2; Interlude; Vocal, v. 3; Interlude; Vocal, v. 4; Interlude; Vocal, v. 5; Interlude; Vocal, v. 6; Coda (instrumental fade-out).

Concept DURATION: Rhythm patterns are made up of long and short tones.

Discover LISTEN! WHAT IMPORTANT WORDS IN THIS SONG MATCH THIS RHYTHM PATTERN? Play this pattern on a drum, or on another instrument which will sustain the long tones:

Play the first verse and refrain until children hear the words:

ZOO, ZOO, ZOO: ▬▬▬ ▬▬ ▬▬

you, you, you: ▬▬▬ ▬▬ ▬▬

too, too, too: ▬▬▬ ▬▬ ▬▬

ZOO, ZOO, ZOO: ▬▬▬ ▬▬ ▬▬

This song is quite long, and it is important that children listen many times to the song before they attempt to sing it. You might also play the recording and lower the volume as children join in on the refrain, so they learn to sing it without help.

Extend Invite children to plan an imaginary trip to the ZOO. WHAT MUSIC MIGHT WE USE TO DESCRIBE OUR ENTRANCE TO THE ZOO? (Perhaps "Parade," from *Divertissement*, p. 53.) CAN YOU PLAN A PARADE OF ANIMALS AFTER YOU REACH THE ZOO, AS YOU SING ABOUT EACH IN THE STORY? Each "animal" should make appropriate motions which match the beat. CAN SOMEONE ELSE PLAY THE PATTERN OF LONG TONES EACH TIME IT IS REPEATED? (They might choose a different instrument to play the refrain after each new animal is repeated.) WHAT MUSIC SHOULD END OUR TRIP? (Perhaps "Goodnight," page 18, or other "sleepy" music.)

1. Dad-dy's tak-in' us to the zoo to-mor-row, ___
2. See the el-e-phant with the long trunk swing-in', ___
3. See ___ all the mon-keys ___ scritch, scritch, scratch-in', ___
4. Big ___ black ___ bear all ___ huff, a-puff-in', ___
5. Seals ___ in the pool all ___ honk, honk, honk-in', ___
6. We ___ stayed all day, and I'm get-tin' sleep-y, ___

28

zoo to-mor-row,__ zoo to-mor-row,__ Dad-dy's tak-in' us to the
Great big ears and__ long trunk swing-in',__ Sniff-in' up__ pea-nuts with the
Jump-in' round__ scritch, scritch, scratch-in',__ Hang-in' by their long tails__
Coat's too heav-y,__ he's a-puff-in'. Don't__ get too near the__
Catch-in' fish and__ honk, honk, honk-in',__ Lit-tle__ seals honk,__
Get-tin' sleep-y,__ get-tin' sleep-y,__ Home__ al-read-y, and I'm

zoo to-mor-row,__ We can__ stay all day.
long trunk swing-in',__ We can__ stay all day.
scritch, scritch, scratch-in',__ We can__ stay all day.
huff, a-puff-in',__ You can't__ stay all day.
honk, a-honk-in',__ We can__ stay all day.
sleep, sleep, sleep-y,__ We have__ stayed all day.

Refrain

We're go-in' to the zoo, zoo, zoo. How a-bout you, you,

you? You can come too, too, too. We're go-in' to the zoo, zoo, zoo.

29

Loud–Soft (8–9)

Concept MUSICAL CONTROLS: Sounds may be loud or soft.

Discover The recorded narration provides environmental and musical sounds which correspond to the student's page. Play the recording as the children look at pages 8–9 in their books.

Narration:

There are many sounds in our world . . .
   . . . in the city (Cars, sirens, paging in department store.)
   . . . in the country (Cows, rooster, peeping chicks.)
   . . . in our school room (Voices, pencil sharpener, buzzer.)
   . . . in our homes (Electric mixer, vacuum cleaner, doorbell.)

Close your eyes and see if you can guess the sounds you will hear. (Water faucet—drawing a glass of water, door bell, cuckoo clock, jet plane, ice cream vendor.)

Some sounds are very loud and some are very soft. When you hear a loud sound, find the picture it matches on your page. When you hear a soft sound, find the picture it matches on your page.

(Help children point to correct picture in their books as sounds are played: loud drum played with beaters, soft drum played with brushes, dog barking, dog growling, soft creak of rocking chair, yowl of injured cat.)

Sounds can be louder than other sounds because there are more of the same sounds. (One duck quacking . . . many ducks quacking.)

Listen again to one duck. Listen to many ducks. Place your finger on the ducks. Which are the loudest? (Repeat duck sounds.)

Listen to one car . . . to many cars. (One car . . . many cars.)

Listen again to one car. Listen to many cars. Place your finger on the car sounds which are the loudest. (Repeat car sounds.)

Musicians can play music which is loud and music which is soft. ("Oh, When the Saints Go Marching In.")

Listen to other instruments play loud and soft. (Short phrase.)

Instruments playing loudly and softly are used by composers when they are expressing musical ideas in their pieces. The next time you hear a recorded piece of music, do you think you could hear how the composer used loud sounds and soft sounds?

8

Extend Play Speer's "Fanfare," page 31, for children. Ask them to raise their hands each time they hear the music played softer. (The music alternates from loud to soft each time a phrase is played by the brass.) Children may wish to express the loud and soft sounds through large body movements such as marching.

Record 2   Side A   Band 3

Fanfare for Three Trumpets, Three Trombones, and Timpani

by Daniel Speer
BORN 1636   DIED 1707

Concept   MUSICAL CONTROLS: Sounds may be loud or soft.

Discover   Discuss the meaning of "Fanfare." (Remind children of the Stravinsky fanfare, p. 20). THIS MUSIC WAS WRITTEN FOR "TOWN MUSICIANS" WHO LIVED LONG AGO. THEY ANNOUNCED THE ARRIVAL OF IMPORTANT VISITORS WITH THE TRUMPETING OF HORNS. THIS MUSIC SEEMS JUST RIGHT FOR WELCOMING A VERY IMPORTANT NOBLEMAN OR KING. THE BRASS INSTRUMENTS SEEM TO BE ECHOING ONE ANOTHER AS THEY PASS THE NEWS TO ALL THE VILLAGE.

A   The first group plays an exciting fanfare that loudly proclaims, "Everyone, look! Here comes someone very important" (loud).

A   The second group of instruments picks up the tune and echoes it from far away (soft).

B   The brass instruments loudly play a fanfare, but this time it is a slightly different melody.

B   From far away it is echoed (soft).

A   The first group completes the piece by playing both
B   fanfares (A and B) in a very loud, stately manner, reminding us that this is music for a grand affair (loud).

You may wish to cut bugles of different sizes from construction paper to illustrate the loud and soft sections, as shown above.

Extend   Upon repeated listenings, ask children to make up movements reflecting the style and dynamic changes of the music. They may wish to walk in a stately manner when they hear the loud sections and stop when the music is soft.

Record 9   Side A   Band 2
The London Brass Players,
Joshua Rifkin, director.
TIME: 1:09

31

Winnie the Witch

Words and Music by Barbara Andress

Key: D Minor   Starting Tone: D(1)

Meter: $\frac{3}{4}$ $\left(\begin{smallmatrix}3\\ \downarrow\end{smallmatrix}\right)$

DT/ **Record 2   Side A   Band 4** VOICES: children's choir.
ACCOMPANIMENT: synthesizer.
FORM: Introduction; *v. 1;* Interlude; *v. 2;* Coda.

Concept TIMBRE: When an instrument is played in different ways, it produces different qualities of sound.

Discover Learn the song "Winnie the Witch." Ask children to take turns creating an introduction, interlude, and coda for the song on an autoharp.

Hold the **Dm** chord throughout the introduction as one child makes up scary sounds. He might use a pencil to tap strings with eraser; tap strings with wooden end of pencil; drop pencil gently across strings (soft bounce); drag eraser across strings; slowly run metal part of pencil on lowest wire-wrapped string, making a scratchy sound. The child signals whenever he completes his introduction. Ask the child to strum throughout the song as the teacher changes the chords. (He should strum once per measure, on the strong beat.) Make up an interlude and coda.

Extend Dramatize "Winnie the Witch." Select a "witch" and a few children to act out the parts. Add instruments to help suggest sounds in the story ("tapped at the door," "rattled the roofs").

32

DT/ Record 2 Side A Band 5 VOICES: children's voices.
ACCOMPANIMENT: percussion.
FORM: Instrumental; *v. 1;* Interlude; *v. 2;* Interlude; *v. 3* (fade out).

Black and Gold

Music by Charlotte Odgen
Words by Nancy Byrd Turner

Key: D Minor   Starting Tone: A(5)

Meter: 4/4 (4/♩)

Concept   TIMBRE: Sounds may be used to suggest a mood.

Discover   Read the words of the song as a poem. WHAT SOUNDS MIGHT YOU USE TO SUGGEST BLACK? WHAT TO SUGGEST GOLD? Invite children to make a selection from the instruments available.

Listen to the music. DO YOU THINK IT SUGGESTS "BLACK" OR "GOLD"? Play only the instrumental introduction. (Accept children's suggestions; there is no "right" answer.)

Play the complete song. Compare the sounds heard in the introduction (xylophone, whip, castanets) with those heard during verse two (orchestra bells). Encourage children to think of words to describe the different sounds they hear.

The class may select their own "black" and "gold" instruments to play. Choose a different group of instruments for each verse. Play at the end of each two-measure phrase (on "gold," "night," "moon," and "light").

Other Concept   PITCH: High and low tones may be combined to create harmony.

Discover   Children may play the following patterns as an accompaniment. They may wish to choose one instrument to be "black" and another "gold."

alto metallophones:

bass xylophone

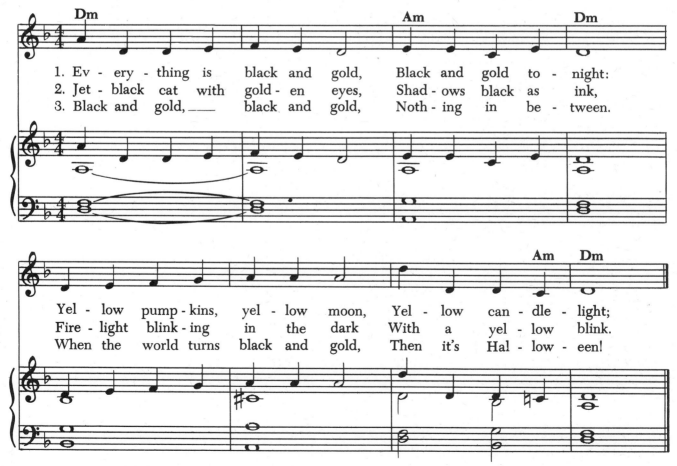

1. Ev - ery - thing is black and gold, Black and gold to - night:
2. Jet - black cat with gold - en eyes, Shad - ows black as ink,
3. Black and gold, ___ black and gold, Noth - ing in be - tween.

Yel - low pump - kins, yel - low moon, Yel - low can - dle - light;
Fire - light blink - ing in the dark With a yel - low blink.
When the world turns black and gold, Then it's Hal - low - een!

Five Little Pumpkins

Music by Charles Winter
Words Traditional

Key: C Starting Tone: C(1)

Meter: $\frac{4}{4}$ ($\frac{4}{\downarrow}$)

DT/ Record 2 Side A Band 6 VOICES: children's voices.
ACCOMPANIMENT: trumpet, clarinet, viola, trombone, percussion.
FORM: Introduction; Vocal; Coda.

Concept PITCH: Melodies are based on a specific group of tones such as a major scale.

Discover Precede the discovery lesson with several hearings of the song on different days. When the class can sing the song well, choose five children, one to sing the part of each pumpkin.

Put out the bells for the C scale. Play the descending pattern for the first phrase: "Five little pumpkins sitting on a gate, The first one said, Oh, my, it's getting late."

OUR SONG IS ABOUT FIVE LITTLE PUMPKINS, BUT HOW MANY BELLS DID I NEED TO PLAY THE MELODY? (Eight.)

Choose a child to play the following pattern as the class sings. Guide the class to discover that his melody matches theirs.

CAN YOU FIND ANOTHER PLACE TO PLAY THIS PATTERN? (Last phrase.) Some children may also be able to find the pattern for the middle phrases. Play one bell as each pumpkin is mentioned.

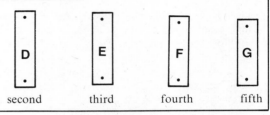

Extend Begin another day's activities by showing the melodic and rhythmic picture of the first phrase:

CAN YOU TELL WHAT SONG I AM SHOWING? WHAT HELPS YOU KNOW? WHAT SONG CAN YOU REMEMBER THAT BEGINS HIGH AND MOVES DOWN STEP BY STEP? As children offer suggestions, play each song they name, until they agree that their ideas match the picture.

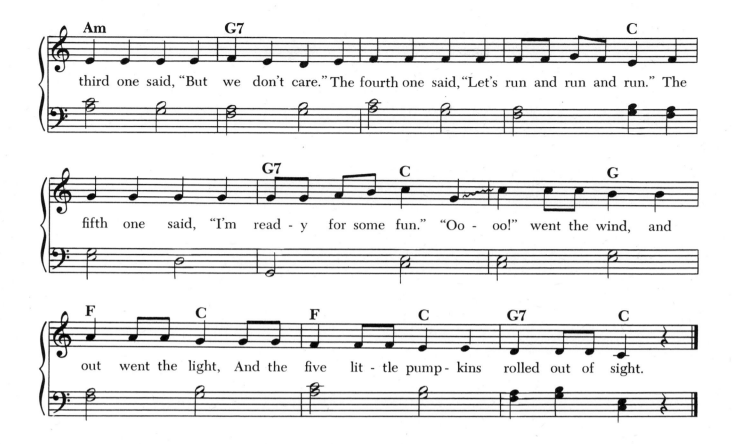

third one said, "But we don't care." The fourth one said, "Let's run and run and run." The

fifth one said, "I'm read-y for some fun." "Oo - oo!" went the wind, and

out went the light, And the five lit-tle pump-kins rolled out of sight.

Record 9   Side A   Band 3
The New York String Quartet with
Gilbert Kalish, pianist.
TIME: 2:12

Hallowe'en

By Charles Ives
BORN 1874   DIED 1954

Concept EXPRESSIVE TOTALITY: Rhythms, melody, tempo, volume, timbre combine to communicate musical ideas or extra-musical feelings.

Discover WHAT DO YOU SEE AT HALLOWEEN? (Ghosts, witches, goblins, devils.)

HOW DO THESE SCARY CREATURES MOVE? (Creep about, hop, run and hide, scuttle, dance.)

LISTEN TO SOME HALLOWEEN MUSIC. DO YOU THINK IT IS DESCRIBING THE CREATURES WE TALKED ABOUT? DO THEY MOVE IN THE WAYS WE THOUGHT THEY SHOULD?

Extend On subsequent occasions, draw attention to the way certain elements of music help to create the mood.

The music begins with strings scampering up and down—first one, then two, then more and more join in.

The piano plays loud, strong, percussive chords. At first the sounds are far apart in time, then they occur more frequently.

Near the end, the strings scamper about alone once more. Bass drum and piano join in for an exciting ending.

Children might draw a picture of the music. Suggest that they choose two colors—one for the scampering strings, another for the strong sounds of piano. Play the composition through while children draw the way they think the scampering strings are moving (up and down). Repeat the composition while children add strong marks with a brighter color to represent the piano. WILL YOU HAVE THESE COLORS ALL OVER YOUR PICTURE? (No, only part, because the piano isn't heard all of the time.)

I Am a Tiger

Words and Music by Gregory Kosteck

No key signature, free form of C Minor
Starting Tone: G(5)

Meter: ¢ (²⁄₂)

Concept EXPRESSIVE TOTALITY: Musical elements combine to communicate ideas or feelings.

Discover IF YOU MET A TIGER IN THE NIGHT, WHAT DO YOU SUPPOSE HE MIGHT SAY TO YOU? HOW WOULD HE MOVE? WHAT WOULD YOU SAY TO HIM?

Listen to the song. Talk about the words. Guide children to notice things in the music that help to suggest the scary tiger: the "roar" on the piano, the stealthy footsteps played by the piano while the tiger is singing, the scary voice of the man, the contrasts between soft and loud sections.

Invite children to move as they listen to the music. CAN YOU MOVE WITH THE SOUND OF THE TIGER'S FOOTSTEPS?

WHAT WILL YOU DO EACH TIME HE ROARS? (Move head from side to side.)

Extend Children may create their own tiger story on the piano. FIND SOME LOW TONES FOR THE TIGER'S ROAR. WHERE WILL WE FIND LOW TONES? Allow a child to experi-

Record 2 Side A Band 7 VOICE: man.
ACCOMPANIMENT: piano.
FORM: Introduction; Vocal.

ment and decide that the low tones are at the left end of the piano. Suggest that he play on the black keys, up and then back down.

CAN SOMEONE ELSE FIND TWO BLACK KEYS IN THE "MIDDLE" TO MAKE THE SOUND OF THE TIGER WALKING?

Give two children time to work together to plan their music. WILL SOMEONE PLAY FIRST, THEN THE OTHER ONE, OR WILL YOU BOTH PLAY ALL OF THE TIME? WILL YOU PLAY FAST OR SLOW? LOUD OR SOFT?

The two patterns might be something like this:

Similar patterns might be played on the bass and alto xylophones.

36

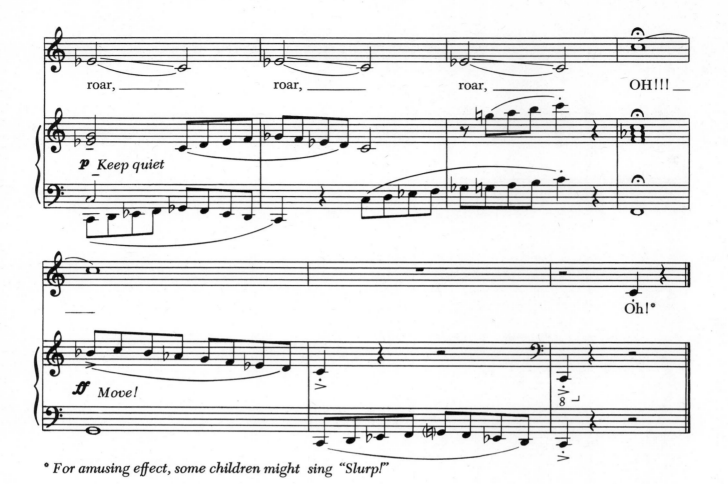

roar,_____ roar,_____ roar,_____ OH!!!_____

p _Keep quiet_

Oh!*

ff _Move!_

* _For amusing effect, some children might sing "Slurp!"_

Les Diablotins (The Little Devils)

by Charles-Henri Valentin Alkan
BORN 1813   DIED 1888

Record 9   Side A   Band 4
Raymond Lewenthal, pianist.
TIME: 2:18

Concept   MUSICAL CONTROLS: Sounds may be loud or soft. Sounds may move from one to the next smoothly or in a "detached" manner.

Discover   AT HALLOWEEN TIME, IMPS AND DEVILS MAY BE OUT, DOING MISCHIEVOUS TRICKS! CLOSE YOUR EYES AND LISTEN TO SOME MUSIC. CAN YOU IMAGINE HOW THIS LITTLE DEVIL IS MOVING? WHAT PRANK IS HE PLAYING? Play the complete composition for the class.

CAN YOU BE THE IMP? HOW WILL YOU MOVE? Give children ample opportunity for experimentation. Repeat sections of the composition several times, until children have had time to explore different modes of response. As children move, draw attention to those whose movements are particularly expressive of the music. Ask leading questions to direct children's attention to the music: DID YOU SHOW THE "QUESTION-ANSWER" BETWEEN HIGHER AND LOWER SOUNDS? CAN YOU STEP THE RHYTHM WITH YOUR FEET? HOW WILL YOU SHOW LOUD SOUNDS? SOFT SOUNDS? WILL YOUR MOVEMENTS BE SMOOTH, "IN A CIRCLE," OR STRAIGHT AND JERKY?

Extend   When children have enjoyed being "imps" on several different days, guide them to verbalize reasons for their movements. Avoid overemphasis on "What is the imp doing?" and stress "Why?" Help children use simple musical terminology: **higher-lower, smoother-"jerkier," faster-slower, louder-softer, even-uneven.**

The Music

Introductory passage: Fanfare-like figures are answered by higher "clusters" of sounds.

Second section: This rhythm (♩ ♩ ♫ ♫), repeated in the low register, is interrupted with loud, percussive chords. Brief passages alternate between high and low.

Third section: Sustained, low sounds introduce a quieter, smoother section, which is interrupted in turn with sharp, percussive chords.

Fourth section: Similar to the third section, but the sustained passage is higher. A gentler version of the percussive music returns.

Fifth section: A loud, fast, exciting coda ends the work.

A Long Movement

Concepts   DURATION: Sounds may be long or short.
   MUSICAL CONTROLS: Sounds may be sustained or detached.

Discover

TAKE A BREATH.

LET IT OUT SLOWLY.

MOVE AS LONG AS YOU ARE LETTING OUT THIS BREATH · · · · THEN FREEZE!

WHEN YOU ARE IN "FREEZE" POSITION, COUNT TO YOURSELF: 1 2 3 4 5 6 7 8 9 10—THEN REPEAT YOUR LONG MOVEMENT AGAIN.

Remind the child that he should breathe while he counts.

Help children become aware that they will not always move at the same time as their neighbors do.

Ask one child to perform an accompaniment for the sustained movements. (Since all are moving at different times, this will need to be a continuous sound.) Use resonator bells or metallophone. The child may use two mallets and play any two sounds simultaneously. Ask him to let the sound "spin all the way out" (fade away completely) before he plays another pair of sounds.

Help children sense that the long sounds of the instruments help describe their long movements.

Contrast the long, sustained sounds of the bell or metallophone with short sounds by asking the bell performer to change the position of the mallets so that he is holding the "ball" and playing with the end of the stick. Ask him to play any quick, short sounds.

Ask the class to listen to the short sounds and make up a movement which reflects them.

HOW IS THIS DIFFERENT FROM YOUR FIRST MOVEMENT? (A short, sharp movement is indicated.)

Extend   Listen to "Dreaming" from *Scenes from Childhood,* page 156. WILL YOU USE LONG OR SHORT MOVEMENTS TO SHOW THE WAY THE MELODY MOVES? (Long, sustained movements.)

Autumn Leaves Now Are Falling

German Folk Tune
Words Traditional

Key: F   Starting Tone: A(3)

Meter: $\frac{3}{4}$ $\left(\frac{3}{\downarrow}\right)$

DT/ Record 2   Side A   Band 8   VOICES: children's choir.
ACCOMPANIMENT: trumpet, clarinet, viola, trombone, percussion.
FORM: Introduction; v. 1; Interlude; v. 2; Coda.

Concept   STRUCTURE: A phrase ends when it "comes to rest."

Discover   When children have heard the song and discussed the words, ask them to show how a leaf floats to the ground. WILL YOU SINK DOWN SLOWLY AND GENTLY? OR QUICKLY AND STIFFLY?

LISTEN CAREFULLY. IN THIS SONG SEVERAL LEAVES FLOAT DOWN. CAN YOU SHOW WHEN EACH ONE REACHES THE GROUND? After children have shown that they sense the "resting places," choose four children to be the four leaves. Each may start on tiptoe, with hands overhead, and gradually sink to the ground as they twirl around. One child may start to move at the beginning of each new phrase.

Extend   Play "Entreating Child" from *Scenes from Childhood,* page 156. CAN YOU SHOW THE RESTING PLACES IN THIS MUSIC AS YOU MOVE?

1. Au - tumn leaves now are fall - ing, Red and yel - low and
2. Au - tumn leaves from the tree - tops Flut - ter down to the

brown. Au - tumn leaves now are fall - ing, See them flut - ter - ing down.
ground. When the wind blows his trum - pet, They go whirl - ing a - round.

Refrain
Tra la la la la la la, Tra la la la la la, Tra la

la la la la la, Tra la la la la la la.

Record 2 Side B Band 1 VOICES: woman, man.
ACCOMPANIMENT: woodwind quartet, percussion.
FORM: Introduction; Vocal, *v. 1;* Interlude; Vocal, *v. 2;* Interlude; Vocal, *v. 3;* Interlude; Vocal, *v. 4;* Coda.

Can You Dance?

Traditional Singing Game

Key: F Starting Tone: F(1)

Meter: $\frac{6}{8}$ ($\frac{2}{\text{♩.}}$)

Concept MUSICAL CONTROLS: Sounds may be short and detached or sustained and smooth.

Discover Review activities in "Response to Duration and Timbre, No. 1," page 4, before you play the recording of "Can You Dance?" LISTEN TO THE MUSIC. WILL YOU DANCE WITH SHORT, BRISK MOVEMENTS, OR WITH LONG, SMOOTH ONES? The crisp sounds of the instruments on the recording suggest short movements. Invite children to plan movements for their dance, following the suggestions of the words.

Review "Autumn Leaves Now Are Falling," page 40. WHAT KINDS OF MOVEMENTS FIT THIS MUSIC? DO YOU MOVE THE SAME WAY THAT YOU DO FOR "CAN YOU DANCE"? (No, the sounds in "Autumn Leaves Now Are Falling" suggest a more sustained movement.)

Other Concepts PITCH: Melodies have contour.

Discover On another day, show children a picture of the melody of the first three phrases, without naming the song. CAN YOU TELL ME SOMETHING ABOUT HOW THIS MELODY WILL SOUND BY LOOKING AT ITS PICTURE?

Guide children to notice that the contour of each phrase is the same: at first it stays the same, then it moves down. Each phrase, however, begins a little higher than the previous one. WHO CAN THINK OF A SONG WE KNOW THAT BEGINS THIS WAY? Play each suggestion until the children determine the correct title.

Place the F A C bells in a row (leave space for "missing" bells). Ask one child to play a different bell at the beginning of each new phrase. WHICH BELL WILL HE PLAY FIRST? (The lowest.)

PITCH: Groups of tones sounded simultaneously may support the melodic line.

Discover Play the autoharp to accompany the song. RAISE YOUR HAND WHEN THE SOUND OF THE AUTOHARP CHANGES. (On the last phrase.)

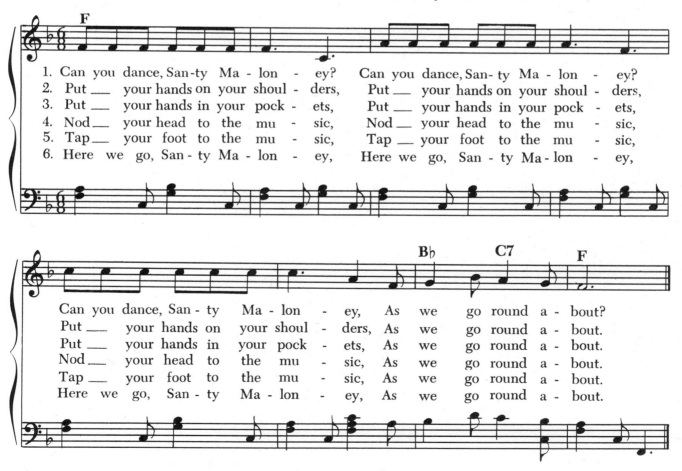

1. Can you dance, San-ty Ma-lon - ey? Can you dance, San-ty Ma-lon - ey?
2. Put __ your hands on your shoul - ders, Put __ your hands on your shoul - ders,
3. Put __ your hands in your pock - ets, Put __ your hands in your pock - ets,
4. Nod __ your head to the mu - sic, Nod __ your head to the mu - sic,
5. Tap __ your foot to the mu - sic, Tap __ your foot to the mu - sic,
6. Here we go, San-ty Ma-lon - ey, Here we go, San-ty Ma-lon - ey,

Can you dance, San-ty Ma-lon - ey, As we go round a - bout?
Put __ your hands on your shoul - ders, As we go round a - bout.
Put __ your hands in your pock - ets, As we go round a - bout.
Nod __ your head to the mu - sic, As we go round a - bout.
Tap __ your foot to the mu - sic, As we go round a - bout.
Here we go, San-ty Ma-lon - ey, As we go round a - bout.

Grinding Corn

Pueblo Indian Song

Pentatonic   Starting Tone: D♭

Meter: $\frac{2}{4}$ $\left(\frac{2}{\downarrow}\right)$

Concept   PITCH: Melodies move up and down by steps or skips.

Discover   Show this pattern on a chart:

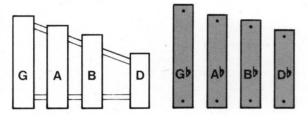

WHO CAN DECIDE HOW THIS WILL SOUND? WHEN WILL IT MOVE DOWN? UP? WHEN WILL IT SKIP? STEP?

Put out the alto xylophone or resonator bells with only four pitches showing, arranged in the following order:

G   A   B   D   G♭   A♭   B♭   D♭

One or two children may play this part. Help a child locate the melody, beginning on D♭ (or D).

Ask the class to sing the pattern, using the words "grinding corn, grinding corn." Draw attention to the rhythm pattern shown in the picture (short short long short short long). LISTEN! CAN YOU FIND THE PATTERN YOU PLAYED IN THIS SONG? DO YOU HEAR IT MORE THAN ONCE? (Yes, twice.)

Other Concepts   TIME AND PLACE: The expressive totality of a piece of music is influenced by its time and place of origin.

Discover   WHO DO YOU THINK FIRST SANG THIS MUSIC? WHAT HELPS YOU DECIDE? Listen again to the music and encourage children to express their observations. They may notice the drum and the words about grinding corn.

DID YOU NOTICE THAT WE COULD PLAY THE WHOLE SONG WITH ONLY FIVE BELLS? MANY INDIAN SONGS CAN BE PLAYED WITH JUST FIVE DIFFERENT TONES.

TEXTURE: Music may have a melody and an accompaniment.

Discover   Guide children's attention to the introduction. Notice the sounds of the different instruments.

Children may play an accompaniment on bass xylophones or on the black keys of the piano.

Another child may play the steady drum beat.

(*no accent*)

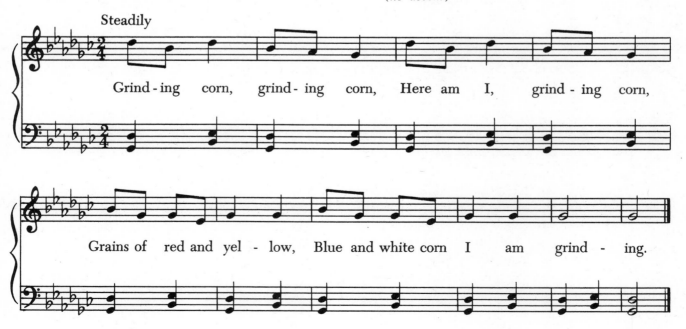

Grind - ing   corn,   grind - ing   corn,   Here   am   I,   grind - ing   corn,

Grains   of   red   and   yel - low,   Blue   and   white   corn   I   am   grind - ing.

Steadily

xylophone

DT/ Record 2   Side B   Band 2   VOICES: children's choir. ACCOMPANIMENT: percussion. FORM: Introduction; Vocal; Interlude; Vocal; Coda.

Record 2 Side B Band 3 VOICE: woman.
ACCOMPANIMENT: flute, koto, percussion.
FORM: Introduction; Vocal; Instrumental; Vocal; Coda (instrumental fade-out).

Mooki, Mooki

Hopi Indian Lullaby
English words by Eunice Boardman

Key: F   Starting Tone: C(5)

Meter: $\frac{4}{4}$ $\left(\frac{4}{\quad}\right)$

Concept EXPRESSIVE TOTALITY: Musical elements may be combined in different ways to suggest a mood or feeling.

Discover Play the recording for the children. WHAT KIND OF MUSIC IS IT? (A lullaby.) WHAT HELPS YOU KNOW? Listen again to notice the gentle "rocking" motion of the melody as it moves up and down, the soft voice of the singer, and the quiet, even rhythm of the accompaniment.

DO YOU THINK THIS IS A LULLABY TO A LIZARD? Discuss the fact that "little lizard" is a term of endearment. LIZARDS LIVE IN THE SOUTHWEST WHERE THE HOPI INDIANS LIVE. THIS IS A LULLABY SUNG TO A HOPI BABY.

Extend Review the lullabies "Sleep, Baby, Sleep," p. 8, and "Goodnight," p. 18. DO YOU HEAR THE SAME KIND OF MUSIC IN ALL THREE SONGS? ARE THEY ALL SOFT AND QUIET?

DO ALL THREE HAVE MELODIES THAT SEEM TO "ROCK"? WHY WOULD LULLABIES ALL BE SOFT AND GENTLE, WITH "ROCK-ING" MELODIES? (To help the baby go to sleep.)

Other Concept STRUCTURE: Phrases may be the same or different.

Discover Ask children to pretend they are holding a baby. CAN YOU PRETEND TO PUT YOUR BABY DOWN AT THE END OF EACH PHRASE? (Every two measures.) When children have sensed the six-phrase form, draw attention to similarities and differences between phrases. Each phrase is repeated; the words sometimes change.

Make six charts to show the contour of each phrase. Scramble the order of the charts and ask children to place them in the correct sequence as they listen. (Make two of each chart.)

Moo - ki, moo - ki, Moo - ki, Moo - ki, moo - ki, moo - ki, Let the liz - ard sleep, While a watch I keep. Sleep now my lit - tle one, On your rock in the sun.

43

Grandpa's Turkey

Traditional

Key: F Starting Tone: C(5)

Meter: $\frac{4}{4}$ ($\frac{4}{4}$)

DT/ **Record 2 Side B Band 4** VOICES:
children's choir.
ACCOMPANIMENT: electric guitar, bass
harmonica, electric bass, percussion.
FORM: Introduction; Vocal; Interlude;
Instrumental; Interlude; Vocal; Coda
(fade).

Concept DURATION: Music moves with steady beats, some of which may be stressed.

Discover Play the recording for the class and give them time to enjoy the story of the turkey and the interesting sounds in the accompaniment.

WHO CAN STRUT LIKE GRANDPA'S TURKEY? Notice the way each child moves, as you play the recording again, or as the class sings.

Some may step with the **beat**:

Some may step on the **accents**:

Show the difference with lines.

Other Concept STRUCTURE: Phrases may be the same or different.

As children strut to the basic beat, suggest that they show how the turkey moves about the barnyard. TURN WHEN HE PAUSES AT THE FENCE EACH TIME. HOW CAN YOU TELL? (There is a long tone or a pause at the end of the phrase.)

HERE IS A PICTURE OF A PUMPKIN. THE PUMPKIN WILL STAND FOR PHRASE ONE. LISTEN CAREFULLY. DO WE NEED ANOTHER PUMPKIN OR AN EAR OF CORN FOR PHRASE TWO? (A pumpkin, because it sounds the same.) Help the children decide that phrases three and four should have different pictures because each phrase sounds different.

girls and boys, He thinks he's sing - ing when he makes that noise. He'll

sing that song an - oth - er way up - on Thanks-giv - ing Day!

DT/ Record 2 Side B Band 5 VOICE: male folk singer.
ACCOMPANIMENT: harmonica, banjo, double bass.
FORM: Introduction; *v. 1;* Interlude; *v. 2;* Interlude; *v. 3;* Interlude; *v. 4;* Coda.

The Squirrel

American Folk Song

Key: F   Starting Tone: A(3)

Meter: $\frac{4}{4}$ $\left(\frac{4}{\text{♩}}\right)$

Listen to the recording. Have the children find out what each animal does. Draw attention to the instruments on the recording. The accompaniment is played by harmonica, banjo, and double bass. The first two instruments are often heard with American folk music.

Concept PITCH: A repeated pitch pattern may be sounded simultaneously with a melody.

Discover Play this pattern on the bells, glockenspiel, or soprano xylophone.

WHAT DO WE SING TO THIS MELODY PATTERN? ("hides it on the rail.") WHO CAN PLAY THIS PATTERN FOR US, OVER AND OVER, AS WE SING? Give children the appropriate bells, or place only the bars needed on the glockenspiel. (The glockenspiel will sound an octave higher.) Allow a child to practice until he can sustain the pattern independently. Then use it as an accompaniment for the song.

Extend Put these bars on the bass xylophone.

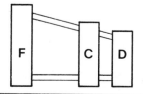

Ask a second child to develop a pattern such as the following to use as an accompaniment. This may be combined with the soprano xylophone pattern previously given.

F   C   D   C

Other Concept DURATION: Rhythm patterns include long and short sounds.

Discover After children have completed the activities described in "Use New Sounds" pages 12-13, find patterns of rhythm in "The Squirrel." Tap this rhythm pattern:

▬ ▬ ▬ ▬ ▬▬▬

WHAT WORDS MATCH THIS PATTERN? ("funny little thing.") Invite children to describe the pattern in terms of short and long. **(Short short short short long.)**

Show the pattern on the chalkboard. Put the pattern for "hides it on the rail" beneath it. Talk about similarities and differences between the two. Chant the pattern for "hides it on the rail" **(long long long long lo-ong)**

▬▬ ▬ ▬ ▬ ▬▬▬

▬▬ ▬ ▬ ▬ ▬ ▬▬▬

Let the children choose appropriate instruments to play these patterns as an accompaniment to the song.

Song on next page.

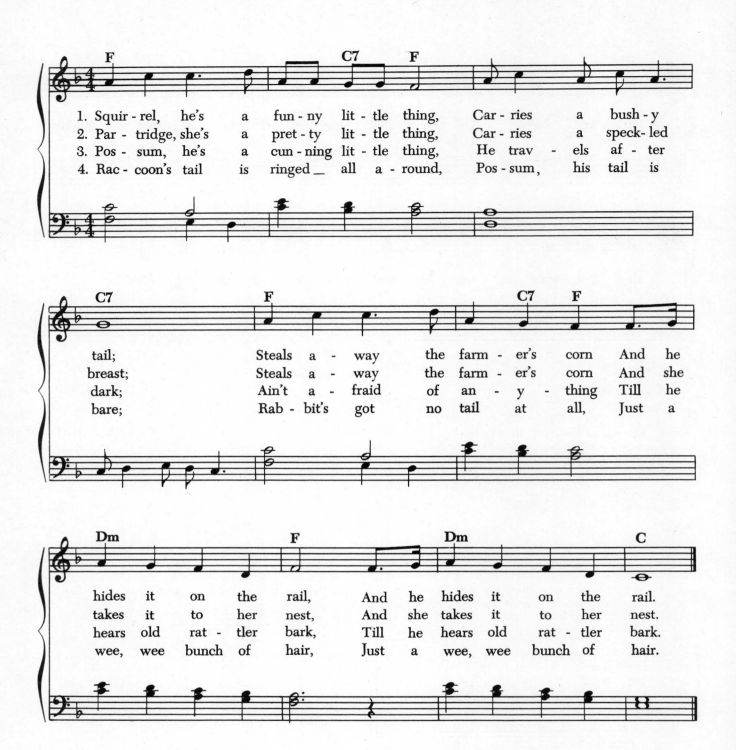

1. Squir - rel, he's a fun - ny lit - tle thing, Car - ries a bush - y
2. Par - tridge, she's a pret - ty lit - tle thing, Car - ries a speck - led
3. Pos - sum, he's a cun - ning lit - tle thing, He trav - els af - ter
4. Rac - coon's tail is ringed __ all a - round, Pos - sum, his tail is

tail; Steals a - way the farm - er's corn And he
breast; Steals a - way the farm - er's corn And she
dark; Ain't a - fraid of an - y - thing Till he
bare; Rab - bit's got no tail at all, Just a

hides it on the rail, And he hides it on the rail.
takes it to her nest, And she takes it to her nest.
hears old rat - tler bark, Till he hears old rat - tler bark.
wee, wee bunch of hair, Just a wee, wee bunch of hair.

DT/ Record 2 Side B Band 6 VOICES: boys' choir.
ACCOMPANIMENT: harp, oboe, French horn, cello.
FORM: Introduction; Vocal; Interlude; Vocal; Coda.

Since Others Do So Much For Me

American Folk Tune
Words by V. B. Silliman

Key: F   Starting Tone: A(3)

Meter: $\frac{4}{4}$ ($\frac{4}{\downarrow}$)

Play the recording. Discuss the meaning of the words. WHAT THINGS DO OTHERS—YOUR MOTHER, FATHER, BROTHERS, SISTERS, FRIENDS—DO FOR YOU? WHAT CAN YOU DO FOR OTHERS?

Learn this song at Thanksgiving time. Sing it together the rest of the year.

Concept   STRUCTURE: A phrase is a complete musical idea.

Discover   As children listen to the song, ask them to mirror your movements as you move your arm in an arc to show each **phrase.**

begin phrase   end phrase

HOW MANY PHRASES DID WE SHOW? (TWO.) WHAT HELPED US KNOW WHEN WE SHOULD COMPLETE ONE PHRASE AND BEGIN ANOTHER? (The long tone at the end of each phrase.)

Extend   Help children sense similarities and differences in phrases. Show the rhythmic pattern for each phrase:

– – – – – – – – – – – – –

– – – – – – – – – – – – –

Notice that one phrase moves evenly. The other has an uneven rhythm on the word "happiness."

Since oth-ers do so much for me, I, too, will free-ly give, And

help to fill with hap-pi-ness This world in which I live.

Explore Long and Short Sounds (10–11)

Concepts DURATION: Sounds may be long and short.
TIMBRE: Sounds may be used expressively because of their distinctive qualities.

Discover Engage the class in the following activity. CLOSE YOUR EYES AND LISTEN TO MY SOUND. LISTEN AGAIN. (Play long ringing sounds on the finger cymbals.) OPEN YOUR EYES AND LOOK WHEN YOU HEAR MY SOUND. MAKE A FIST WITH ONE HAND.

I WILL PLAY MY SOUND. AS LONG AS YOU HEAR THE SOUND, LET YOUR FINGERS OPEN SLOWLY . . . FREEZE WHEN YOU NO LONGER HEAR THE SOUND.

CLOSE YOUR EYES AGAIN AND LISTEN TO MY SOUND. (Play a short sound on the finger cymbals. Stop the sound by touching the cymbal with your finger immediately after striking it.)

MAKE A FIST WITH ONE HAND. I WILL PLAY MY SOUND. AS LONG AS YOU HEAR MY SOUND, LET YOUR FINGERS OPEN SLOWLY . . . FREEZE WHEN YOU NO LONGER HEAR THE SOUND.

DID YOUR HAND OPEN VERY MUCH? DID IT OPEN AS MUCH AS BEFORE? (No.) Give children time to discuss the differences they heard and felt as they moved.

Play a hand cymbal or gong with a soft mallet. HOW IS THIS SOUND DIFFERENT FROM THE OTHER SOUNDS WE HEARD? (Bigger, louder, rings longer.) WHAT PART OF YOUR BODY COULD YOU MOVE TO SHOW THAT IT IS A BIGGER SOUND? (Arm, head, whole body.)

LET'S BEGIN WITH A "CLOSED" FEELING. (The child should crouch down or curl up.) WHEN YOU HEAR MY SOUND, OPEN UNTIL YOU NO LONGER HEAR THE SOUND, THEN FREEZE!

(A gong sound may be obtained from a metal soap barrel lid. These are often available at laundromats at no cost. Drill holes for the string to hold it by. Use a soft beater and strike it with a glancing blow.)

After children have experienced these activities, ask them to open their books to page 10.

Help them to chant "The Butterfly" together. Then follow these steps.

Explore **LONG** Sounds

Sleeping
On a big bell,
A golden butterfly—

10

48

Explore SHORT Sounds

Chirping
In the tall grass,
A busy cricket—

11

1. Speak the verse chorally while in a "closed" position.
2. Strike the gong; the children may open slowly as the sound rings on and on.
3. When the gong sound has died away, play a slow rocking pattern on the C G A bells. The children may make graceful swaying motions like butterflies.

When the boys and girls have fully explored their movement ideas, ring the gong again, and let the "butterflies" fold slowly in, stopping their movements when they no longer hear the sound.

Follow a similar procedure and explore the short sounds of the wood block or rhythm sticks. Learn to say the poem about the cricket together. The children may then chant the poem, standing in a stiff position. Play a sequence of sounds on the wood block. The children should make short movements, one to each sound.

Talk about the differences in the sounds they heard and about the ways they moved in response to the sounds of the butterfly and the cricket.

Extend Children will need many opportunities to respond to long and short sounds as they gain an understanding of this musical concept. In the activity that follows, the children sing and move appropriately as a percussion sound is played. As children respond, stress the importance of extending the movement only as long as they hear the sound of the instrument.

Children sing:

Look at me, Look at me.

Leader speaks:
"I'm a straight stick!"   Drum:

(Repeat "Look at Me . . ." between each image; the percussion sounds may be played by the teacher or by one or two children.)

"I'm a green rainbow . . ."   Finger cymbals:

"I'm a sliding door . . ."   Tambourine:

"I'm a GIANT HIC-CUP!"   Drum:

"I'm a shining light bulb . . ." Finger cymbals:

"I'm a table leg!"   Drum:

Response to Patterns of Sound, No.1

Concept DURATION: Patterns of rhythm may include sound and silence.

Discover Play the following rhythm on the rim of the drum or on a triangle:

Invite the children to move in each of the following ways:

1. The children step only when they hear the sound.
2. The children step only when they do not hear the sound (during the measure rest).
3. Encourage children to explore many different directions with their movements in space.

Play this rhythm on a drum:

1. The children move only when they hear the sound.
2. The children step only when they do not hear a sound (during the measure rest).

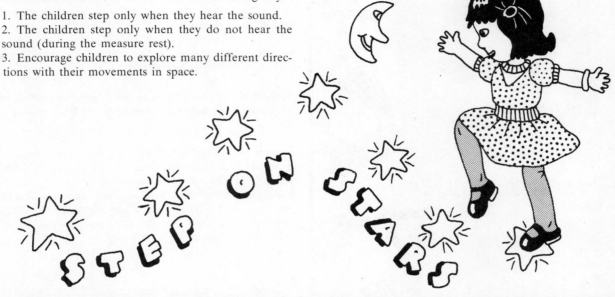

STEP ON STARS

Extend Play "Bright Stars, Light Stars," page 51, and "One Misty, Moisty Morning," page 52, without telling the children the name of the songs.

Play only the instrumental of each piece. Ask children to decide which of their movements would be most appropriate for each song. Invite them to experiment.

FIND AN EMPTY PLACE AND SIT DOWN. LISTEN TO ALL OF THE SONG. DID YOUR MOVEMENTS SHOW ANYTHING ABOUT THE WORDS OF THE SONG?

CAN WE LEARN TO SING THESE SONGS? CAN WE MOVE AND SING AT THE SAME TIME?

Bright Stars, Light Stars

Music by Irving Lowens
Words by Rhoda W. Bacmeister

Key: E Starting Tone: B(5)
Autoharp Key: F Starting Tone: C(5)

Meter: $\frac{2}{4}$ $\left(\begin{smallmatrix} 2 \\ \downarrow \end{smallmatrix}\right)$

Concept DURATION: Rhythms may include sounds and silences which are long and short.

Discover Listen to the instrumental of this song. DOES THIS MUSIC SUGGEST "STEPPING ON STARS" OR "CARRYING

DT/ Record 2 Side B Band 7 VOICES: children's choir.
ACCOMPANIMENT: harp, oboe, French horn, cello, celesta.
FORM: Instrumental; *v. 1;* Instrumental; *v. 2;* Coda.

A CLOUD"? Encourage children to base their answers on what they hear in the music. Some might notice a steady rhythm that sounds like stepping from one star to the next. Others might notice the bell-like sound of the celesta.

Give all children time to move with the sound of the celesta during the instrumental. BE SURE YOU ARE ONLY MOVING WHEN YOU HEAR THE "STAR-STEPPING" SOUND!

Extend Invite children to plan a "star-stepping" introduction and coda, using any of these pitches on the bells or glockenspiel.

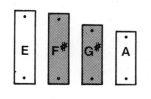

Other Concept PITCH: Tones may be combined to make pleasing sounds.

Discover Put out the bells E F♯ G♯ A. CAN YOU MAKE A PATTERN THAT SKIPS DOWN, STARTING WITH THE HIGHEST

TONE? (A F♯) WITH THE NEXT HIGHEST TONE? (G♯-E) Give the two "skipping patterns" to two children. With the help of the rest of the class, ask them to decide when each pattern should be played as an accompaniment.

To help children remember when to play, make a "score." Show the bells G♯ E on red paper, the bells A F♯ on green paper. Have extra pieces of paper in each of the two colors. While children sing and experiment with the pitch combinations, a third child may put the paper of the appropriate color in the chalk tray. (Choose one "skipping" pattern for each measure.) The completed "score" would look like this.

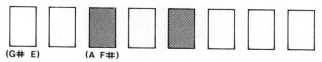

Play the complete "score" while the class sings the melody. One child might serve as a conductor by pointing to each paper when it is time for that pattern to be played.

Lightly

1. Bright stars, light stars, Shin-ing-in-the-night stars,
2. Yel-low stars, red stars, Shine-when-I'm-in-bed stars,

Lit-tle twin-kly win-kly stars, Deep in the sky!
Oh, how man-y blink-y stars, Far, far a-way!

51

One Misty, Moisty Morning

Music by W. S. Haynie
Words from Mother Goose

Melody Pentatonic   Starting Tone: D(1)

Meter: $\frac{4}{4}$ ($\frac{4}{\downarrow}$)

Record 3   Side A   Band 1 VOICE: woman.
ACCOMPANIMENT: string quartet, clarinet, celesta.
FORM: Instrumental; Vocal; Instrumental (voice on last four measures).

Concept   DURATION: Sounds and silences may be long or short.

Discover   Play the instrumental of this song. Compare it with the instrumental of "Bright Stars, Light Stars." As children listen they may decide that the **long** sounds of the accompaniment and the "gloomy" sound of the music suggest a cloudy day.

When children have demonstrated appropriate movements for the introduction, play the complete song. Talk about the words; decide that when there is mist in the morning, it is like being "inside a cloud."

Extend   Invite children to follow the same suggestions made for "Bright Stars, Light Stars" and plan their own "cloud-carrying" introduction. Use a cymbal, a gong, or the bells C D F G A.

Other Concept   PITCH: Tones may be combined to create pleasing sounds.

Draw attention to the bell-like sound of the celesta. Notice the accompaniment. Help two children play this pattern on bells or glockenspiel.

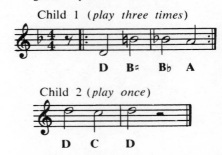

Another time, invite them to improvise their own accompaniment, using the tones from the pentatonic scale on which the melody is based: C D F G A.

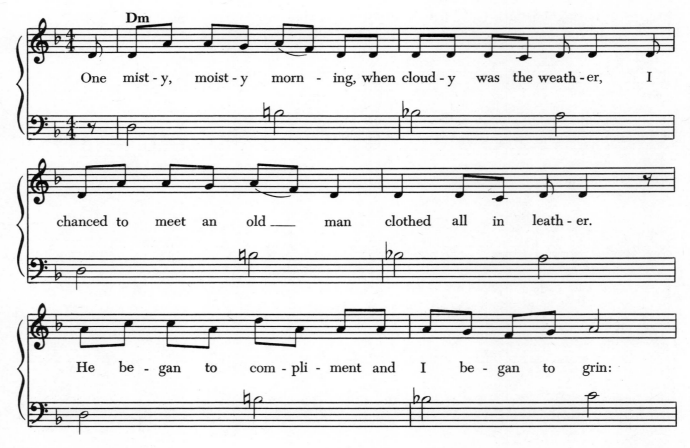

52

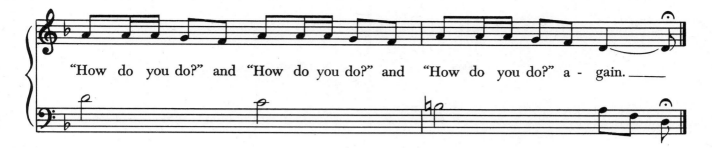

"How do you do?" and "How do you do?" and "How do you do?" a - gain. _____

Exploring Music: the Second Quarter

Record 9   Side A   Band 5
The Philadelphia Orchestra,
Eugene Ormandy, conductor.
TIME: 4:30

Divertissement
"Parade" and "Nocturne"

by Jacques Ibert (ee-bayr')
BORN 1890   DIED 1962

Parade

Concept   MUSICAL CONTROLS: Music may become loud and soft.

Discover   LET'S LISTEN TO A PARADE. FIRST YOU'LL HEAR A CHORD THAT SAYS "ATTENTION." YOU'LL HEAR MARCHING FEET AND A QUIET TRUMPET FANFARE, THEN HERE COMES THE PARADE, CLOSER AND CLOSER. RAISE YOUR HAND WHEN YOU THINK THE PARADE IS GOING AWAY. PLAY THE RECORDING.

HOW DID YOU KNOW THE PARADE WAS GOING AWAY? (The music became softer.) DID THE PARADE BEGIN RIGHT IN FRONT OF US, OR DID IT COME FROM FAR AWAY? (Far away.)

HOW COULD YOU TELL? (The music started softly, then became louder.)

LISTEN AGAIN. RAISE YOUR HAND WHEN THE PARADE IS THE VERY LOUDEST.

Extend   SHOW ME, BEGINNING WITH YOUR HAND BEHIND YOUR BACK, HOW THE PARADE MOVES. LET YOUR HAND KEEP TIME WITH THE BEAT. WHEN YOU HEAR THE PARADE COMING CLOSER, MOVE YOUR HAND TO THE FRONT. WHEN THE PARADE IS IN FRONT OF YOU, PRETEND YOU ARE PLAYING THE CYMBALS. THEN, WITH YOUR OTHER HAND, SHOW THE PARADE GOING AWAY.

Nocturne

Concept   EXPRESSIVE TOTALITY: Musical elements may be combined to suggest a mood or idea.

Discover   Listen once to the recording, then draw faces on the board. Ask questions as you draw. (Do not encour-age children to answer until they listen to the music a second time.) Do you think this music is

sad?   happy?   peaceful?

exciting?   scary?

(Children may think it is sad, peaceful, or even slightly scary.)

WHAT TIME OF DAY COULD THIS MUSIC BE DESCRIBING? (Night.)

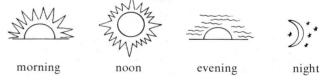

morning   noon   evening   night

Listen again and decide which pictures express the mood of the music. Help children develop a vocabulary that describes music. WHY DOES THIS MUSIC FEEL QUIET AND PEACEFUL? WERE THE MUSICAL SOUNDS LOW AND SLOW OR HIGH AND FAST? (Low and slow.) WERE THEY SMOOTH OR JERKY? (Smooth.) DID THE MUSIC END LOUDLY OR SOFTLY? (Softly.)

The Music   The following outline lists the main musical events in the work.

Low strings play unison tones interrupted by crescendo–decrescendo of other instruments.

Clarinet plays legato melody over the low sounds.

Piano enters with fast rippling sounds.

Clarinet plays four descending tones.

Low strings end the piece.

Play Long and Short Sounds (12–13)

Concept DURATION: Rhythm patterns are made up of long and short sounds.

Discover Discuss the pictures of sound shown in the pupil's book in terms of **long** and **short**. Experiment with the sounds of the rhythm sticks and the triangle. Help the children decide that the sound of the triangle is **longer** than the sound of the rhythm sticks. Ask two children to use the appropriate instrument and play what the "picture of the sounds" indicates.

First let them play each line separately. When children can play each line, have them play the first line and then the second line without interrupting the beat.

Read the two verses in rhythm.

Long	John		Brown	
car-ried his	saw	in - to	town.	He
sawed,	sawed,	sawed,	sawed, so	the
King and his court would	all	ap - plaud.	But the	
King said, "Stop! I'll	not	ap - plaud.	For the	
leg of my chair	is	what	you	sawed!"

Lit - tle	Nif - ty	Nick	said,	
"This	I'll	fix!	A	
ham - mer	and a	nail	will	
do	the	trick."	With a	
tap, tap,	tap, tap,	tap, tap,	tap, tap,	
rip, rap,	rip, rap,	rip, rap,	rap!	
"Oh,"	said the	King,	"I	
know that	you have	tried,	but	
won't you	please	learn	on	the
wood- pile	out		side?"	

Ask children to rhythmically chant the lines:

He sawed, sawed, sawed, sawed

With a tap tap tap tap tap tap tap tap

LOOK AT THE SOUND PICTURE IN YOUR BOOK (page 13). WHICH MATCHES THE SOUND OF YOUR VOICES WHEN YOU CHANT "SAWED, SAWED"? (The picture for long sounds.) WHICH MATCHES "TAP, TAP, TAP, TAP"? (The picture for short sounds.)

Have two children play the sound picture, using the instruments suggested on the pupil's page 13. Divide the class into two groups. Ask Group I to swish their hands to join the person playing the tone blocks. Group II may tap their pencils on the desk tops in time to the sound of the wood block.

54

Here is a picture of long and short sounds.

Which instrument can make a long sound? A short sound?

Long   John   Brown
Carried his saw into town.
He sawed, sawed, sawed, sawed,
So the King and his court
    would all applaud.
But the King said, "STOP!
    I'll not applaud,
For the leg of my chair is
    what you 'sawed'!"

12

The challenge for the student is to follow the sound picture. Put the two pictures on a large chart or use the Jumbo Book. To help everyone to play together, point to each line picture as the group plays.

Johnny Works with One Hammer

American Folk Song

Tonality: Pentatonic   Starting Tone: F

Meter: $\frac{6}{8}$ ($\frac{2}{}$)

Record 3 Side A Band 2 VOICE: man.
ACCOMPANIMENT: clarinet, trumpet, trombone, viola, percussion.
FORM: Introduction; Instrumental; Vocal, *vv. 1-4;* Coda.

Little Nifty Nick said, "This I'll fix!
A hammer and a nail will do the trick."
With a tap, tap, tap, tap, tap, tap, tap, tap,
Rip, rap, rip, rap, rip, rap, rap!
"Oh," said the King, "I know that you have tried,
But won't you please learn on the woodpile outside?"

Play this sound picture.

Choose other instruments to play this sound picture.

13

Concept DURATION: Rhythm patterns are made up of long and short sounds.

Discover After children have explored long and short sounds (pages 12–13 in their books), invite them to sing this song.

WILL JOHNNY'S HAMMER MAKE LONG OR SHORT SOUNDS? (Short.) LET'S SEE IF WE CAN PLAY THE PATTERN OF SHORT SOUNDS THAT IS SHOWN IN YOUR BOOK WHILE SOME OF US SING THE SONG. Use the Jumbo Book or draw the pattern on the chalkboard. Point to each part of the sound picture as the class plays.

The children might use their pencils to tap on their desks in this rhythm:

Children will also enjoy doing motions as suggested by the words. Notice that, as Johnny works with additional hammers, additional motions are added.

Two hammers—pound both fists on knees.

Three hammers—tap right foot, both fists.

Four hammers—tap both feet, both fists.

Five hammers—move head back and forth along with other movements.

Extend Contrast the short sounds of the pattern the children have tapped with longer sounds which move with the accented beat. LET'S SING NEW WORDS TO OUR SONG. ("Johnny works with one saw," for example.) CAN YOU MAKE LONG SOUNDS? Swish hands together, or play the triangle or cymbal in this rhythm:

Divide the class into two groups. One group may tap short sounds while the other one makes long sounds.

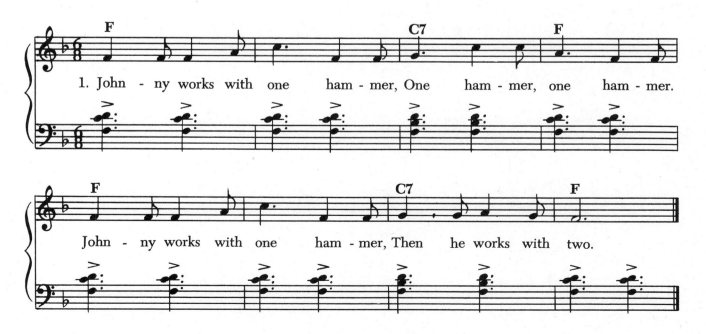

1. John-ny works with one ham-mer, One ham-mer, one ham-mer.

John-ny works with one ham-mer, Then he works with two.

Tap Long and Short (14–15)

Concept DURATION: Rhythm patterns are made up of long and short sounds.

Discover Draw children's attention to the pictures at the top of pupil's page 14. Discuss the picture in terms of **short** and **long.** Clap the picture of sounds:

Follow the suggestions on the pupil's page: chant the word patterns as someone taps on the appropriate item. Help children discover that the words match the sound picture. Invite children to think of other items in their room that they can tap which will make the same pattern of sounds (desk-top, chalkboard, etc.). If a child suggests a one-syllable word such as "book," show him the picture of its sound pattern and discuss the difference.

tap-ping on the book

— — — —

Read the questions at the bottom of page 15. Help children discover that the first part of the pattern tells them to play **short** sounds, because those are the **shorter** lines; the last part of the pattern has **longer** lines, therefore that pattern should sound with **longer** tones.

Extend On another day, help children discover that the same rhythm pattern is in the songs "Who's That Tapping at the Window?" and "Chatter with the Angels," pages 58–59.

Give children additional experience in feeling long and short tones by learning the following chant:

Verse 1

swish:

        swish your hands,   long   long.

clap:

        Clap your hands ___ short short short short

swish, clap:

        Swish them   long.   clap them short

step:

        March your feet to the sol - dier's fort.

TAP LONG AND SHORT

Here is a pattern of long and short sounds.

Play this pattern on many things in your classroom.

Tapping on the room door,
Tapping on the tile floor.

14

Verse 2

clap:

        Clap your hands, ___ short short short short

swish:

        Swish your hands.   long   long

clap, swish:

        Clap them short. ___ swish them long.

step:

        March back home where you be - long.

When children have enjoyed the chant, show them sound pictures. WHICH TELLS US TO SWISH OUR HANDS? WHICH SAYS TO CLAP?

Which part of the pattern told you to play
short sounds? Long sounds?
Can you hear this pattern in music?

15

Who's That Tapping at the Window?

American Folk Song

Pentatonic   Starting Tone: D(1)
Autoharp Key: C   Starting Tone: C(1)

Meter: $\frac{2}{4}$ ($\frac{2}{\quad}$)

DT/ Record 3   Side A   Band 3   VOICES:
children's choir.
ACCOMPANIMENT: trumpets, clarinet, viola,
trombone, percussion.
FORM: Instrumental; Vocal; Instrumental;
Vocal; Coda.

Concept   DURATION: Rhythm patterns are made up of long and short sounds.

Discover   Introduce this song after children have tapped the patterns on pupil's pages 14–15. Play the recording or sing the song. CAN YOU HEAR THE PATTERN WE'VE BEEN TAPPING? RAISE YOUR HANDS WHEN YOU HEAR IT. LOWER THEM WHEN YOU DO NOT HEAR IT. WHICH WORDS MADE THE PATTERN? ("tapping at the window.") Invite children to tap the pattern at appropriate times as they listen to the song.

Extend   THIS SONG HAS TWO QUESTIONS. ONE OF THEM ASKS "WHO'S THAT TAPPING AT THE WINDOW?" WHAT DOES THE OTHER ONE ASK? ("Who's that knocking at the door?") LISTEN. I AM GOING TO PLAY ONE OF THE PATTERNS ON THE WOOD BLOCK. CAN YOU TELL WHETHER I AM TAPPING AT THE WINDOW OR KNOCKING AT THE DOOR?

Play "knocking at the door." Guide children to select the correct answer. They might count the number of syllables in each pattern as they chant the words, then count the number of sounds you are playing. "Tapping at the window" ends with two long sounds; "knocking at the door" ends with only one.

Turn the song into a singing-playing dialogue:

Class sings:	Someone plays:
"Who's that	tapping at the window?"
"Who's that	knocking at the door?"

WHO CAN PLAY THE RHYTHM PATTERN FOR "WHO'S THAT" ON THE FINGER CYMBALS? HOW MANY SOUNDS WILL YOU MAKE? (Two.) WILL THEY BE LONG OR SHORT? (Very long.)

The children might perform the song as a percussion composition.

finger cymbals
(swish hands) $\frac{2}{4}$

wood block $\frac{2}{4}$

drum $\frac{2}{4}$

Other Concepts   PITCH: Tones within a melody may move by steps or skips. Put out the bells D E F♯ G A. Ask one child to find the pattern for "Who's that." WILL WE NEED BELLS THAT ARE CLOSE TOGETHER OR FAR APART? Guide children to experiment until they discover that the two "outside" bells (D A) are needed. Perform the percussion composition again, adding bells to the finger cymbals.

Song on page 58.

57

(Who's That Tapping at the Window)

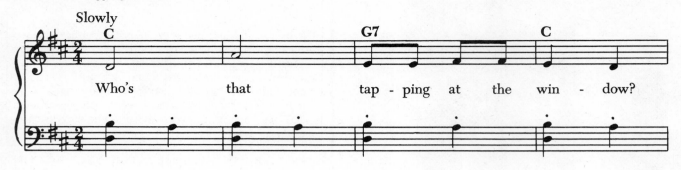

Who's   that   tap - ping at the win - dow?

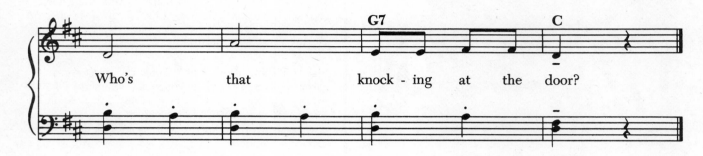

Who's   that   knock - ing at the door?

Chatter with the Angels

Spiritual
Traditional Words

Tonality: Pentatonic   Starting Tone: F

Meter: $\frac{4}{4}$ ($\frac{4}{\text{♩}}$)

Concept DURATION: Rhythm patterns are made up of long and short tones.

Discover Review the activities on pages 14–15 of the pupil's book. DO YOU RECALL A SONG WE HAVE LEARNED THAT USES THAT PATTERN. ("Who's That Tapping at the Window?" page 56–57.)

LISTEN. CAN YOU FIND THE PATTERN IN THIS NEW SONG? Ask children to listen for the words that match the rhythm. WHICH PATTERN DID YOU FIND? ("Chatter with the angels.")

HOW MANY TIMES DID YOU HEAR THAT PATTERN? One child may put a mark on the chalkboard each time the pattern is repeated. COUNT THE MARKS. (Six: play only the first verse and refrain.)

Extend Help children hear and play the rhythm patterns of the words. Divide the class into two groups. Ask one group to clap:

DT/ **Record 3** **Side B** **Band 4** VOICES: children's choir, baritone.
ACCOMPANIMENT: electric organ, piano, guitar, bass, drums.
FORM: Introduction; *v. 1;* Interlude; *v. 2;* Interlude; *v. 3;* Interlude; *v. 4;* Coda.

Chat - ter with the an - gels

Ask another group to clap:

Soon in the morn - ing

Two children may play these rhythms on the tambourine and claves as the class sings the song.

Other Concept PITCH: Certain tones may be sounded simultaneously to support the melodic line.

Discover Patterns such as the following may be used on the xylophone or metallophone as an accompaniment. Give the child ample opportunity to practice his patterns.

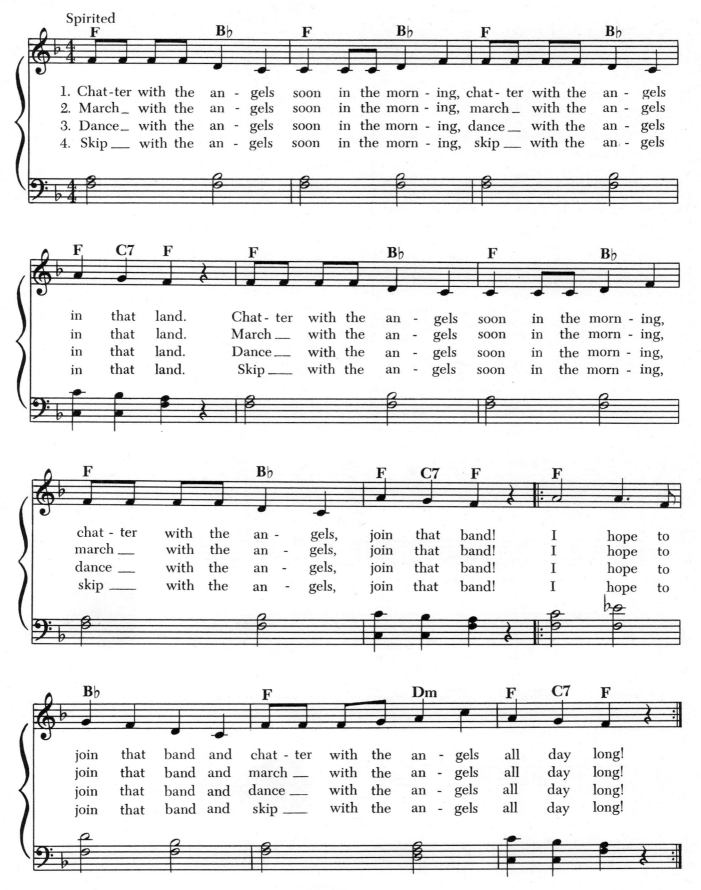

I'm a Little Teapot

Traditional

Key: C   Starting Tone: C(1)

Meter: $\frac{2}{4}$ $\left(\frac{2}{\sphericalangle}\right)$

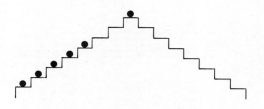
DT/ Record 3   Side A   Band 5   VOICE: man.
ACCOMPANIMENT: flute, bassoon, violin, cello, percussion, trumpet, trombone.

Concept   STRUCTURE: Music is made up of sections which may be the same or different.

Discover   The instrumental of this song includes a middle section which uses the traditional song "Polly, Put the Kettle On." Play the instrumental for the class. Listen to the music. RAISE YOUR HAND WHEN SOMETHING BRAND NEW STARTS TO HAPPEN! (At the beginning of "Polly, Put the Kettle On.") CAN YOU HEAR SOMETHING THAT SOUNDS LIKE THE FIRST MUSIC YOU HEARD? (At the return of "I'm a Little Teapot.")

Extend   When children have listened to the song "I'm a Little Teapot," invite them to make up movements for the different sections. Some may be teapots, with one arm akimbo and the other out to show the spout. Others may be "Polly" and hold arms out as though carrying a heavy teakettle. Each group moves at the appropriate time.

At another time, children will enjoy planning their own movements for the song "I'm a Little Teapot."

Other Concept   PITCH: Melodies move by steps and skips.

Discover   When children know the melody, put out the step bells. WHO CAN FIND THE MELODY FOR "I'M A LITTLE TEAPOT"? Ask the class to help decide when the melody moves by **steps** and when it **skips**. Show the pattern on stairsteps on the flannelboard.

WHICH OTHER WORDS USE THIS SAME MELODY PATTERN? ("When I get all steamed up.")

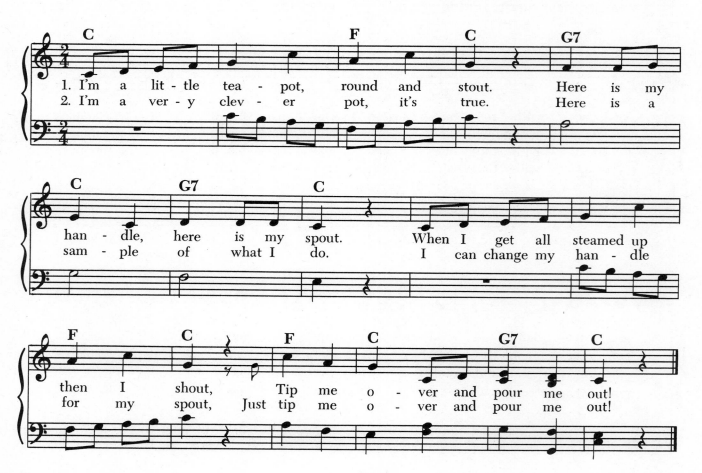

Record 3 Side A Band 6 VOICES:
woman, man.
ACCOMPANIMENT: accordion, guitar,
double bass, percussion.
FORM: Introduction; Vocal, *vv. 1-6*.

Looby Loo

English Singing Game

Key: F   Starting Tone: F(1)

Meter: $\frac{6}{8}$ ($\frac{2}{\downarrow.}$)

Children will enjoy reviewing or learning this singing game. The traditional game is as follows. All dance in a circle during phrases one and two (each phrase is four measures long). Then, during phrases three and four, everyone stands in place and does motions as indicated by the words.

Concept DURATION: The rhythm of a melody may move evenly or unevenly.

As children dance the game, draw attention to those who are skipping in the circle in response to the **uneven** rhythm of the melody. LET'S ALL SKIP AS WE LISTEN TO THE MUSIC. (Galloping is equally appropriate, and some children may find it easier.)

THIS TIME, LET'S WALK ALONG, MOVING THE WAY JUAN WAS MOVING. (Help everyone move to the underlying **even** pulse.)

61

Bingo

American Folk Song

Key: G   Starting Tone: D(5)

Meter: $\frac{2}{4}$ ($\frac{2}{\downarrow}$)

DT/ Record 3   Side A   Band 7   VOICES: children's choir.
ACCOMPANIMENT: guitar, bass, percussion, banjo.
FORM: Instrumental; Vocal; Interlude, Vocal; Coda.

Concept DURATION: Rhythm patterns are made up of short and long sounds.

Discover Put this pattern on the chalkboard. Discuss it in terms of **long** and **short.**

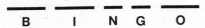

Let the class practice clapping the pattern.

THE LETTERS SPELL THE NAME OF SOMEONE'S PET. LISTEN TO THE SONG AND DECIDE WHAT KIND OF ANIMAL THE PET IS, AND WHAT NAME THESE LETTERS SPELL! (A dog named Bingo.) LISTEN AGAIN. HOW MANY TIMES DID THE SINGER SPELL BINGO'S NAME? (Three times.) CAN YOU TAP THE PATTERN EACH TIME YOU HEAR IT?

Extend Help children develop rhythmic coordination by playing a game. Put the letters B I N G O on the board five times. Play or sing the song. Each time the song is repeated, circle an additional letter; children must clap on the circled letters and remain silent on the others. Ask children to show the picture of each new pattern with felt lines on the flannel board.

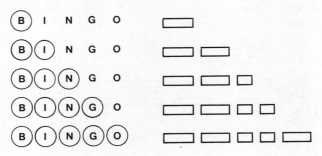

There was a farm-er had a dog, And Bin-go was his name - O.

B - I - N - G - O,   B - I - N - G - O,

B - I - N - G - O,   and Bin-go was his name - O.

62

DT/ Record 3 Side B Band 1 VOICES: boys' choir.
ACCOMPANIMENT: flute, bassoon, violin, cello, percussion, trumpet, trombone.
FORM: Introduction; Vocal; Instrumental; Vocal; Instrumental; Vocal; Instrumental; Vocal; Instrumental.

Anton Firulero

Costa Rican Folk Song

Key: C   Starting Tone: G(5)

Meter: $\frac{3}{8}$ ($\frac{3}{♪}$)

Concept TIMBRE: Individual instruments have distinctive qualities of sound.

Discover Listen to the recording and learn to sing the song. Then play a listening game to help children demonstrate their awareness of changes in instrumental sounds. On the recording, the singing alternates with various instrumental duets in the following order: **woodwinds** (flute, bassoon); **strings** (violin, cello); **percussion** (snare drum, timpani); **brass** (trumpet, trombone). As children listen, encourage them to show with appropriate body movements their awareness of contrasts between high and low sounds.

Later, help them associate the sound with a picture of the instrument. Obtain pictures of each instrument; one child may hold up each picture as that instrument is heard.

Other Concept DURATION: Music moves with a steady beat which may be organized by accents into groups of two or three.

Discover Guide children to clap as they sing, emphasizing the **heavy** light light sequence. Next, clap only the **heavy** beat. One child may play a G bell on this heavy beat.

Lively

An - ton,   An - ton,   An - ton Fi - ru - le - ro,   Each

one,   each one   will   play   his   own   way,   oh,   And the

one,   and the one   who does - n't   o - bey,   oh,   Must do,   must

do   what An - ton,   what An - ton   will   say,   oh.

Even—Uneven (16–17)

Concept DURATION: Patterns of rhythm may move evenly or unevenly.

Discover Look at the pictures on page 16 of the pupil's book. Invite children to demonstrate the different ways they jump rope. Look at the three "sound pictures." Talk about the differences in the pictures; encourage children to describe each with **long** and **short**. Help them to decide that the first and third patterns are **even** and the second pattern is **uneven**. Tap each pattern with the class.

Read the instructions in the pupil's book aloud. Chant the jump-rope rhyme given below.

Blue bells, cockle shells, (Pantomime gentle swinging of rope, "rocking the cradle.")

E-v-i-v over. (Pantomime full swing of rope over head.)

DO YOU KNOW THE JUMP-ROPE GAME "ROCK THE CRADLE"? HOW IS IT PLAYED? WHAT HAPPENS TO THE ROPE? (The rope sways gently, the feet move with small hops until the big hop at the end.)

Ask children to chant the rhyme with you as they pat their thighs with both hands to make the sound of jumping feet. Point to the first sound picture **(long long long long)** over and over again so that the children's eyes follow the picture of sounds as they chant. (Use the Jumbo Book, or put the pattern on the chalkboard or flannel board.)

(Continued next page.)

EVEN UNEVEN

Here is a picture of the ways your feet move
  when you jump rope.
Listen to a jump-rope chant.
How would your feet move to this chant?
Which picture shows the way your feet move?

16

Kuma San (Mr. Bear)

Japanese Folk Song

Pentatonic   Starting Tone F

Meter: $\frac{2}{4}$ $\left(\frac{2}{\downarrow}\right)$

This song comes from northern Japan, where it is very cold; the children there wear padded clothing that makes them look as chubby as little bears. The song "Kuma San," or "Mr. Bear," is a rope-jumping song.

DT/ Record 3   Side B   Band 2   VOICES: children's choir.
ACCOMPANIMENT: harp, wood flute, percussion.
FORM: Introduction; Vocal; Interlude; Vocal: Coda.

Concept DURATION: Rhythm patterns may move evenly or unevenly.

Discover Listen to this song. Girls and boys in Japan sing this song as they jump rope. ARE THEY JUMPING EVEN-LY OR UNEVENLY? (Evenly.) CLAP YOUR HANDS WHEN YOU THINK THE ROPE IS STRIKING THE GROUND.

Ku - ma   san,   Ku - ma   san   right   turn   a - round,
Ku - ma   san,   Ku - ma   san,   hands   touch the   ground.

When did your feet jump even? Uneven?
When did your feet jump fast? Slow?
Jump rope with a friend.
Which picture of sounds will be for you?
Which will be for your friend?

17

Chant the next rhyme, "Cinderella."

Cinderella, dressed in yellow,
Went upstairs to kiss a fellow.
By mistake she kissed a snake.
How many doctors did it take?
1 2 3 4 5 - - - -

HOW IS THIS GAME PLAYED? WHAT HAPPENS TO THE ROPE?
(The rope swings over the head, the feet move in a "jump-bounce" pattern.) Ask children to pat their hands on their thighs to make an uneven rhythm as they chant the words.

HERE IS A THIRD CHANT, "HOT PEPPERS." HOW IS IT PLAYED?
WHAT HAPPENS TO THE ROPE? (The rope swings over and under rapidly; the feet must move quickly. On the word "pepper," the rope is swung very fast.)

My mother sent me to the store,
And this is what she sent me for:
Salt, vinegar, mustard, pepper!

Children may pat their hands on their thighs again to make **short** sounds as they follow the sound picture with their eyes and chant the words.

After children have enjoyed each chant, answer the questions on page 17 of the pupil's book. The sound of the feet would be **even** when jumping to "Rock the Cradle" and "Hot Peppers," **uneven** when jumping to "Cinderella." The pattern is fast on "Hot Peppers," slow on "Rock the Cradle."

In response to the suggestions in the pupil's book, ask children to plan a rope-jumping game with a friend. WHO WILL SWING THE ROPE? WHICH PICTURE OF SOUND WILL BE FOR HIM?

WHO WILL JUMP ROPE? WHICH PICTURE OF SOUND WILL MATCH THE SOUND OF HIS FEET?

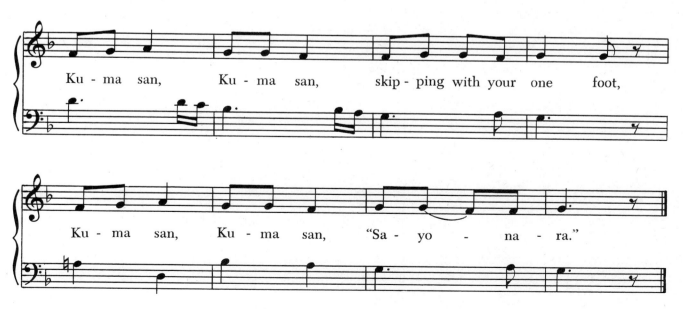

Clapping Land

Danish Folk Song

Key: C Starting Tone: C(1)

Meter: $\frac{2}{4}$ $\left(\frac{2}{\downarrow}\right)$

DT/ Record 3 Side B Band 3 VOICES: children's choir.
ACCOMPANIMENT: flute, bassoon, violin, cello, percussion, trumpet, trombone.
FORM: Introduction; *v. 1;* Interlude; *v. 2;* Instrumental (in 6/8); *v. 3;* Interlude; *v. 4;* Interlude; *v. 5;* Instrumental; *v. 6;* Interlude; *v. 7;* Coda.

Concept DURATION: The rhythm of a melody may be even or uneven.

Discover After children have listened to the song, invite them to move to the music. Play verses one and two and the interlude following verse two. Notice children who change movements to match the **even** and **uneven** patterns in the music.

Refer to the pictures in the pupil's book, page 16. WHICH MATCHES THE WAY YOU MOVED DURING VERSE ONE? (Even.)

WHICH MATCHES THE WAY YOU MOVED DURING THE INTERLUDE? (Uneven.)

As children listen to the remainder of the song and move with appropriate actions, they will also sense a change in tempo after verse five.

Extra verses: 2. Skipping Land 3. Tapping Land 4. Hopping Land 5. Nodding Land 6. Pointing Land 7. Stamping Land

Gaily

1. I traveled over land and sea, I met a man and old was he, I said to him, "Where do you live?" And this is what he told me:

Refrain

"Come with me to Clapping Land, Clapping Land, Clapping Land; If you wish to live with me, Come with me to Clapping Land."

66

Expressive Movement, No. 1

Concept EXPRESSIVE TOTALITY: A mood may be expressed through a combination of musical elements.

Discover This lesson provides an opportunity for children to reflect many different types of movement, such as **heavy, long, short, swaying, hopping.** The teacher must be an active participant in this experience. She will need to communicate the ideas by speaking the poems expressively and by being a "model" as she moves.

Dibble-dee-dop
A-hop! A-hop!
One foot down
The other is not!
. . . a-hop . . . a-hop . . . a.

A worm wiggles and makes himself go
by pushing a swallow down to his toes.

Big, Heavy,
Down, Down,
Low, Low,
Oh__ Oh__!

Down a dark hole
The light is at the top.
Deeper and deeper
'Til the light is a dot!

Dry wind blows . . . hot is the sun,
the flower bends 'cause it cannot run.

Black, black
Walking in black!

Pink, pink
Walking in pink!

Extend Give children the opportunity to respond to recorded music, using some of the ideas they explored when moving to the poems. For example, listen again to "Dream March," by Copland, page 87. After children have reviewed the composition, introduce them to the idea of moving with it.

CAN YOU GET INSIDE A PIECE OF MUSIC?

I am music!
Move when you hear me play!
Listen to my sounds . . .
You may want to be me when I'm
low low oh   low (speak with appropriate pitch levels)
         so

You may want to be me when I'm
                ta
             ta
          ta
ta ta ta   (imitate brass fanfare)
or when I'm
         brrum-m pum pum   (snare drum)
Or you may want to be all of me—all at the same time!

Play the recording, and invite children to move to the instrumentation and the changes in tempo and dynamics.

If You're Happy (18-19)

Traditional

Key: F   Starting Tone: C(5)

Meter: $\frac{4}{4}$ $\left(\frac{4}{\quad}\right)$

Concept DURATION: Rhythm patterns may be made up of long and short sounds.

Discover The purpose of this lesson is to help girls and boys begin to transfer their visual information from "sound pictures" (line notation) to musical notation. At this time, the names of the notes need not be identified; the activities on these pages simply give students an opportunity to associate new symbols with the aural concepts of **long** and **short.**

Discuss the questions on the student's pages as you read them with the class. Listen to the song all the way through, even though only the first line appears on the student's page. Help students to decide that, except for the last note of each phrase, the melody of this song is made up entirely of **short** sounds.

Sing the song, using a finger-tip clap to accompany the melody, and two hand claps where the words indicate.

"If you're happy and you know it, clap your hands!" (Clap! Clap!)

Listen to the sad version of the song. Help children decide that now most of the sound pictures are long because the sounds are longer. Discuss the differences in the two songs.

If You're Happy

When you are happy,

do you smile?

do you laugh?

do you get the giggles?

Do you think "giggles" would be

long   ——
or
short?   — —

Here is a happy song that has many short sounds.
— — — — — — — — — — — —
If you're hap-py   and   you   know it,   clap your hands!

18

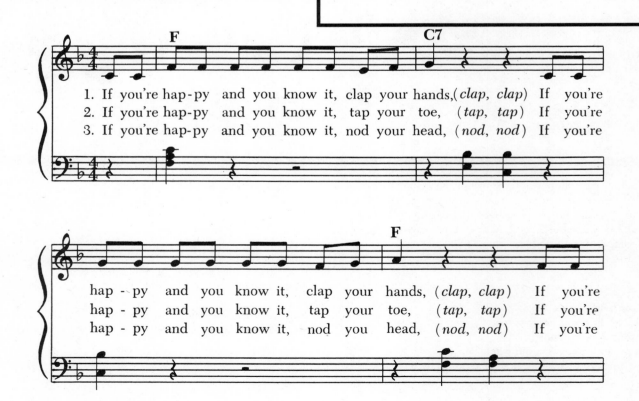

1. If you're hap-py and you know it, clap your hands, (*clap, clap*) If you're
2. If you're hap-py and you know it, tap your toe, (*tap, tap*) If you're
3. If you're hap-py and you know it, nod your head, (*nod, nod*) If you're

hap-py   and   you   know it,   clap   your   hands, (*clap, clap*)   If you're
hap-py   and   you   know it,   tap   your   toe, (*tap, tap*)   If you're
hap-py   and   you   know it,   nod   you   head, (*nod, nod*)   If you're

ere is another way to make a picture of short and long sounds.

short short long

Softly clap this picture of sounds as you sing.

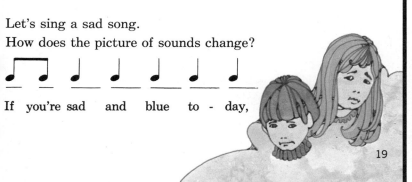

If you're hap-py and you know it, clap your hands!

Which part of the picture is not a short sound?

Let's sing a sad song.
How does the picture of sounds change?

If you're sad and blue to-day,

19

In the "happy" song the sounds are short and the music moves quickly. In the "sad" song the sounds are longer and the music moves more slowly.

Extend Review other songs in which children have discussed the rhythm patterns in terms of **long** and **short.** Show these patterns now, in rhythmic notation.

WHO REMEMBERS A SONG THAT USES THIS RHYTHM PATTERN?

("Who's That Tapping at the Window," page 57, "Chatter with the Angels," page 58, "I'm a Little Teapot," page 60.)

WE CAN USE OUR NEW NOTES TO SHOW THIS RHYTHM. Have construction paper or felt notes available. Ask children to help you put the notes on the flannel board. WHICH PICTURE WILL WE USE FIRST? WHO REMEMBERS THE NOTE THAT SOUNDED THE SHORTEST? THE LONGEST?

When the sound picture is complete, invite children to tap the pattern. Give them freedom to rearrange the notes to make up new patterns.

Two Versions
Happy
DT/ Record 3 Side B Band 4 VOICES: children's choir.
ACCOMPANIMENT: string quartet.
FORM: Introduction; *v. 1;* Interlude; *v. 2;* Interlude; *v. 3;* Coda.

Sad
DT/ Record 3 Side B Band 4 VOICES: children's choir.
ACCOMPANIMENT: string quartet.
FORM: Introduction; Vocal; Coda.

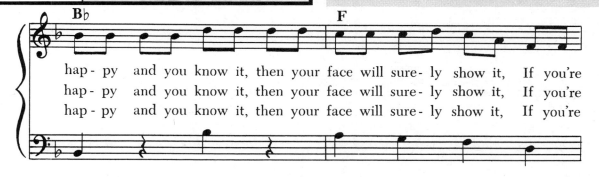

hap-py and you know it, then your face will sure-ly show it, If you're
hap-py and you know it, then your face will sure-ly show it, If you're
hap-py and you know it, then your face will sure-ly show it, If you're

hap-py and you know it, clap your hands. (*clap, clap*)
hap-py and you know it, tap your toe. (*tap, tap*)
hap-py and you know it, nod your head. (*nod, nod*)

Seven Steps

German Folk Song

Key: F Starting Tone: C(5)

Meter: $\frac{2}{4}$ $\left(\frac{2}{\quad}\right)$

Record 3 Side B Band 5 VOICE: woman.
ACCOMPANIMENT: clarinet quartet, percussion.
FORM: Introduction; Vocal (English); Interlude; Vocal (German).

Concept DURATION: Rhythm patterns are made up of long and short sounds.

Discover Show the pattern below with notes.

WHO CAN REMEMBER HOW THESE NOTES WILL SOUND? WHICH ONES WILL BE LONGER, WHICH WILL BE SHORTER? Guide children to tap and chant the pattern, using "short" and "long."

LISTEN! CAN YOU FIND THAT PATTERN IN OUR MUSIC? Play the first verse; guide children to decide that they hear the pattern four times, on the words "One, two, three, four, five, six, seven" and "Swing your partner merrily!"

CAN YOU FIND A PATTERN THAT SOUNDS SHORT SHORT LONG? ("Step with me," "one, two, three.") WHO CAN MAKE A SHORT SHORT LONG PICTURE WITH NOTES?

Play the complete song: tap the patterns the children have found. Listen for the German words of the second verse. NOW YOU CAN COUNT TO SEVEN IN ANOTHER LANGUAGE!

Pronunciation for the German numbers follows.

ahyns tsvahy drahy feer fuynf zex zeebn

Other Concept DURATION: Music moves with steady beats which may be grouped by accents.

Discover Help children learn the dance.

Measures 1–2 Take seven steps to the right.

Measures 3–4 Reverse direction.

Measures 5–6 Three steps into center; three steps back to place.

Measures 7–8 Swing partner once around.

Measures 9–12 Repeat actions for measures 5–8.

Record 3 Side B Band 6 VOICE: man.
ACCOMPANIMENT: English horn, violin, harp.
FORM: Introduction; Vocal; Coda.

Little Cabin in the Woods

German Folk Song
Words by Betty Welsbacher

Key: F   Starting Tone: C(5)

Meter: $\frac{4}{4}$ $\left(\frac{4}{\,\rlap{\char"0E}}\right)$

Concept STRUCTURE: Music is made up of phrases.

Discover As children learn the words, help them develop actions to "tell the story." Plan the actions so that a new motion begins with each two-measure **phrase.** Actions might be:

1. Form a peaked roof with hands, fingertips touching.

2. Shade eyes with hands, peer out the "window."

3. Middle and forefinger up for rabbit's ears, other fingers tucked under thumb; make rabbit "hop."

4. Pantomime knocking on door.

5. Wave hands in air on each "help!"

6. Pantomime shooting a gun.

7. Beckon rabbit to come near.

8. Warm hands at the fire.

71

For the Tiny Child

French Folk Tune
Words by Elva S. Daniels

Key: G   Starting Tone: D(5)

Meter: $\frac{2}{4}$ $\left(\begin{smallmatrix} 2 \\ \end{smallmatrix}\right)$

DT/ Record 3   Side B   Band 7   VOICES: boys' choir.
ACCOMPANIMENT: flute, bassoon, violin, cello, percussion, trumpet, trombone.
FORM: Introduction; *v. 1*; Interlude; *v. 2*; Interlude; *v. 3*; Coda.

Concept   TIMBRE: Sounds with different qualities may help to express extra-musical ideas.

Discover   Sing the song. Add the sounds of instruments to help suggest words such as "bells" and "drum."

Play the bells with the rhythm of the words in the first verse.

ring tong ting tong ting tong

Pantomime playing the flute in the second verse each time the following is heard.

Play the drum with the rhythm of the words on the third verse each time the following is heard.

rat tat tat

Extend   Children may wish to dramatize this song, selecting someone to be Mother, Father, and the three visitors who bring "gifts of music" to the baby. They might improvise on instruments or "just pretend."

Make up new words and verses to the song mentioning other "performance gifts" for the baby.

"I will dance around with a twirly, twirly, twirly."

"I will play my sticks with a click-a click-a click-a!"

1. For the tin - y child ly - ing in the man - ger low - ly, I will
2. For the moth - er mild watch - ing o'er the sleep - ing bab - y, I will
3. For the fath - er strong, who is guard - ing babe and moth - er, I will

play my bell with a ring, tong, ting, tong, ting. I will
play my flute with a sleep - y sil - ver - y tong. I will
play my drum with the soft - est rat - tat - tat. I will

play my bell with a ring, tong, ting, tong, ting, tong. I will
play my flute, oo. _____ I will
play my drum with the soft - est rat - tat - tat. ____ I will

play my bell with a ring, tong, ting, tong, ting.
play my flute, oo. _____
play my drum with the soft-est rat-tat-tat.

In the Window

Hasidic Folk Song
Words by Judith K. Eisenstein

Key: F Minor   Starting Tone: F(1)
Autoharp Key: G Minor   Starting Tone: G(1)

Meter: 3/4 (♩)

When children have heard the song, discuss the tradition of the Festival of Lights (Hanukah) which is celebrated each winter by the Jews. It lasts for eight nights; each evening an additional candle on the menorah is lit.

Concept PITCH: Tones may be combined to form chords.

Discover Play the autoharp as children sing the melody. CAN YOU TELL ME WHEN I HAVE CHANGED THE SOUNDS (played a different chord) ON THE AUTOHARP? RAISE YOUR HAND EACH TIME YOU HEAR A DIFFERENT SOUND; THEN PUT YOUR HAND DOWN AGAIN SO YOU ARE READY TO RAISE IT THE NEXT TIME I CHANGE.

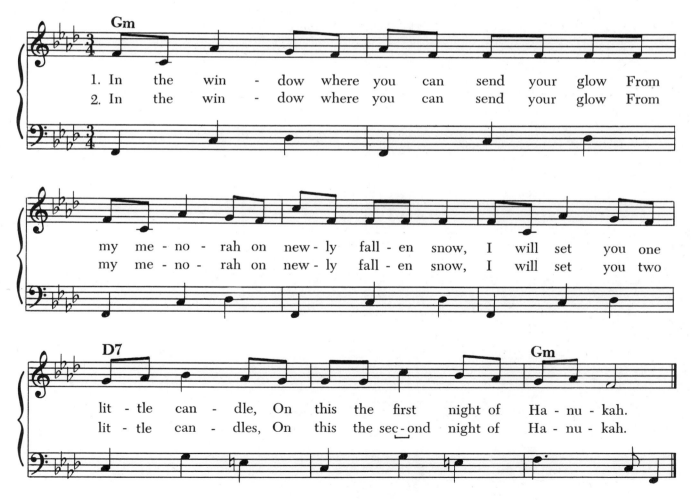

1. In the win - dow where you can send your glow From
2. In the win - dow where you can send your glow From

my me - no - rah on new - ly fall - en snow, I will set you one
my me - no - rah on new - ly fall - en snow, I will set you two

lit - tle can - dle, On this the first night of Ha - nu - kah.
lit - tle can - dles, On this the sec - ond night of Ha - nu - kah.

Jingle Bells

Words and Music by James Pierpont

Key: F Starting Tone: C(5)

Meter: $\frac{2}{4}$ $\left(\begin{smallmatrix} 2 \\ \end{smallmatrix}\right)$

DT/ Record 4 Side A Band 2 VOICES: children's choir.
ACCOMPANIMENT: electric guitar, electric bass, piano, drums, percussion.
FORM: Introduction; Vocal; Instrumental verse; Vocal refrain; Coda.

Concept DURATION: The rhythm of a melody moves in relation to an underlying beat.

Discover Many children will know the refrain; they may sing softly with the recording and listen to the verse.

Invite children to imagine they are driving a horse and sleigh while sitting at their desks. They may pretend to pull lightly on the reins as they sing. Encourage them to pull on each **beat.**

Ask others to be the trotting horse. Notice that some will step with the beat (♩ ♩) others may move with shorter steps (♫ ♫).

Choose an instrument to suggest the sound of the horse hooves and another to play the sound of the jingling harness bells.

high

low

Jingle bells:

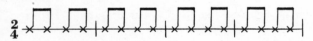

Show the picture of the two patterns and discuss the differences. One pattern moves **with the beat;** the other is made up of shorter sounds.

Extend Find other patterns of rhythm in the music. ("Dashing through the snow" and "Jingle bells," for exam-

ple.) Draw the patterns on the chalkboard. Show the patterns in relation to the steady beat. Notice when the pattern sounds with tones **shorter than the beat** and when it sounds with tones that are **the same as the beat.**

Jin - gle bells	**Dash - ing through the snow**

Other Concept PITCH: Melodies may move by steps or skips.

Discover Put out the bells F G A B♭ C. CAN YOU PLAY THE MELODY FOR THE FIRST PHRASE OF OUR REFRAIN? YOU WILL NEED TO BEGIN WITH THE BELL MARKED "A". Use appropriate questions to guide the children as they experiment. WILL YOU MOVE UP, DOWN, STAY THE SAME? DOES THE PATTERN YOU PLAY SOUND LIKE THE MELODY YOU SING? DO YOU NEED TO STEP OR SKIP?

When children have found the complete phrase, count the bells. HOW MANY BELLS ARE IN OUR ROW? (Five.) WHICH ONE DID WE BEGIN WITH? (The third one, A.) As children decide the number for each bell, write them on a chart; include the letter names as well.

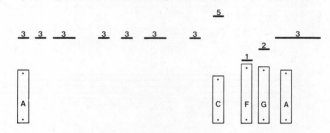

Have the class sing the melody with numbers as someone plays the bells.

Dash - ing through the snow   In a   one - horse o - pen sleigh,

O'er· the fields we go,   Laugh - ing all the way;

Bells on bob-tail ring, Making spir-its bright, What
fun it is to ride and sing A sleigh-ing song to-night!

Refrain

Jin-gle bells, jin-gle bells, jin-gle all the way!

Oh, what fun it is to ride in a one-horse o-pen sleigh!____

one-horse o-pen sleigh!

Concept PITCH: Melodies may be based on a specific group of tones, such as a major scale.

Discover Teach "The Snow Man" to the children. Let them chant it in rhythm. CAN WE MAKE A MELODY FOR OUR POEM? Put the bells for the C major scale in order. FIRST, LET'S MAKE OUR SNOWMAN GET "BIGGER AND BIGGER." Sing each line of the poem on one note, beginning with C and moving up one note for each new line. Repeat the high C on line 9, then move back down, step by step.

Ask children to name the bells with numbers. Sing the "melody" of the new song with numbers and letters. There are eight different numbers and seven different letters.

The Snow Man
Unknown

Once there was a Snow Man
Stood outside the door.
Thought he'd like to come inside
And run around the floor;
Thought he'd like to warm himself
By the firelight red.
Thought he'd like to climb
Upon the big white bed;
So he called the North Wind,
"Help me now I pray,
I'm completely frozen
Standing here all day."
So the North Wind came along
And blew him in the door—
Now there's nothing left of him
But a puddle on the floor.

Up on the Housetop

Traditional

Key: E♭ Starting Tone: B♭(5)
Autoharp Key: F Starting Tone: C(5)

Meter: 4/4 (4/♩)

Record 4 Side A Band 3 VOICES: woman, man.
ACCOMPANIMENT: 2 flutes, French horn, tuba, percussion.
FORM: Introduction; Vocal, *v. 1;* Interlude; Vocal, *v. 2;* Interlude; Vocal, *v. 3;* Coda.

Concept TIMBRE: Sounds have distinctive qualities which can help suggest ideas.

Discover After children have enjoyed listening to this song, which will be familiar to many, place a variety of classroom instruments in view. Include among them instruments heard in the recording, such as the **triangle, jingle bells, wood blocks,** and **xylophone.** Include others, such as sand blocks, drums, and resonator bells, which are not heard.

WHAT INSTRUMENTS THAT YOU HAVE PLAYED CAN YOU HEAR IN THE MUSIC? LISTEN CAREFULLY! WHEN YOU THINK YOU RECOGNIZE AN INSTRUMENT, RAISE YOUR HAND. After children have listened, choose a boy or girl to come to the instrument table and find one of the instruments he has heard.

Verse 1: xylophone and triangle

Refrain: jingle bells and wood blocks

Invite children to plan their own accompaniment, using these or other instruments. WHY ARE THESE GOOD INSTRUMENTS TO USE? WHAT SOUNDS DO THEY SUGGEST? Decide that the **xylophone** slithers up and down, like Santa climbing down and up the chimney; the **jingle bells** might be the bells on the reindeer harnesses; the **wood blocks** sound like reindeer hooves.

Listen again for other instruments. SOMETIMES YOU WILL HEAR INSTRUMENTS THAT SOUND LOW; SOMETIMES YOU WILL HEAR HIGH INSTRUMENTS. WHICH DO YOU HEAR DURING THE FIRST VERSE? (Mostly low; the tuba and horn.) RAISE YOUR HAND WHEN YOU HEAR A HIGH INSTRUMENT BEGIN. (During the refrain the flute is heard.)

Extend Have the children dramatize this song. They might pantomime the actions as suggested by the words. Santa may even have a solo part for "Ho, ho, ho!" in the refrain.

Costumes are never necessary for girls and boys to enjoy a dramatization. However, if you would like quick, simple costumes for the reindeer and Santa, use paper bags and construction paper and follow the directions shown with the diagrams on page 77.

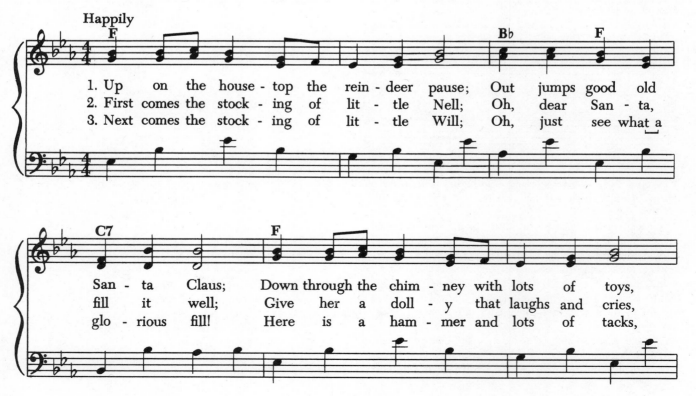

Happily

1. Up on the house-top the rein-deer pause; Out jumps good old
2. First comes the stock-ing of lit-tle Nell; Oh, dear San-ta,
3. Next comes the stock-ing of lit-tle Will; Oh, just see what a

San-ta Claus; Down through the chim-ney with lots of toys,
fill it well; Give her a doll-y that laughs and cries,
glo-rious fill! Here is a ham-mer and lots of tacks,

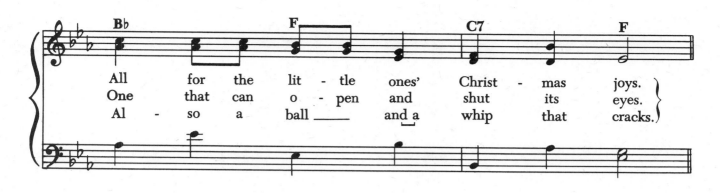

All for the lit - tle ones' Christ - mas joys.
One that can o - pen and shut its eyes.
Al - so a ball ____ and a whip that cracks.

Refrain

Ho, ho, ho! who would-n't go? Ho, ho, ho! who would-n't go?__

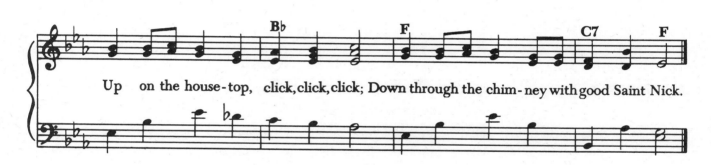

Up on the house-top, click, click, click; Down through the chim-ney with good Saint Nick.

Use construction paper for antlers,
eyes, and a red nose for Rudolph.

Cut the top
out to here.

To form a nose,
fold in sides and staple.

Cut away as marked.

Cut ears from the scraps
and staple on.

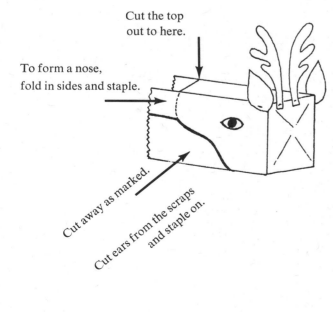

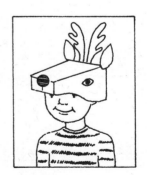

Cut out a round hole for the face,
and arches on the bottom for shoulders.

Use cotton and construction paper
for beard, eyebrows, and a cap.

Away in a Manger

Traditional

Key: F Starting Tone: C(5)

Meter: $\frac{3}{4}$ $\left(\frac{3}{\unicode{x2669}}\right)$

DT/ Record 4 Side A Band 4 VOICES: children's choir.
ACCOMPANIMENT: recorder, electric harpsichord, acoustic guitar, marimba, percussion.
FORM: Introduction; Vocal; Interlude; Vocal; Coda.

Concept EXPRESSIVE TOTALITY: Musical elements may be combined to suggest a feeling or an idea.

Discover Review lullabies that the children have learned, such as "Sleep, Baby, Sleep," page 8 and "Goodnight," page 18. WHAT KIND OF MUSIC DO WE USUALLY SING FOR LULLABIES? (Quiet, gently rocking melodies that do not move too quickly.)

LISTEN TO THIS SONG ABOUT THE BABY JESUS. WOULD IT MAKE A GOOD LULLABY? WHY?

Some children may pretend to rock the baby, responding to the movement in threes. Add to the "rocking" feeling of the song by letting one child play the following pattern on the glockenspiel.

(play four times)

1. A - way in a man - ger, no crib for a bed, The lit - tle Lord
2. The cat - tle are low - ing, the ba - by a - wakes, But lit - tle Lord

Je - sus laid down his sweet head. The stars in the sky____ looked
Je - sus, no cry - ing he makes. I love Thee, Lord Je - sus, look

down where he lay, The lit - tle Lord Je - sus a - sleep on the hay.
down from the sky, And stay by my cra - dle till morn - ing is nigh.

DT/ Record 4   Side A   Band 5 VOICES:
duet - soprano and alto.
ACCOMPANIMENT: 2 trumpets, percussion,
guitar, bass, drum.
FORM: Introduction; *v. 1;* Interlude;
Instrumental; Interlude; *v. 2.*

Christmas Song

Puerto Rican Folk Song
Adapted by Ruth DeCesare

Key: F Minor   Starting Tone: C(5)

Meter: $\frac{2}{4}$ ($\begin{smallmatrix}2\\ \end{smallmatrix}$)

THIS IS A CHRISTMAS SONG FROM PUERTO RICO. THE CHIL-
DREN WHO LIVE THERE SING ABOUT GIFTS WHICH THEY
FIND IN THE OCEAN NEAR THEIR HOMES AND BRING TO
THEIR FRIENDS.

Concept   STRUCTURE: Music is made up of sections.

Discover   Help children sense the four phrases. Ask them
to "mirror" each **phrase** by moving their right arms in an
arc. Start with the arm across the waist, pointing to the
left.

Other Concept   PITCH: High and low melody patterns
may be sounded simultaneously.

Discover   Ask children to listen carefully to the recording
and compare the sound of the voice during verse one and
verse two. Help them to hear that two voices are singing
verse two, and that one voice is a little lower than the
other one.

To help children sense the differences, ask one child to
play this pattern on the bells.

Ask another child to play this pattern. (Use two sets of
bells.)

Have them play the two patterns, one after another. Then
help them play their two patterns at the same time.

1. We greet   you for Christ - mas, this hol - i - day gay.
2. We're here   with a gift   from the o - cean so blue,

We come   with a song   and a pres - ent to - day.
With bright   pearls and sea - shells the o - cean once knew.

pres - ent to - day.
o - cean once knew.

Santa Claus Is Comin' to Town

Music by J. Fred Coats
Words by Haven Gillespie

Key: C   Starting Tone: G(5)

Meter: $\frac{2}{2}$ ($\frac{2}{\text{♩}}$)

Many children will be somewhat familiar with this popular Christmas song. However, urge them to listen carefully to the recording until they are sure of the words and melody before they attempt to sing it.

Concept STRUCTURE: Music is made up of sections which are the same or different.

Discover Ask children to sing the first part of the song (through the first "Santa Claus is coming to town"). As they sing, draw a face on the chalkboard.

Ask them to sing the second part through the second "Santa Claus is coming to town." Draw a face that is the same as the first.

WHO CAN TELL ME WHY I DREW TWO FACES EXACTLY ALIKE TO SHOW OUR MUSIC? WHY DIDN'T I DRAW TWO DIFFERENT FACES? Help children sense that these two parts have exactly the **same melody,** even though the words are different. If necessary, sing each part on a neutral syllable. CAN YOU TELL WHICH PART I'M SINGING? SHALL I DRAW A NEW FACE FOR THE NEXT PART OF OUR MUSIC? OR CAN I DRAW THE SAME ONE AGAIN? (New, because the music is different.) Decide that the last face could be like the first two faces. The design will be:

DT/ **Record 4   Side A   Band 6**   VOICES: children's choir.
ACCOMPANIMENT: alto sax, trumpet, French horn, trombone, percussion, celesta, guitar, bass, drums.
FORM: Introduction; Vocal; Instrumental; Vocal.

Other Concept TEXTURE: A melody pattern may be used to accompany another melody.

Discover Children may add an accompaniment to learn that more than one thing can "happen at once" in music.

For sections 1, 2, and 4

Bass xylophone (Phrase 1):

Alto xylophone (Phrase 2):

Wood block or rhythm sticks:

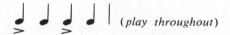 (*play throughout*)

For section 3 (mm. 17–24)

Glockenspiel:

Triangle or finger cymbals:

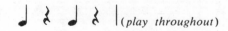 (*play throughout*)

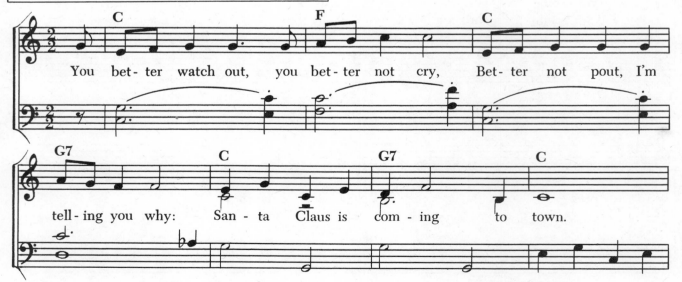

You bet-ter watch out, you bet-ter not cry, Bet-ter not pout, I'm tell-ing you why: San-ta Claus is com-ing to town.

80

Scatter the Bon Bons
Echen Confites

Mexican Folk Song
English words by Barbara Andress

Key: C   Starting Tone: E(3)

Meter: $\frac{3}{8}$ $\left(\frac{3}{\flat}\right)$

DT/ Record 4   Side A   Band 7   VOICES: children's choir.
ACCOMPANIMENT: 2 trumpets, marimba, guitar, bass.
FORM: Introduction; *v. 1* (English); Interlude; *v. 1;* (Spanish) Interlude; *v. 2;* Interlude; *v. 3;* Interlude; *v. 4;* Coda.

This song is sung by boys and girls in Mexico as they break the piñata. The piñata is a gaily decorated cardboard or paper container, usually in the shape of an animal. It is filled with nuts and candies and suspended in the middle of the room. Each child is blindfolded in turn and given one chance to break the piñata by striking it with a stick. When the piñata is broken, the candies scatter all over the floor and everyone scrambles to get his share.

Concept   DURATION: Rhythms move with steady beats, some of which are accented.

Discover   Listen to the music and talk about the meaning of the words.

PRETEND YOU ARE THE ONE WHO IS STRIKING THE PIÑATA. CAN YOU "SWING" WITH YOUR STICK AT THE HANGING PIÑATA? Help children swing with the **accented beat** by playing the finger cymbals on the first beat of each measure.

Choose two children to accompany the class as they sing. One may play the **steady beat** on the rhythm sticks while the other plays the finger cymbals on the **accented beats.**

Extend   Children may take turns swinging at the piñata as they might do at a Mexican Christmas party. Line up four children. The rest stand in a circle, clapping with the accented beat. With the first statement of the melody, the first child steps to center of the ring and tries to strike the piñata. The second child must be ready to start his turn when the next verse begins, and so on until the music is ended. Be sure you strike "with the music," or you will lose your turn!

Other Concept   PITCH: Groups of pitches may sound simultaneously to support a melodic line. Accompany the song on the autoharp. RAISE YOUR HAND WHEN I NEED TO CHANGE THE SOUNDS OF THE AUTOHARP SO THAT IT WILL SOUND RIGHT WITH THE MELODY YOU ARE SINGING.

Pronunciation for the Spanish follows.

eh-tchen cawn-fee-tays

eeh cah-nay-loh-nays

pah-rah lohs neen-yohs

kay sohn mui trah-go-nays

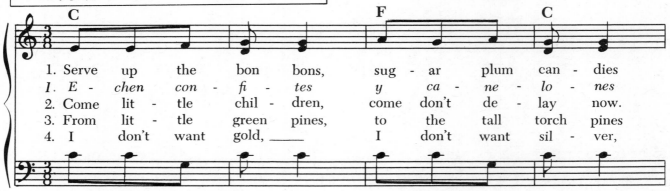

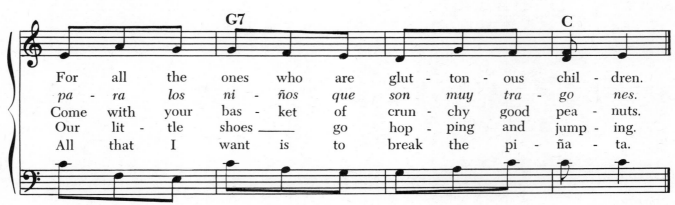

1. Serve up the bon bons, sug-ar plum can-dies
1. E-chen con-fi-tes y ca-ne-lo-nes
2. Come lit-tle chil-dren, come don't de-lay now.
3. From lit-tle green pines, to the tall torch pines
4. I don't want gold, ___ I don't want sil-ver,

For all the ones who are glut-ton-ous chil-dren.
pa-ra los ni-ños que son muy tra-go-nes.
Come with your bas-ket of crun-chy good pea-nuts.
Our lit-tle shoes ___ go hop-ping and jump-ing.
All that I want is to break the pi-ña-ta.

82

Record 4 Side B Band 1 VOICE: man
ACCOMPANIMENT: string quartet, flute.
FORM: Introduction; Vocal, *v. 1;*
Instrumental (vocal on "Tiddely Pom");
Vocal, *v. 2.*

Pooh's Song

Music by W. S. Haynie
Words by A. A. Milne

Key: F Starting Tone: C(5)

Meter: $\frac{6}{8}$ $\left(\frac{2}{\bullet.}\right)$

Concept PITCH: Melodies move up and down by steps and skips.

Discover Show these pictures on charts.

HOW DO YOU THINK EACH PATTERN WILL SOUND? WHEN WILL IT MOVE UP? DOWN? WHICH ONE WILL MOVE BY STEPS, WHICH BY SKIPS? Describe the pattern of each.

1. start-skip-skip-skip or start-up-down-down
2. start-same-step-step or start-same-up-down

LISTEN TO THIS SONG. CAN YOU FIND PATTERNS THAT MOVE THE WAY THE SOUND PICTURES MOVE? ("The more it snows" and "Tiddely pom".)

Invite children to join in on the "Tiddely pom" pattern

each time it is sung. Then encourage them to sing the complete song without assistance.

Extend Put out these bells, or use only these bars on the alto xylophone:

C D E F G A B♭ C

WHO CAN FIND THE PATTERN FOR "TIDDELY POM"? WILL YOU USE LOW BELLS OR HIGH ONES? WILL YOU STEP OR SKIP? Look at the chart to help you decide. A child may play the pattern each time it appears in the song.

Some children may be able to find the pattern for "The more it snows." It might be helpful to remind them that they must make a **big skip** up, then **smaller skips** down.

The words of this song appear in the story "Pooh Builds a House" from *The House at Pooh Corner,* by A. A. Milne. You may wish to read the story to the children after they have learned the song.

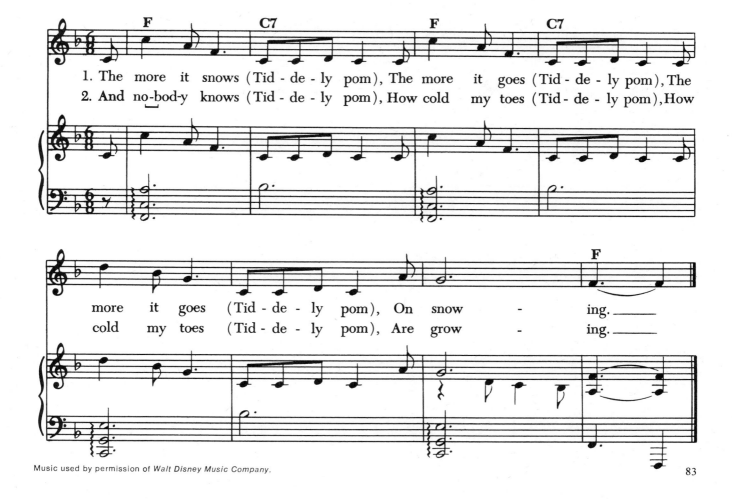

Music used by permission of *Walt Disney Music Company.*

Animal Crackers in My Soup

Music by Ray Henderson
Lyrics by Ted Kochler and Irving Caesar

Key: C   Starting Tone: G(5)

Meter: $\frac{2}{2}$ ($\frac{2}{\text{♩}}$)

DT/ Record 4   Side B   Band 2 VOICES: children's choir
ACCOMPANIMENT: flute, trumpet, trombone, French horn, percussion, piano, bass, guitar, drums.
FORM: Introduction; Vocal; Instrumental; Vocal.

Concept STRUCTURE: Music is made up of phrases which are the same or different.

Discover Listen to the entire song and enjoy the amusing words. Identify the different animals that are mentioned. Make a simple mask of each animal. The mask should be large enough so that the child can hold it in front of his face.

WE CAN MAKE OUR OWN ANIMAL CRACKER GAME! WHO WILL BE OUR MONKEY TO MARCH DURING THE FIRST PHRASE? Give one child a monkey mask and let him step to the music during the first phrase. (Measures 1-4.)

LISTEN CAREFULLY. DO WE NEED ANOTHER MONKEY, OR A DIFFERENT ANIMAL TO JOIN OUR PARADE? THIS MUSIC WILL HELP YOU DECIDE. Since the music is **different,** a new animal is needed. (A rabbit.)

Follow a similar procedure until eight animals have been chosen, each with an appropriate mask to show **same** and **different phrases.**

| monkey | rabbit | monkey | rabbit |
| lion | tiger | monkey | rabbit |

Suggest that all the "rabbits" work together to plan similar dance movements. The "monkeys" should also plan their motions together. The "lion" and "tiger" may plan their dances individually.

Extend Listen to "Circus Music" from *The Red Pony*, p. 87, and find the **same** and **different** sections in this music. Children may wear the masks used for "Animal Crackers" or make new ones to suggest various circus characters.

Other Concept DURATION: Rhythm patterns are made up of long and short sounds.

Discover Play this rhythm on drum or triangle.

Ask children to describe the pattern in terms of **short** and **long.** Help them to decide that the last sound should be "lo-ng" because it is the longest sound of all.

HOW MANY TIMES DO YOU HEAR THIS PATTERN AS WE SING THE REFRAIN OF OUR SONG? (The pattern is heard exactly in measures 1–2, 3–4, 9–10, 11–12, 25–26, 31–32. Measures 15–16, 27–28 are similar.)

Invite children to tap this pattern each time it is repeated.

An - i - mal crack - ers in my soup, mon - keys and rab - bits loop the loop.

Gosh, oh gee, but I have fun, swal - low- in' an - i - mals one by one.

In ev-ery bowl of soup I see, li-ons and ti-gers watch-ing me. I make 'em jump right thru a hoop, those an-i-mal crack-ers in my soup. When I get hold of the "Big bad wolf," I just push him un-der to drown. Then I bite him in a mil-lion bits, and I gob-ble him right down. When they're in-side me where it's dark, I walk a-roun' like "No-ah's ark." I stuff my tum-my like a "Goop," with an-i-mal crack-ers in my soup.

Trot, Pony, Trot

Chinese Folk Song

Pentatonic   Starting Tone: B♭ (5)
Autoharp Key: D minor   Starting Tone: A(5)

Meter: 2/4 (♩)

Record 4   Side B   Band 3   VOICES: children's choir.
ACCOMPANIMENT: percussion.
FORM: Instrumental; Vocal; Instrumental.

Concept TIMBRE: Sound sources can be identified by their distinctive qualities.

Discover After listening to the complete song, ask children to listen carefully to the introduction. WHICH INSTRUMENTS DO YOU HEAR THAT WE HAVE PLAYED IN THE CLASSROOM? Children might mention the wood block, xylophone, bells, drum.

The introduction begins with the **wood block,** joined by the **bells** and **xylophones.** The **finger cymbals** may also be heard.

Extend Invite children to develop their own accompaniment, based on patterns they have heard.

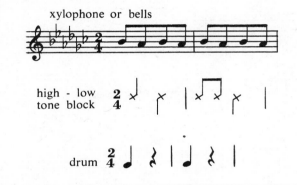

Other Concepts DURATION: Rhythm patterns are made up of long and short sounds.

Discover As children plan their own instrumental introduction and accompaniment, help them make their own "score." Listen to each instrument and challenge the children to express its rhythm in terms of **long** and **short** as shown.

tone block

▬ ▬▬ ▬▬ ▬▬ ▬▬ ▬

xylophone or bells

▬ ▬ ▬ ▬ ▬ ▬ ▬ ▬ ▬ ▬ ▬ ▬

PITCH: Melodies move by steps and skips.

Discover When children have determined the rhythm pattern for each part, help them determine the **melody patterns.** Put out the appropriate instrument, with only the needed bars showing. Help children show the pattern first with line notation, then with numbers.

xylophone or bells

5   5 5

1   1

5   4   5   4   5   4   5   4

Trot, trot, po-ny trot, Trot to Grand-ma's gate-way,

She comes out and calls the dog, And then we ride on,

   Used by permission of Mrs. Mabel L. Fitzhugh.

jog - a - jog. Trot, trot, trot, trot, trot, trot.

Record 9 Side A Band 6
St. Louis Symphony Orchestra,
André Previn, conductor.
TIME: 4:40

Dream March and Circus Music
from *The Red Pony*

by Aaron Copland
BORN 1900

These compositions are from a suite composed originally as background music for the film *The Red Pony*, based on a tale by John Steinbeck. It is a story of a ten-year-old boy, Jody, and his life on a California ranch. In the scene accompanied by these compositions, Jody is daydreaming. He first imagines that he is leading an army of knights, all dressed in silver armor. During the second composition he is the ringmaster at a circus.

You will wish to introduce the two compositions on different days and allow children to become familiar with each. Later, children will enjoy listening to both during the same lesson and comparing the moods of the two movements.

Dream March

Concept   MUSICAL CONTROLS: Contrasts in loud and soft help to communicate a musical idea.

Discover   LISTEN TO SOME MUSIC. IS THIS A MARCH OR A LULLABY? (A march, because of the use of trumpet, brass and drums; the music moves with a strong beat in twos.) THE TITLE OF THIS MUSIC IS "DREAM MARCH." WHY DO YOU THINK THIS MUSIC IS CALLED A "DREAM MARCH"? (The quiet beginning and ending.)

Extend   Children may dramatize the march. One child may be Jody and begin to march as the trumpet announces the fanfare. He should step with the rhythm of the beat heard in the tuba part. Other children may join, one at a time, as the fanfare theme is heard in other instruments. With the sound of the snare drum, all begin marching together behind Jody. At the end children might cease marching, a few at a time, and sink to a sleeping position until only Jody is left.

WHAT DO YOU SUPPOSE JODY WAS PRETENDING TO BE AS HE WAS DREAMING? WHAT WERE YOU PRETENDING?

The entire composition is based on musical ideas drawn from the trumpet's fanfare theme.

Circus Music

Concept   EXPRESSIVE TOTALITY: Musical elements can be combined to suggest a mood or a feeling.

Discover   IN THIS MUSIC, JODY DREAMS OF A CIRCUS. CLOSE YOUR EYES AND IMAGINE YOU ARE AT A CIRCUS, WATCHING THE ACTS IN THE BIG RING. ARE THE SAME ACTS GOING ON ALL THE TIME? (Probably not, because the music changes.)

As children listen again, help them notice the different sections of the music. Each section is distinguished by different instrumentation and melodies. (See "The Music" for details.)

Extend   Children may plan their own circus. The general plan might be:

I.   Triumphal entrance of all circus performers, led by the Ringmaster. (As children dance and bow, guide them to notice that the phrase lengths vary.)

II.   Different performers present their acts.

III.   The performers repeat their triumphal march around the ring and end with a grand bow.

The Music:

Section I: Trumpet announces the entrance of performers (8 measures). Woodwinds play a melody which is broken up into patterns of different lengths. The section ends with a sustained chord.

Section II: In three parts.

1. Woodwinds play a rapidly moving melody; trumpets play a descending pattern.

2. Woodwinds play a new melody; snare drum announces the end of this part.

3. Woodwinds and trumpet play a melody which "scoops" down and up.

Section III: The same as Section I.

Use Your Own Sounds (20–21)

Concept DURATION: Patterns of rhythm include long and short sounds.

Discover Examine the illustrations on page 20 of the pupil's book. Encourage children to experiment and discover many different body sounds in addition to those illustrated.

Invite the children to use the body sounds suggested on page 21 and follow the notation. CAN YOUR FOOT TAP LONG AND SHORT? Discuss which notes represent **long** and **short sounds.** Use the Jumbo Book or show the notation as each child makes a tapping sound with his foot. Give children a clue as to when you will begin, such as "Ready, begin." (Chant in the tempo you expect them to tap.) You may need to continue to use words such as "tap tap—tap tap tap."

Repeat the pattern over and over. When children can tap the pattern easily, begin to chant:

One, two, show your shoe.
Three, four, shut the door.
Five, six, pick up sticks.
Seven, eight, lay them straight.
Nine, ten, big fat hen!

CAN YOUR TONGUE CLICK? WILL IT MAKE SHORT OR LONG SOUNDS? Look at the notation of the second pattern and compare it with the **long** and **short** lines in the first pattern. Decide that the tongue-clicking sounds will all be **short.**

When children can maintain the clicking pattern easily, divide the class into two groups. Begin the clicking sound with one group. The other group may sing or chant:

Cobbler, cobbler, mend my shoe.
Get it done by half past two.
Do it neat, and do it strong,
I will pay you when it's done.

LOOK AT YOUR BOOKS AGAIN. CAN YOU CLAP YOUR HANDS AS YOU SEE THE PICTURES OF SOUND? Guide them to clap the four "long" sounds (represented by quarter notes). Make up simple rhymes to help the children clap together as they follow the notation.

One two three four
Listen and I'll clap some more.

CAN YOU NOT CLAP YOUR HANDS WHEN THERE IS NO PICTURE OF SOUND? Help children remember not to clap by making up simple chants such as:

One two out three
I will watch so you can't catch me!

Invite children to substitute other body sounds and repeat the patterns shown on the page. Cut quarter and eighth notes from felt or construction paper and arrange new patterns for children to perform with different body sounds.

Extend Introduce "This Old Man." Encourage children to use different body sounds to accompany each verse.

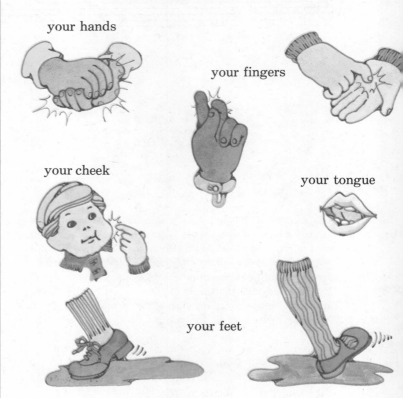

USE YOUR OWN SOUNDS

Make different sounds with

your hands

your fingers

your cheek

your tongue

your feet

How many different sounds can you make with your body?

20

DT/ Record 4 Side B Band 4 VOICES: children's choir.
ACCOMPANIMENT: flute, bassoon, violin, cello, percussion, trumpet, trombone
FORM: Introduction; *v. 1*; Interlude; *v. 2*; Interlude; *v. 3*; Interlude; *v. 4*; Interlude; *v. 5*; Interlude; *v. 6*; Interlude; *v. 7*; Interlude; *v. 8*; Interlude; *v. 9*; Interlude; *v. 10*; Coda.

This Old Man

Traditional

Key: F   Starting Tone: C(5)

Meter: $\frac{2}{4}$ $\left(\frac{2}{\quarternote}\right)$

Additional verses:

4. This old man, he played four,
   He played nick-nack on my door.

5. This old man, he played five,
   He played nick-nack on my hive.

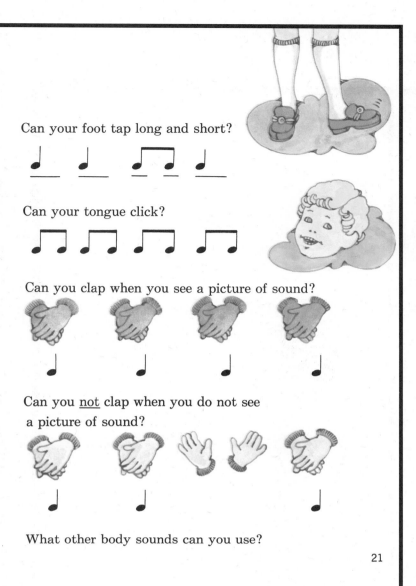

Can your foot tap long and short?

Can your tongue click?

Can you clap when you see a picture of sound?

Can you <u>not</u> clap when you do not see a picture of sound?

What other body sounds can you use?

21

6. This old man, he played six,
   He played nick-nack on my sticks.

7. This old man, he played seven,
   He played nick-nack up to heav'n.

8. This old man, he played eight,
   He played nick-nack on my pate.

9. This old man, he played nine,
   He played nick-nack on my spine.

10. This old man, he played ten,
    He played nick-nack back again.

Concept RHYTHM: Music moves with a steady beat over which a pattern of long and short tones may sound.

Discover As children learn the many verses, suggest that they plan actions which move with the **steady beat.** For example:

measures 1–2   Clap hands.

measures 3–6   Tap appropriate part of body on each beat.

    1. Tap thumbs together.

    2. Tap on shoes.

    3. Tap on knees.

    4. Tap on forehead.

    5. "Chase bees away."

    6. Tap index finger.

    7. Wave hands above head.

    8. Tap top of head.

    9. Tap on backbone.

    10. Tap on thumbs.

measures 7-8   Move hands around each other in a rolling motion.

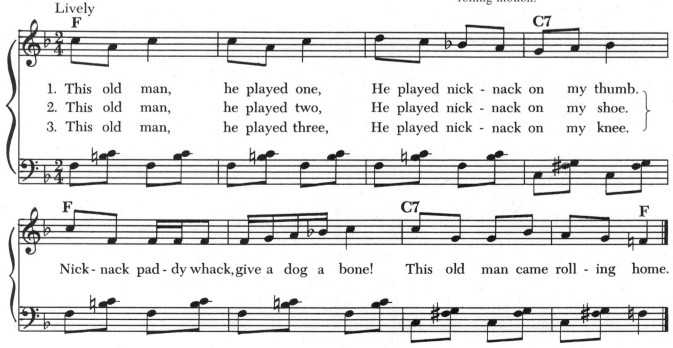

Lively

1. This old man, he played one, He played nick-nack on my thumb.
2. This old man, he played two, He played nick-nack on my shoe.
3. This old man, he played three, He played nick-nack on my knee.

Nick-nack pad-dy whack, give a dog a bone! This old man came roll-ing home.

Response to Patterns of Sound, No. 2

Concept   DURATION: Rhythm patterns are made up of long and short sounds.

Discover   Introduce this activity by giving the following instructions and playing the patterns on the tambourine.

LISTEN TO MY SOUNDS.

 tambourine:

LISTEN TO ANOTHER SOUND.

tr 〰〰

Ask children to stand in pairs, side by side, and to place the palms of their hands together like this:

WALK WHEN YOU HEAR:

STOP AND MOVE THE HANDS THAT ARE TOUCHING IN A CIRCLE FOR AS LONG AS YOU HEAR MY SOUND:

CHANGE THE DIRECTION OF YOUR CIRCLE EACH TIME YOU HEAR THE LONG SOUND.

LISTEN AND MOVE.

WHO WOULD LIKE TO TELL THE GROUP HOW TO MOVE BY PLAYING THE SOUNDS?

Extend   Play the recording. Ask children to use **long** and **short** movements as they respond to the music. WILL YOU USE THE SAME MOVEMENTS THROUGHOUT THE ENTIRE PIECE? (No, the middle section is different.) Encourage children to vary their movement responses by seeking different levels (in space) and directions. Children may wish to work in pairs or individually.

Record 4   Side A   Band 5

DT/ Record 4   Side B   Band 6 VOICES: woman, man.
ACCOMPANIMENT: harpsichord, recorder, viola, cello.
FORM: Instrumental; Vocal; Coda.

Nothing But Sing

Traditional

Key: D   Starting Tone: D(1)
Autoharp Key: C   Starting Tone: C(1)

Meter:

Concept DURATION: Music moves with steady beats which may be grouped by accents.

Discover After children have engaged in the activities described on page 90, help them transfer their feeling for long and short sounds to $\frac{3}{4}$ meter. Play the triangle. Dampen the sound at the end of the first pattern.

STEP WHEN YOU HEAR:

POINT WITH YOUR TOE WHEN YOU HEAR:

(left toe)

Repeat the following pattern over and over until the children can sense the **movement in threes.**

Extend Play the instrumental to "Nothing but Sing." CAN YOU HEAR THE PATTERN IN THE MUSIC? CAN YOU STEP WITH IT?

WHO CAN PLAY THE PATTERN WHILE SOME SING AND OTHERS MOVE? The child may choose an appropriate instrument.

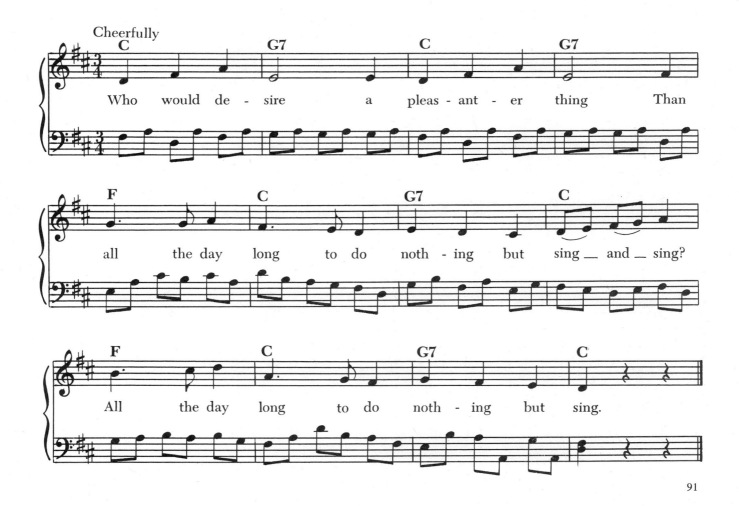

Cheerfully

Who would de-sire a pleas-ant-er thing   Than
all   the day   long   to do   noth-ing   but   sing __ and __ sing?
All   the day   long   to do   noth-ing   but   sing.

Let's Have a Parade (22–23)

Concept DURATION: Rhythm patterns include sound and silence and move in relation to an underlying beat.

Discover Ask children to look at the picture at the top of page 22 in the book (or use the Jumbo Book).

HERE ARE PICTURES OF YOUR HANDS CLAPPING . . . AND NOT CLAPPING . . . . (Point to the first box.)

HERE IS A PICTURE OF SOUNDS THAT SAY "MAKE A SOUND" AND "DO NOT MAKE A SOUND." (Point to the second box.)

CAN YOU CLAP THESE PICTURES OF SOUND? READY BEGIN! You may need to say:

clap out clap out clap clap clap out

LET'S HAVE A PARADE! As children clap the rhythm pattern or play it on a drum, speak Robert Louis Stevenson's poem "Marching Song."

Bring the comb and play up-on it, Marching here we come.
 Willie cocks his highland bonnet, Johnny beats the drum.
(*Make up a tambourine part; continue throughout piece.*)

Mary Jane com - mands the party, Peter leads the rear;
Feet in time a - lert and hearty, Each a gren-a- dier.
(*Make up a cymbal part; continue throughout piece.*)

All in a most martial manner, Marching double quick
While the napkin, like a banner, Waves up-on a stick.

> **DT/ Record 4 Side B Band 7** VOICES: children's choir.
> ACCOMPANIMENT: trumpet, trombone, French horn, piccolo, xylophone, piano, bass, guitar, drums.
> FORM: Introduction; *v. 1;* Interlude; *v. 2;* Interlude; Instrumental; *v. 3;* Interlude; *v. 4;* Coda.

Can you clap this?

Now clap this

22

After the poem has been chanted, suggest that children bring their parade to a halt by:

1. stopping all sounds or
2. getting softer as the parade fades away down the street.

Have the class answer the questions in the pupil's book, page 23.

With spirit

1. Kick   your knees up,   step   in   time!   Kick   your knees up,   step   in   time!
2. Link   your el - bows,   step   in   time!   Link   your el - bows,   step   in   time!
3. Spin   a - bout and   step   in   time!   Spin   a - bout and   step   in   time!
4. 'Round   the chim - ney   step   in   time!   'Round   the chim - ney   step   in   time!

Let's have a parade!

When was our parade loudest? Softest?

23

Step in Time

Words and Music
By Richard M. Sherman
and Robert B. Sherman

Key: C   Starting Tone: E(3)

Meter: $\frac{2}{2}$ $\left(\frac{2}{\d}\right)$

Concept   DURATION: Music moves with a steady beat.

Discover   After children have created their own parade (as suggested in their books, pages 22–3), play this song for them.

WHAT KIND OF MUSIC IS THIS? WHAT HELPS YOU TO KNOW? Decide that it is a march, because it moves with a **steady beat.** Also, the instruments on the recording sound like a marching band.

Extend   Invite children to march around the room as they listen to the recording. When they know the melody, they may wish to use the percussion sounds they planned for their parade as an accompaniment to this marching song.

Other Concept   PITCH: Melodies move up and down by steps or skips.

Discover   This melody has a limited range and uses six tones of the C major scale (E F G A B C). Some children may be able to find the needed pitches and learn to play the complete melody.

Begin by helping children draw the melodic contour of each phrase, noticing when the melody **goes up, down,** or **stays the same** and when it steps or skips. Put each phrase on a separate chart. Notice the similarities between phrases one and two.

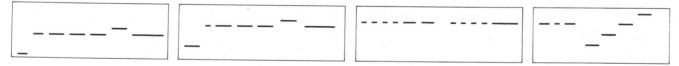

Put the charts in the Music Learning Center with the necessary bells (E F G A B C). Give individuals time to work by themselves to discover the melody.

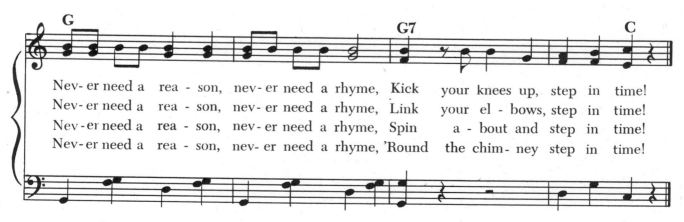

Nev-er need a rea-son, nev-er need a rhyme, Kick your knees up, step in time!
Nev-er need a rea-son, nev-er need a rhyme, Link your el-bows, step in time!
Nev-er need a rea-son, nev-er need a rhyme, Spin a-bout and step in time!
Nev-er need a rea-son, nev-er need a rhyme, 'Round the chim-ney step in time!

Children's March

By Edwin Franko Goldman
BORN 1878   DIED 1956

Record 9   Side A   Band 7
Northeast Louisiana State College
Concert Band, Joe Barry Mullins,
conductor.
TIME: 2:43

Concept STRUCTURE: Music is made up of sections.

Discover This march for band includes many familiar nursery melodies. Play the march in its entirety. Ask the children to raise their hands when they hear a melody they recognize. After they have listened, ask them to name the songs they know.

The other melodies may be identified for them at this time. Their order of appearance is as follows:

> Introduction
>
> Mary Had a Little Lamb
>
> Jingle Bells
>
> Sing A Song of Sixpence
>
> Farmer in the Dell
>
> (trumpet and drum interlude)
>
> Lazy Mary
>
> Hickory, Dickory, Dock
>
> Three Blind Mice
>
> Rockabye Baby

> Pop! Goes the Weasel
>
> London Bridge

Prepare a series of pictures to illustrate the songs. The sketches below could be used as a guide.

Select ten children. Give one picture to each child. Each child is to hold up his picture when he hears "his music" begin and put his picture down when his music ends.

Extend Divide the class into ten groups, one for each song. Each group is to march only when its melody is heard. IS THERE ANY TIME WHEN TWO GROUPS WILL MARCH AT THE SAME TIME? Help children hear that "Pop! Goes the Weasel" and "London Bridge" are combined at the end of the march.

Children may plan their own march, singing the songs they know, one after another, in any order they choose. Interludes between some songs might be played on drums and cymbals. Wood blocks, triangles, or other instruments might be played to keep a steady beat during the singing of the songs.

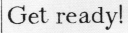

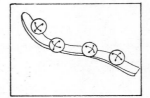
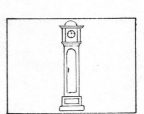

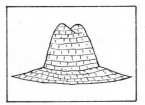

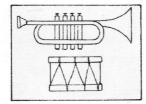

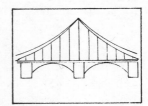

Record 4 Side B Band 8 VOICE: man.
ACCOMPANIMENT: woodwind quintet.
FORM: Introduction; Vocal, *v. 1*;
Instrumental; Vocal, *v. 2*; Coda.

Six Little Ducks

American Folk Song

Key: F   Starting Tone: A(3)

Meter: $\frac{4}{4}$ ($\frac{4}{\downarrow}$)

Concept DURATION: Rhythm patterns move in relation to an underlying beat.

Discover HERE IS ANOTHER PARADE! WHO IS "MARCHING"? Play the recording. Discover that this is a "duck parade." Choose six "ducks" to march in the parade. As the class sings or listens to the recording, suggest that the ducks parade down to the river bank in a single line. Notice how the children move as they "wibble, wobble, wibble, wobble." Some will move with each **beat:**

Some will move with the **accented beats:**

One child may choose to play either the **beat** or the **accented beats** on an instrument of his choice while the others move.

Extend WHICH WORDS MATCH THIS PATTERN?

Clap: short—short—long. Ask children to tap and chant the pattern: "quack, quack, quack."

Choose a child to play this pattern. A guiro might suggest the quacking sound of a duck. Show on the chalkboard the different patterns the children have reflected in their movement and sounds. Point out similarities and differences:

steady beat:

pattern:

accented beats:

Divide the class into three groups. Group 1 claps the **steady beat;** group 2 adds the **pattern,** then group 3 joins in on the **accents.** LISTEN TO THE WAY YOUR PATTERN SOUNDS IN RELATION TO THE OTHERS!

1. Six lit-tle ducks that I once knew, Fat ones, skin-ny ones,
2. Down to the riv-er they would go, Wib-ble,wob-ble, wib-ble,wob-ble,

fair ones too,
to and fro, } But the one lit-tle duck with a feath-er in his back,

He ruled the oth-ers with a quack, quack, quack, quack, quack, quack.

Poor Bird

Japanese Singing Game

Pentatonic   Starting Tone: A

Meter: $\frac{2}{4}$ ($\frac{2}{\downarrow}$)

Record 5   Side A   Band 1   VOICES: children's choir.
ACCOMPANIMENT: recorder, koto, flute, percussion.
FORM: Introduction; Vocal; Interlude; Vocal; Coda (instrumental fade-out).

Concept   PITCH: Melodies move up and down by steps or skips.

Discover   Put the following patterns on individual charts:

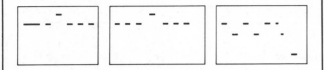

Talk about the "sound pictures." Describe each picture using terms such as "step up," "step down," "skip down."

LISTEN TO THIS SONG. CAN YOU FIND THE WORDS THAT MATCH THE FIRST PICTURE YOU SEE? Hold up only Chart 1. Help children decide that the first phrase ("Poor bird, you are so sad,") matches this picture.

Listen to the complete song; point to each picture as the children listen.

Extend   Some children will be able to learn to play the complete song. Put the charts (in the correct order) in the Music Learning Center with the bells E G A B.

Other Concepts   PITCH: Tones may be combined to create harmony.

Discover   The following patterns may be played to accompany "Poor Bird."

metallophone   alto xylophone

Add a percussion accompaniment to help children sense the movement in twos. Give one instrument to each child; play one after another, on the accented beat. The pattern is played three times.

drum   wood block   triangle   finger cymbals

TIME AND PLACE: Distinctive timbres may reflect the origin of the music.

Discover   Draw attention to the accompaniment played by **recorder, flute, koto,** and **percussion.** (A koto is a large stringed instrument; it is played by plucking the strings.) THIS SONG IS SUNG BY JAPANESE BOYS AND GIRLS. THE INSTRUMENTS YOU HEAR ARE OFTEN USED WITH THE MUSIC OF JAPAN.

Children may learn the Japanese game. All stand in a circle with hands joined. The person who is "it" sits in the center with eyes covered. As the class walks around the circle singing, one player goes quietly to the center and stands behind the seated player. On the words "All together, now fall down," everyone drops down. The player standing in the center sings "Who's behind you? Can you guess?" If the person who is "it" guesses correctly he returns to the circle and the second player becomes "it." If he misses, he remains in the center.

Poor bird, you are so sad, Sitting in your bamboo cage.

Will you sing a song for me, If I come and set you free?

All to - geth - er, now fall down. Who's be - hind you? Can you guess?

Small Group Event, No. 2

Concept MUSICAL CONTROLS: Sounds may be loud and soft, depending upon the materials used. Loud and soft sounds may express ideas.

Discover Help children to explore degrees of **loud** and **soft** with rattling sounds. Provide the following materials:

several paper cups with lids,

a portion each of dried rice, dried beans,

salt, and unpopped corn;

masking tape (to secure lids on cups).

Ask a small group of children to place equal portions of the various materials into separate paper cups. (A small amount will suffice.) Seal the cups with masking tape. Children should shake cups and decide which is the loudest and which is the softest. Ask children to place the cups in order from those having the **softest** sounds to those having the **loudest** sounds. Children may tell a sound story about something that is far away and comes closer. TELL ANOTHER SOUND STORY ABOUT SOMETHING THAT IS FAR AWAY, COMES CLOSER, THEN GOES FAR AWAY AGAIN.

Suggest that children plan their ideas together and then choose a leader to tell each child when to play. The groups may perform for the class. Discuss whether the class could or could not follow the sound story.

Extend Children may review "Parade" from *Divertissement* by Ibert, page 53. Remind children that this is a parade. Listen first. Play it a second time and ask the children to make a picture of the sound when it is far away, close, and far away again. WHEN IT IS FAR AWAY, USE TINY DOTS; WHEN IT COMES CLOSER, MAKE THE DOTS AND CIRCLES BIGGER AND BIGGER.

Have children fold a 12″ x 18″ sheet of paper twice lengthwise so that there are four spaces in which they may make their dots and circles. Tell the children to keep the dots fairly close together so they will have room for all of the music.

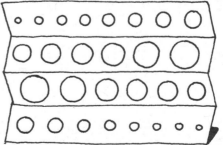

Ringo, Rango, Jingo

Words and Music by Janet Eucher

Key: C   Starting Tone C(1)

Meter: $\frac{2}{2}$ ($\frac{2}{\downarrow}$)

DT/ **Record 5   Side A   Band 2**   VOICES: children's choir.
ACCOMPANIMENT: trumpet, clarinet, viola, trombone, percussion.
FORM: Introduction; Vocal; Instrumental; Vocal; Coda.

Concept DURATION: The rhythm of a melody moves in relation to an underlying beat.

Discover Listen to the recording; invite children to comment about their own dreams of owning a pony to take care of.

As you play the recording again, ask the children to tap the **rhythm of the melody.** Next, play the **rhythm of the beat.** (This is tapped by the temple block on the recording.) Which rhythm seems to suggest the sounds of the pony's hooves? (The temple block pattern because it moves steadily and evenly.)

Children may add an accompaniment by tapping on a high-low tone block to give a clip-clop effect.

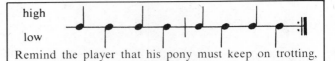

Remind the player that his pony must keep on trotting, even when the melody pauses at the end of phrases.

Other Concept STRUCTURE: Music is made up of phrases.

Discover Invite a few children to trot around the room while others sing and the accompanist plays the wood block. CAN YOU SHOW ME THE END OF EACH PHRASE BY TURNING YOUR PONY AROUND? (Children should turn on long tones "-ly," "me," "hay," "way.")

Rin - go, ran - go, jin - go, a - rid - ing mer - ri - ly

Up and down on my po - ny who takes good care of me.

I will cur - ry my po - ny and feed him oats and hay, A

lump of sug - ar nice and sweet, then we will ride a - way.

Exploring Music: the Third Quarter

Response to Accent

Concept DURATION: Music moves with steady beats, some of which may be accented.

Play the following sounds on the drum. Invite children to take a walk in the room. Children may go anywhere they wish but they "may not use the space that their neighbor is in!"

Ask children to step each time they hear the drum beat.

drum: ♩ ♩ ♩ ♩ ♩ ♩

LET'S MAKE A SOUND PATTERN FOR OUR WALK. (The teacher adds an accent on the first beat to form a pattern.) Ask children to count aloud as they walk with the drum.

$\frac{4}{4}$ ♩ ♩ ♩ ♩ :‖

Eliminate the counting aloud. Ask children to continue to walk with the beat while responding to the strong beat in one of the following ways:

step: ‖: ♩ ♩ ♩ ♩ :‖

other response (clap, stamp, "ho" "hup") ‖: ♩ 𝄾 𝄾 𝄾 :‖

KEEP ON WALKING WITH THE DRUM BEAT. WHEN YOU HEAR THE STRONG BEAT, CHANGE DIRECTION.

MAKE A STRAIGHT STICK.

ALTERNATE OPEN-CLOSE.

DISCOVER HOW YOUR FEET MOVE DIFFERENTLY WHEN YOU "OPEN AND WALK" AND "CLOSE AND WALK." WILL YOUR STEPS BE THE SAME? (Open—larger steps; close—smaller steps.)

Extend Listen to Schumann's "Soldier's March," page 5. Invite children to use their many movement ideas to respond to this music.

Humpty Dumpty (24–25)

Traditional Melody
Words from Mother Goose

Key C: Starting Tone: C

Meter: $\frac{6}{8}$ ($\left.\begin{smallmatrix}2\\ \text{♩.}\end{smallmatrix}\right.$)

Concept DURATION: Patterns of rhythm may move evenly or unevenly.

Discover In response to the question in the pupil's book, divide the class into two groups. Ask Group 1 to chant the pattern in the first box and Group 2 to chant the pattern in the second box. Ask them to clap the rhythm of the words as they chant them.

ONE OF OUR GROUPS IS CLAPPING AN EVEN PATTERN. THE OTHER GROUP IS CLAPPING AN UNEVEN PATTERN. WHICH GROUP IS CLAPPING AN UNEVEN PATTERN? (Group 1.) WHICH GROUP IS CLAPPING AN EVEN PATTERN? (Group 2.) CAN YOU CLAP YOUR PATTERNS AS YOU SING THE SONG?

Extend Invite children to sit on the floor and tap the rhythm of their parts on the floor. The purpose of this activity is to help children develop the left-right concept necessary for reading notation.

Ask each child to raise his left hand. When you are sure he has identified "left," ask him to place that hand slightly on the side, on the floor.

CAN YOU TAP YOUR RHYTHM WITH YOUR RIGHT HAND? MAKE YOUR TAPS TRAVEL FROM LEFT TO RIGHT FOR EACH PHRASE. Guide children to begin with right hand close to left and "travel" to the right. They must return their right hands to the left to begin the second phrase, then move to the right again.

Ask groups to exchange patterns. Group 1 will now tap the even rhythm while Group 2 taps the uneven rhythm.

Humpty Dumpty

Can you chant this?

Hump-ty Dump-ty sat on a wall

Hump-ty Dump-ty had a great fall.

All the king's hor-ses and all the king's men,

Could-n't put Hump-ty to-geth-er a-gain.

Clap the patterns.
Sing the song.

24

Hump-ty Dump-ty sat on a wall,   Hump-ty Dump-ty had a great fall.

Make two groups.

Which group begins with even sounds?

Which group begins with uneven sounds?

Tap your patterns on the floor.

_ _ _ _ _ _ _

_ _ _ _ _ _ _

_ _ _ _ _ _ _

_ _ _ _ _ _ _

25

Give children added experience in sensing **even-uneven rhythms** by teaching them the following chants. Decide with the class which move **evenly**, which **unevenly**.

Uneven:
  One po-ta-to, two po-ta-to, three po-ta-to, four;
  Five po-ta-to, six po-ta-to, sev'n po-ta-to, more.

  In-try min-try, cut-rey-corn,
  Ap-ple seed and ap-ple thorn,
  Wire, briar, lim-ber lock,
  Twen-ty geese to make a flock;
  Some flew east, some flew west,
  Some flew over the cuc-koo nest.

Even:
  Bell-horses, bell-horses,
  What time of day?
  One o'clock, two o'clock,
  Off and a-way.

  En-gine, en-gine num-ber nine
  Run-ning down Chi-ca-go line,
  See her spar-kle, see her shine,
  En-gine, en-gine num-ber nine.

DT/ Record 5   Side A   Band 3   VOICES: children's choir.
ACCOMPANIMENT: viola, clarinet, trumpet, trombone, piano, percussion.
FORM: Introduction; Vocal; Interlude; Vocal; Coda.

All the king's hors-es and all the king's men, Could-n't put Hump-ty to-geth-er a-gain.

Have You Seen My Honey Bears?

Traditional Yiddish Tune
Original English Text by Ruth Rubin

Key: D Starting Tone: D(1)
Autoharp Key: C Starting Tone: C(1)

Meter: $\frac{3}{4}$ $\left(\frac{3}{\text{♩}}\right)$

DT/ Record 5 Side A Band 4 VOICES: children's choir.
ACCOMPANIMENT: flute, bassoon, violin, cello, percussion, trumpet, trombone.
FORM: Introduction; *v. 1;* Interlude; *v. 2;* Interlude; *v. 3;* Interlude; *v. 4.*

Concept PITCH: Melodies move up and down by steps and skips.

Discover Put the following sound picture on a chart.

HERE IS A PART OF A NEW SONG. HOW DO YOU THINK IT WILL MOVE? HOW DO YOU THINK IT UP? DOWN? STAY THE SAME? Guide children to describe each movement. (Start—same—same—up—up—same—down—up—same—down.)

CAN YOU DECIDE WHEN IT WILL MOVE UP OR DOWN BY STEPS? BY SKIPS? I'LL GIVE YOU ONE CLUE. THE FIRST TIME THE MELODY MOVES UP IT IS A SKIP. Help them describe the motion, this time using **step, skip,** or **same.** (Start—same—same—skip—skip—same—skip—skip—same—skip.) As children chant these two descriptive phrases, guide them to speak in the appropriate rhythmic pattern. (Short short short short short short long, short short long.)

GOOD! I BELIEVE YOU COULD PLAY THAT PATTERN! HERE ARE FIVE BELLS. WILL WE BEGIN WITH THE LOWEST, THE HIGHEST, OR THE ONE IN THE MIDDLE? (Lowest.)

As one child plays, the others will guide and evaluate. Help children make decisions by asking questions. DOES JOHNNY NEED TO SKIP, OR SHOULD HE STAY ON THE SAME BELL? DID YOU LOOK AT YOUR PICTURE TO HELP YOU DECIDE? WHICH DIRECTION DOES HE NEED TO GO NOW?

After he has played the complete pattern, draw attention to the bells he played. WE BEGAN WITH THE LOWEST, OR "FIRST" BELL. WHICH ONE DID HE PLAY NEXT? (The first one again.) WHEN HE SKIPPED, WHICH BELL DID HE PLAY? (The third.) As children decide on numbers, write them on the chart above the lines.

Help children sing the melody pattern, with numbers or on a neutral syllable.

LISTEN TO A SONG. CAN YOU FIND OUR PATTERN? RAISE YOUR HAND WHEN YOU HEAR IT. (Play the first verse.) WHO KNOWS THE WORDS THAT WERE SUNG TO OUR PATTERN? ("Have you seen my honey bears, honey bears" and "Sitting upon wooden chairs, wooden chairs.")

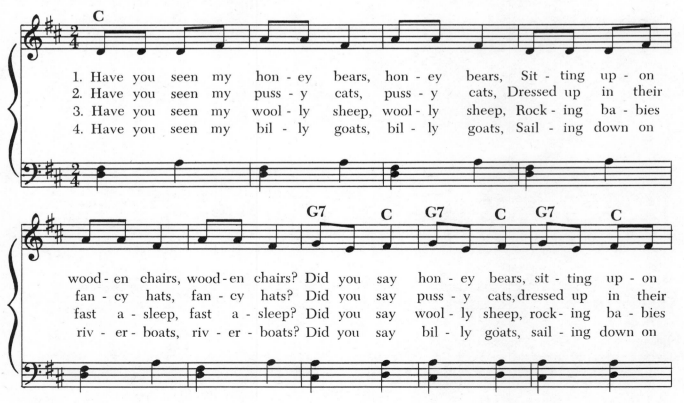

1. Have you seen my hon-ey bears, hon-ey bears, Sit-ting up-on
2. Have you seen my puss-y cats, puss-y cats, Dressed up in their
3. Have you seen my wool-ly sheep, wool-ly sheep, Rock-ing ba-bies
4. Have you seen my bil-ly goats, bil-ly goats, Sail-ing down on

wood-en chairs, wood-en chairs? Did you say hon-ey bears, sit-ting up-on
fan-cy hats, fan-cy hats? Did you say puss-y cats, dressed up in their
fast a-sleep, fast a-sleep? Did you say wool-ly sheep, rock-ing ba-bies
riv-er-boats, riv-er-boats? Did you say bil-ly goats, sail-ing down on

wood - en	chairs?	Oh,	my	dar - ling	dear, _____	Does - n't	it	seem	queer?
fan - cy	hats?	Oh,	my	dar - ling	dear, _____	Does - n't	it	seem	queer?
fast a - sleep?		Oh,	my	dar - ling	dear, _____	Does - n't	it	seem	queer?
riv - er - boats?		Oh,	my	dar - ling	dear, _____	Does - n't	it	seem	queer?

Record 9   Side B   Band 2
New York Philharmonic,
Leonard Bernstein, conductor.
TIME: 2:22

Norwegian Dance, Opus 35, No. 2

by Edvard Grieg (greeg)
BORN 1843   DIED 1907

Concept STRUCTURE: Music is made up of sections which may be the same or different.

Discover Play the first section of "Norwegian Dance." As children listen, quietly mark on the chalkboard, in time with the underlying pulse.

Hand out large pieces of construction paper which have been divided into three sections. YOU MAY MARK AS YOU LISTEN THIS TIME. MARK IN THE FIRST "BOX" ON YOUR PAPER. (Play only the A section again.)

THIS TIME I'M GOING TO PLAY A NEW PART OF THE MUSIC. MAKE YOUR MARKS IN THE MIDDLE BOX OF YOUR PAPER. YOU MAY WANT TO LISTEN FOR A MOMENT BEFORE YOU BEGIN TO MAKE YOUR MARKS. Play the B section. Ask children to show the designs they have created. Comment on differences between the marks they made in the first box and those in the second.

THIS TIME I'M GOING TO PLAY THE MUSIC FROM BEGINNING TO END. AS YOU LISTEN TO THE FIRST TWO PARTS OF THE MUSIC, LOOK AT THE DESIGNS YOU HAVE MADE IN THE FIRST TWO BOXES. WHEN THE THIRD SECTION BEGINS, LOOK AT YOUR PICTURES AGAIN. WHICH ONE MATCHES THIS MUSIC? (The first.) Repeat the entire composition so that the children can complete their pictures. Point out pictures which reveal that the child senses the similarities between part 1 and part 3. The pictures might look something like this.

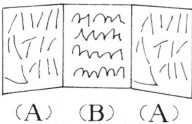

(A) (B) (A)

WHY DID THE PICTURES IN BOXES ONE AND THREE LOOK THE SAME? (The music sounded the same.) WHAT WERE SOME OF THE MUSICAL THINGS THAT WERE DIFFERENT IN THE MIDDLE PART OF THE MUSIC THAT CAUSED YOU TO CHANGE THE WAY YOU MARKED? Help children talk about differences in tempo, rhythm patterns, dynamics, musical controls (smooth—jerky).

Extend OUR MUSIC HAD THREE PARTS. PARTS ONE AND THREE WERE THE SAME, PART TWO WAS DIFFERENT. LISTEN TO ANOTHER COMPOSITION. WOULD THE PICTURES YOU MADE FOR "NORWEGIAN DANCE" MATCH THIS MUSIC?

Play "Dance of the Little Swans," page 185. Help children conclude that the pictures would "match" because this music also has three parts, with parts one and three sounding the **same** and part two sounding **different.** However, they may feel that the pictures need to be different. Some children may wish to draw new designs to match the sound of this music.

Other Concept EXPRESSIVE TOTALITY: Choices of timbres, rhythms, dynamics, melodies, and musical controls help to create different effects.

Invite children to dance what they hear in the music. They might divide into two groups. Group I dances during the A sections; Group II dances during the B section.

After children have danced, talk about differences in the way the two groups danced. Draw attention to gestures used which revealed children's sensitivity to various aspects of the music such as changes in timbres (changes in solo voices, one-many) rhythmic and melodic contrasts, and musical controls.

Oh Mama, Hurry

Brazilian Folk Song

Key: C Starting Tone: G(5)

Meter: $\frac{4}{4}$ ($\frac{4}{\downarrow}$)

DT/ Record 5 Side A Band 5 VOICES: children's choir.
ACCOMPANIMENT: 2 trumpets, percussion, bass, drums, guitar.
FORM: Introduction; Vocal; Instrumental; Vocal.

Concept PITCH: Melodies move up and down by steps and skips.

Discover Review "Have You Seen My Honey Bears?" Remind children of their discovery of the numbers of the **melody pattern.** CAN YOU SING THAT MELODY TODAY, WITH NUMBERS? (Point to the chart as children sing.)

Here is another chart. CAN YOU DECIDE THE NUMBERS FOR THESE PATTERNS?

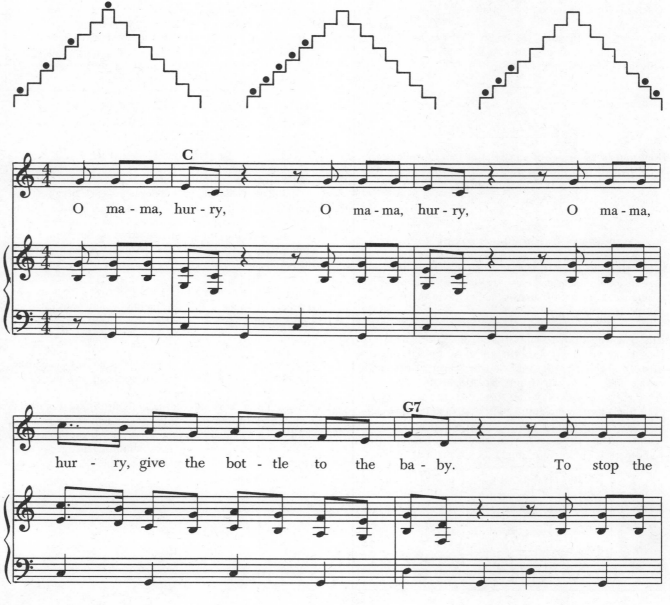

O ma-ma, hur-ry,   O ma-ma, hur-ry,   O ma-ma,

hur-ry, give the bot-tle to the ba-by.   To stop the

104

As children determine the appropriate numbers, ask one child to play the patterns on the bells. Place the bells for the C scale in a single row.

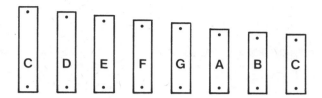

As each pattern is played, ask the class to sing what they have heard.

End the activity by showing them this pattern on the chalkboard or chart.

CAN YOU SING THIS PATTERN? Notice the rhythm as you sing; each sound is "short."

LISTEN TO THE SONG. FIND THE MELODY YOU JUST SANG. WHICH WORDS DID THE SINGER SING WITH THIS PATTERN? ("O mama, hurry.")

Some children may feel that "To stop the crying" is also the same melody. If this suggestion arises, play the two

patterns and show the numbers for the second melody. Ask children to describe the differences.

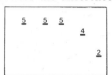

Other Concept PITCH: Chords may be played to accompany a melody.

Discover Help children to play the autoharp. The teacher should press the chord buttons while the child strums the strings. Help the child sense that he must play on the accented pulses, in the following rhythm.

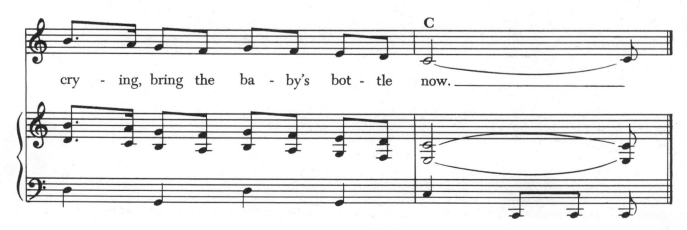

Feeling Your Voice

Concept PITCH: The voice may be used to produce higher and lower tones.

Discover Help children discover that they can "move" their voices up and down by engaging them in the following activities.

Help children to find the dent in the middle of their collarbone.

HOLD TWO FINGERS IN THIS SPOT WHILE YOU HELP ME TELL THE SOUND STORY. THE STORY IS ABOUT A CAR IN THE CITY.

Transfer the diagrams to the chalkboard and guide the children's eyes by using a pointer.

MAKE A LOW "R" SOUND FOR THE CAR'S MOTOR. THE CAR IS WORKING FINE, GOING DOWN THE STREET . . . .

R ——————————————

"OH! OH! TROUBLE!" MAKE THE CAR'S MOTOR STOP AND START EACH TIME I TOUCH A DOT. USE SAME LOW SOUND.

R ——●——●——●——●——●——●——

THE POLICEMAN SAYS IT IS YOUR TURN TO GO . . . DON'T DELAY TRAFFIC. (Sing low-high pitches for "hur-ry.")

HURRY   HURRY   HURRY

BUT THE CAR WAS STILL HAVING TROUBLE.

R ——●——●——●——●——●——●——

WHAT DO YOU THINK THE MAN DID WITH HIS CAR THAT WOULD NOT RUN? (Fixed it himself or took it to the service station.)

WHEN YOU MADE THE SOUND OF THE CAR, WHAT DID YOUR FINGERS FEEL AS YOU TOUCHED YOUR THROAT? (Buzzing.) HOW DID THE DOTS LOOK ON THE CHALKBOARD WHEN YOU WERE THE CAR? (They were in a straight line.) WHEN YOU WERE THE POLICEMAN SAYING "HUR-RY" WHAT DID YOUR FINGERS FEEL? (Buzz on "hur," no buzz on "ry.")

Discuss that the voice went from a low buzz to a higher sound in the head on "Hur-ry." WHAT DID THE DOTS LOOK LIKE WHEN YOU WERE THE POLICEMAN? (Low-high.)

Draw other sounds stories on the chalkboard such as:

Use a pointer to trace the left-right, up-down movement. Ask one child to sing on "loo" without placing his fingers on his throat. He may use any interval as long as he responds to the direction correctly. (Up, down, or stays the same.)

The class echoes the first child's pitches. Later you may wish to draw the five lines of the staff and place these note-heads on lines or spaces. Add stems to complete the notes.

Record 5 Side A Band 6 VOICE: child.
ACCOMPANIMENT: woodwind quartet, percussion.
FORM: Introduction; Vocal, *v. 1;*
Interlude; Vocal, *v. 2;* Interlude; Vocal, *v.*
3; Interlude; Vocal, *v. 4;* Coda.

Had a Little Rooster

American Folk Song

Key: C   Starting Tone: C(1)

Meter: $\frac{3}{4}$ ($\frac{3}{\downarrow}$)

Concept PITCH: Melodies move up, down, or stay the same.

Discover HERE ARE FOUR PICTURES. CAN YOU TELL ME WHICH PICTURE SHOWS THE SOUND OF THE CHICK'S SONG, "CHICK, CHICK, CHICK"? (The second one.) WHICH SHOWS THE BEGINNING OF ROOSTER'S SONG? (The third one.)

Find the two **patterns** on the bells. Play them each time the verse is repeated.

Play the recording on several different occasions until the children understand how to repeat the added verses. A new animal sound is added with each verse; repeat all sounds in reverse order; end with the rooster's call.

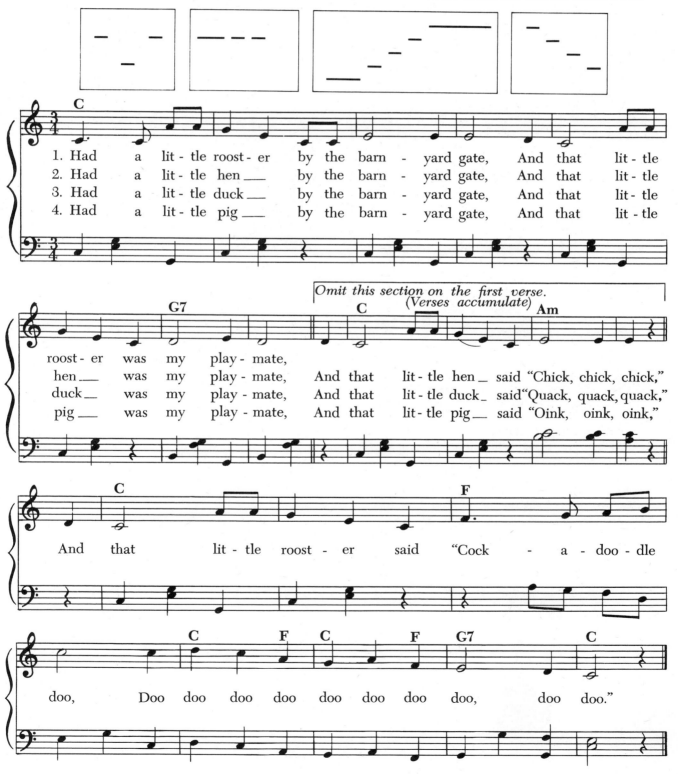

Higher — Lower (26-27)

The concept of "highness-lowness" is a relative one, dependent on the pitch levels used for comparison. Use the terms **high** and **low** to describe the overall pitch level of complete musical patterns rather than for the specific relationship between two pitches. The latter type of discrimination may be too advanced for first-grade children.

Concept PITCH: Tonal patterns may be high, low, or "in the middle."

Discover Look at the pictures in the pupil's book. WHICH ANIMALS DO YOU KNOW THAT MIGHT MAKE LOW SOUNDS? HIGH SOUNDS?

Play the first part of the recording for the children. Ask them to point to the picture in the book which matches the sound they hear. How do you know which animal sound you are hearing? As children suggest a variety of things such as loudness and general sound quality, guide them to become aware that the **highness** or **lowness** of the sound is also an important clue to identification.

Before children hear the remainder of the recording, arrange pairs of **large (low)** and **small (high)** instruments with which they can experiment, such as drums, triangles, wood blocks, finger cymbals, gong.

Ask children to experiment with each pair. WHY ARE THE SOUNDS DIFFERENT ON THE TWO DRUMS? Pose thought-provoking questions that will guide children to notice the difference in size as an important reason for the difference in sound.

Play the second section of the recording; ask children to point to the instrument shown in the book when they hear its sound, or give each child two pieces of colored paper (use contrasting hues). WHEN YOU HEAR A HIGH SOUND, HOLD UP ONE OF YOUR PIECES OF PAPER; WHEN YOU HEAR A LOW SOUND, HOLD THE OTHER DOWN LOW.

Extend Provide children with a variety of environmental sound-producers such as nails and bolts of different sizes, large and small pot lids, and bottles of different sizes. Provide string to tie around small items so that they can vibrate freely. Encourage children to experiment. ON WHICH OF YOUR SOUND-PRODUCERS CAN YOU FIND HIGH SOUNDS? LOW SOUNDS? As children experiment, help them to determine the reasons for the differences in sound: size, shape, type of material.

Play the last part of the recording which consists of musical patterns played in different ranges: **high—middle—low.** Ask children to move appropriately as they hear the sounds. (Stand on tiptoe, arms overhead for high sounds; bend over, hands near toes for low sounds; stand erect, arms swinging by sides for "middle" sounds.)

Find things that make high sounds.
Find things that make low sounds.

26

Record 5   Side A   Band 7

Can you make a pattern of sounds that goes up?
Can you make a pattern of sounds that goes down?
With your voice?
On the bells?

27

Up — Down

Concept PITCH: Tones can move in a sequence which goes up, down, or remains the same.

Discover After children have experimented with sound sources to discover high and low sounds, help them explore instruments which can change pitch, **moving up and down.**

Look at the pictures in the pupil's book. WHO CAN MAKE THE SOUND OF A FIRETRUCK SIREN? A TRAIN WHISTLE AS IT COMES INTO THE STATION? After children have produced the sounds, discuss what happened. DID YOUR SOUND STAY THE SAME? DID IT MOVE UP, FROM LOW TO HIGH? DID IT MOVE DOWN, FROM HIGH TO LOW?

To help children associate the terms **up** and **down** with the appropriate sound pattern, use step bells, or suspend a xylophone so that the highest bars are at the top. Give children the opportunity to play "up" and "down" so that they can experience the direction kinesthetically at the same time that they are hearing the sequence of pitches.

Extend As one child plays a pattern of sounds that go up or down on the bells, as suggested in his book, ask the remainder of the class to show the direction of his pattern with their hands. Can you "mirror" the melody pattern that you hear?

Play "Gavotte" page 5. CAN YOU SHOW WITH YOUR ARMS AND BODY HOW THIS MELODY MOVES UP AND DOWN? CAN YOU LET YOUR FEET STEP THE RHYTHM AS YOU MOVE?

Hush, Little Baby

American Folk Song

Key: F   Starting Tone: C(5)

Meter: $\frac{4}{4}$ ($\frac{4}{\text{♩}}$)

DT/ Record 5   Side A   Band 8   VOICES: soprano, baritone
ACCOMPANIMENT: string quartet
FORM: Introduction; *vv. 1–3;*
Instrumental; *v. 4;* Coda.

Concept   PITCH: Patterns of melody may be low or high.

Discover   Play the recording for the class; let them enjoy the peaceful melody. Listen again. IS THE MELODY PLAYED BY AN INSTRUMENT THAT SOUNDS HIGH OR LOW? Play only the introduction. Decide that the melody is **high,** played by the **violin.** RAISE YOUR HAND WHEN YOU HEAR THE MELODY PLAYED BY A LOW INSTRUMENT. Play the remainder of the recording until children indicate that they hear the **cello.** If possible, show children pictures of the two instruments which reveal their relative sizes. WHICH INSTRUMENT DO YOU THINK PLAYS THE HIGHER SOUNDS? (The smaller one, the violin.)

Draw attention also to the difference between the voice of the man and that of the woman: the woman's voice is **higher;** the man's voice is **lower.**

Extend   If available, use a bass xylophone and a soprano glockenspiel for children to develop their own low and high accompaniments. The same pattern should be played on both instruments. Children may decide which verses should be accompanied by **low** sounds, which by **high.** The pattern might also be played in high and low octaves on the piano.

110

DT/ Record 5 Side B Band 1 VOICES: children's choir.
ACCOMPANIMENT: trumpet, clarinet, viola, trombone, percussion.
FORM: Introduction; Vocal; Interlude; Vocal.

Eency, Weency Spider

Traditional

Key: G   Starting Tone: G(1)

Meter: $\frac{6}{8}$ ($\frac{2}{\text{♩.}}$)

Concept STRUCTURE: Music is made up of sections which may be the same or different.

Discover As children listen to the song, ask them to pretend they are the spider and step forward, then backward, changing direction at the end of each phrase. Observe children's actions as they move to the music and note those children who respond appropriately. DONALD, WHAT HELPED YOU KNOW WHEN TO CHANGE DIRECTION? (The long tone at the end of each phrase.)

CAN YOU MAKE UP AN ACTION TO SHOW WHAT HAPPENS TO OUR SPIDER? Make a new action for each phrase.

Phrase 1 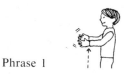   Phrase 2

Phrase 3   Phrase 4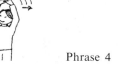

Lightly

Een - cy, ween - cy spi - der went up the wa - ter - spout;

Down came the rain and washed the spi - der out.

Then came the sun and dried up all the rain, And the

een - cy, ween - cy spi - der went up the spout a - gain.

Goldylocks and the Three Bears

The three songs on pages 112-116 and other descriptive music composed to tell the story of the Three Bears are all included on the recording. Enjoy the story with the class. Invite them to give their own ideas about what is happening during each instrumental section. Later, children may want to learn the songs and dramatize the story.

Concept EXPRESSIVE TOTALITY: Melodies, harmonies, rhythms, timbres, and musical controls can be combined in ways to help communicate ideas or "tell a story."

Discover Review the story of the Three Bears with the class, then play the recording. HERE IS SOME MUSIC THAT HELPS TO TELL THE STORY OF THE THREE BEARS! LET'S LISTEN AND SEE IF WE CAN DECIDE WHAT IS HAPPENING.

Overture

This section begins with "early morning sounds" played by percussion, winds, and strings. Then three instruments, one to represent each bear, play a melody, a variation on the song "The Three Bears," below. WHICH INSTRUMENT BELONGS TO THE FATHER BEAR? THE MOTHER BEAR? THE BABY BEAR? DO YOU THINK THESE INSTRUMENTS ARE GOOD CHOICES? WHY?

The **low cello** describes Father Bear and moves "heavily." The brisk, **higher clarinet** describes Mother Bear. Baby Bear's voice, represented by the **piccolo,** is **high.**

The overture continues with a theme from "Goldylocks' Song" page 114, played on the violin, the instrument which will represent Goldylocks in the story. Then the Three Bears' theme returns.

The Three Bears

Each bear sings "good morning" to the others by singing a verse of "The Three Bears." Guide children to notice that the voice qualities are different: Father's voice is **low,** Mother's voice is **high,** and Baby Bear's voice is also **high,** but **lighter** in quality. Notice that the three solos are accompanied by the same instruments that described the bears in the overture.

The Three Bears

Music by Roger Fiske
Words by Jean Sutcliffe

Key: C   Starting Tone: C(1)

Meter: $\frac{4}{4}$ ($\frac{4}{\downarrow}$)

Very steady and cheerful

Father Up in the morn - ing, oh, for me,
Mother Up in the morn - ing, oh, for me,
Baby Up in the morn - ing, oh, for me,

Up in the morn-ing ear - ly, With the bird and the worm and the
Up in the morn-ing ear - ly, With the break - fasts to get for ___
Up in the morn-ing ear - ly, With ___ Dad-dy bear and Mum-my bear and

bus - y buz - zy bee,
one, ___ two, ___ three,
Ba - by bear, that's me,

Up in the morn - ing ear - ly.

CAN YOU TELL BY THE MUSIC WHEN THE THREE BEARS GO FOR A WALK? CAN YOU DECIDE HOW EACH BEAR IS WALKING BY LISTENING TO THE RHYTHM OF HIS INSTRUMENT?

Father Bear walks with big steps:

Mother Bear walks with middle-sized steps:

Baby Bear runs along with tiny steps:

Goldylocks enters

As the bear walk gets softer, a violin melody is heard. Notice the uneven "skipping" rhythm of this music, in contrast to the even "walking" rhythm of the three bears' music. GOLDYLOCKS IS SKIPPING THROUGH THE FOREST. CAN YOU TELL BY LISTENING WHAT SHE IS DOING? The music gets louder as she comes near the house, and slows down as she looks around. Listen for the wood block as she knocks at the door before singing "Goldylocks' Song," page 114.

Goldylocks enters and sings "This soup is too hot," to the melody of her song. She continues around the table, tasting first Father Bear's soup, and then Mother Bear's soup.

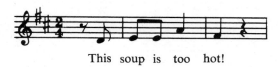

This soup is too hot!

Next Goldylocks goes into the living room and sings:

This chair is too hard.
This chair is too soft.
This chair is just right.

Listen for Baby Bear's chair breaking, as all instruments slide into a resounding "thump."

The same melody is repeated as Goldylocks tries each of the beds:

This bed is too long.
This bed is too short.
This bed is just right.

WHAT HAPPENS TO GOLDYLOCKS WHEN SHE REACHES BABY BEAR'S BED? (She falls asleep.) HOW DOES THE MUSIC HELP YOU KNOW? (It turns into a lullaby, as suggested by the quiet, slow-moving melody.)

Goldylocks' Song

Music by Roger Fiske
Words by Jean Sutcliffe

Key: D   Starting Tone: D(1)

Meter: 2/4 (♩)

Is an - y - bod - y in? Is an - y - one at home? Won't an - y - bod - y an - swer me? I'm lost and all a - lone.

The Bears Return

The Three Bears are heard singing their song as they return. The music gets louder as they near the house, open the door, and enter.

One by one, the three bears discover that someone's been eating their porridge. Here are the three melodies for children to use later, during their own dramatization.

FATHER BEAR

Some-one's been eat - ing my por-ridge!

MOTHER BEAR

Some-one's been eat - ing my por-ridge!

BABY BEAR

Some-one's been eat - ing my por-ridge! ; They've

eat - en it all, they've eat - en it all!

The same melody is repeated, first by the cello, then by the clarinet, then by the flute, as the three bears discover that their chairs have been sat upon. This time the bears sing:

> Someone's been sitting in my chair!
> Someone's been sitting in my chair!
> Someone's been sitting in my chair; they've
> broken it down; they've broken it down!

The Three Bears scurry upstairs. As they discover that their beds have been slept in, they sing:

> Someone's been sleeping in my bed.
> Someone's been sleeping in my bed.
> Someone's been sleeping in my bed and here she
> is now, and here she is now!

Baby Bear's Song

Baby Bear sings the song on page 116. Listen for the scurrying sounds of the violin as Goldylocks awakens and scampers away.

A short instrumental section closes the story. As children listen, ask them to identify the instruments and the characters that are associated with each. Prepare pictures of the characters, and, if possible, pictures of the four instruments. Give the pictures to eight children for them to hold up as their instrument or character is heard. They are heard in the order shown.

Baby Bear's Song

Music by Roger Fiske
Words by Jean Sutcliffe

Key: D minor   Starting Tone: A(5)

Meter: $\frac{2}{4}$ $\left(\frac{2}{\quarternote}\right)$

Song on page 116.

115

BABY BEAR

She eats my por-ridge, And breaks my chair, And lies in my bed And goes to sleep there. How dare she! How dare she! She eats my por-ridge, Oo _____ And

(Cries)

breaks my chair, Oo _____ And lies in my bed And goes to sleep there.

(Cries)

116

Space Walk

Concept   DURATION: Sounds may be long and sustained.

Discover   Help children plan a space walk. HOW DOES A ROCKET BLAST OFF INTO SPACE? Invite the children to explore movement and musical sounds which could express this event.

HOW WOULD YOUR WALK IN SPACE BE DIFFERENT FROM THE WAY YOU WALK ON EARTH? (In space, you feel as though you are weightless.) Ask children to demonstrate their own ideas. Suggest the following means of walking with a weightless feeling. MOVE VERY SLOWLY. LIFT YOUR BODY WITH YOUR BREATH. WHEN YOU BREATHE IN, LET YOUR BREATH PULL YOUR ARMS AND LEGS UP. WHEN YOU BREATHE OUT, MOVE YOUR ARMS AND LEGS DOWN.

Accompany the movement with instruments. Provide the following pitch choices for children. Use resonator bells or metallophone:

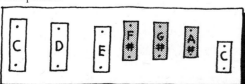

Ask the child who plays the bells to allow each sound to "ring" as long as it can before playing a new sound. He may choose any sounds and play either one or two at the same time.

Extend   FIND AN EMPTY PLACE ON THE FLOOR AND SIT WITH YOUR LEGS CROSSED. CLOSE YOUR EYES AND LISTEN. Play "Underwater Waltz" page 119. Invite children to take another "space walk," this time in response to the recorded selection. After the children have moved to the music, ask them: HOW WERE YOUR MOVEMENTS DIFFERENT FROM THOSE YOU DID WHEN WE MADE UP OUR OWN ACCOMPANIMENT? (Possibly more rhythmic, faster.)

DID THIS MUSIC GIVE YOU NEW IDEAS FOR MOVING IN SPACE? (The music may suggest times to tumble down or be lifted up.)

The Wind (28–29)

Concept PITCH: Tones may be low, high, or "in the middle."

Discover Read the poem in the pupil's book to the children, using appropriate voice levels. Let the children observe the poem and illustrations in their book as you read.

WHO CAN BE THE WIND AND MOVE AS WE CHANT THE POEM TOGETHER? Colored scarves of soft material will help children feel the "swoop" of the wind. As one child pretends to be the wind, others may stand in a circle for him to touch as he goes by.

Remind children of the sound explorations undertaken when studying pupil's book page 26. WHICH LOW SOUND THAT YOU FOUND MIGHT SUGGEST THE SOUND OF THE WIND? WHICH HIGH SOUND? Encourage additional exploration. The **low** and **high** strings on the autoharp may be stroked to suggest the sound of the wind. If possible, open the piano so children can strum **low** and **high** sounds on the piano strings. Two mallets moved rapidly back and forth between two tones on the brass xylophone or metallaphone suggest low wind sounds. A similar pattern might be played on the soprano glockenspiel. WHAT KIND OF SOUNDS MIGHT YOU PLAY AS THE WIND TOUCHES "EVERYTHING"? (Perhaps "middle" sounds, or a pattern which moves rapidly from low to high and back again.)

Extend What other things can be both low and high? Encourage children to stretch their imaginations to think of things that can be sometimes low and sometimes high. They may suggest such things as an airplane, rain, snow, a kite. As children make suggestions, invite them to show the way these things move. Some children might want to improvise appropriate patterns on the piano, autoharp, or other pitched instruments.

The following poem may stimulate additional movement-sound exploration.

Like a Leaf

by Emilie Poulsson

Like a leaf or a feather
In the windy, windy weather,
We'll whirl about and twirl about
and all sink down together.

The Wind

The wind blew low,
The wind blew high,
It touched everything
As it went by.

28

118

Who can be the wind and

blow high

blow low

touch everything?

Find a low sound.
Find a high sound.
Find many sounds.

Play your instruments as the "wind" moves.

29

Underwater Waltz

by Vladimir Ussachevsky (oo-sah-chef'skee)
BORN 1911

Concept   TIME AND PLACE: The choice of timbres and the way they are used can reflect the time and place of origin of a piece of music.

Discover   Children may have moved to this music as part of their "Space Walk" experience, page 117. Now you may wish to discuss the music itself with the class. Explain that the piece was played on a **piano** and that the composer changed the sounds by using a **tape recorder** and other electronic equipment.

THE COMPOSER PLAYED THIS. (Play the melody on the piano.)

THEN HE MADE IT SOUND LIKE THIS. (Play the recording for the class.) HOW DID THE COMPOSER CHANGE THE SOUNDS OF THE PIANO? (He made the tones echo, repeated the same sounds, and added extra tones.)

If your record player has a 16 r.p.m. speed, play the composition at this speed. At this slower speed, it is easier to hear the electronic effects the composer used. DOES THE MUSIC ITSELF CHANGE JUST BY PLAYING IT MORE SLOWLY? (No.) WHAT HAS BEEN CHANGED? (Pitch.) WHAT REMAINS THE SAME? (The up-down contour of the melody.) THIS IS ONE OF THE WAYS COMPOSERS OF TODAY CHANGE MUSICAL SOUNDS. WHAT DO YOU SUPPOSE WILL HAPPEN IF WE PLAY THE COMPOSITION FASTER? (At 78 r.p.m. speed, the pitch will be higher.)

If a tape recorder is available, experiment with changes in speed. Let the children record themselves speaking their names, singing a phrase, or playing a few tones on bells. Replay these fragments at different speeds. Discuss the changes in sound which have occurred.

Record 9   Side B   Band 3
TIME: 1:07

119

The Wind Blow East

Collected, adapted, and arranged
by John A. Lomax and Alan Lomax

Key: F   Starting Tone: F(1)

Meter: $\frac{2}{4}$ $\left(\frac{2}{}\right)$

DT/ **Record 5   Side B   Band 2** VOICES:
children's choir.
ACCOMPANIMENT: harp, oboe, French
horn, cello.
FORM: Introduction; Vocal; Instrumental;
Vocal (fade out).

Concept   PITCH: Melody patterns may move up and down.

Discover   As children listen to the recording, ask them to show the rise and fall of the wind with their arms. They should move on the glissando at the ends of the first two phrases (measures 4 and 8) and during the instrumental.

Next draw two melodic contour charts on sheets of paper. The charts should be roughly the length of a child's arm span. Attach the charts to the bulletin board, or have two children hold them up.

WHICH PICTURE MATCHES THE SOUND OF THE WIND IN OUR SONG? Ask one child to stand in front of the chart and follow first one, and then the other, contour line as he listens to the recording. Guide children to decide that Chart 2 matches the contour of the wind's melody because it rises and falls.

Extend   Put out the bells for the F scale (F G A Bb C D E F); use as many bells as are available and arrange them in order from low to high. As the class sings the song, one child may create the sound of the wind, imitating the sound heard on the recording.

Chart 1

Chart 2

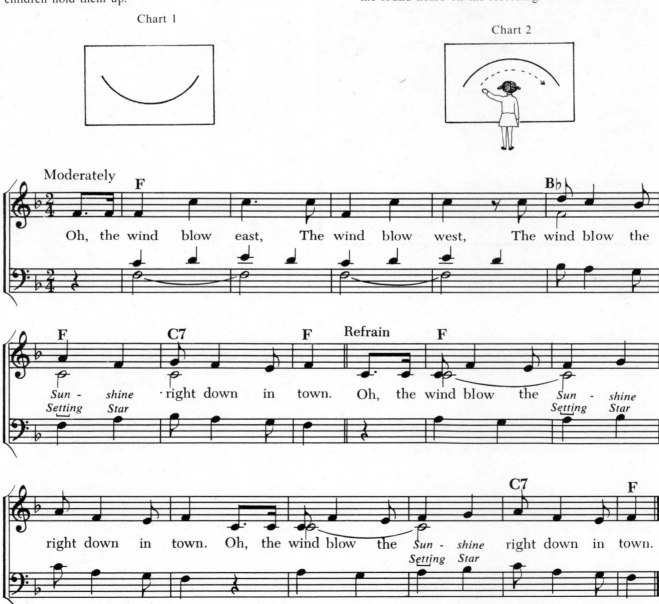

Response to Pitch

Concept PITCH: Melody patterns may be high, low, or in the middle; they may move up, down, or remain the same.

Discover Give children additional experience in associating movement and sound to help them develop concepts of melodic direction. Invite the class to respond with appropriate motions as you speak the following phrases. Improvise an appropriate accompaniment on bells, piano, autoharp or any other pitched instrument.

WHO CAN FIND THE OCEAN FLOOR?

Deep
down
low
Far
be-
low...

WHO CAN TOUCH THE STARS?

touch one!

Stretch.....

glissando

Stretch.....

here's two!

WHO CAN WALK WITH ME?

Where grasses grow . . . (middle sounds)

and blow . .

Nighttime (30–31)

Concept PITCH: Melodies may move up, move down, or remain the same.

Discover Have the class turn to pages 30–31 of the Pupil's Book. Read the poem with them, and allow time to look at the illustrations.

Put the resonator bells in a single row, as shown in the pupil's book. WHO CAN PLAY AN INTERESTING PATTERN THAT SUGGESTS THE LAMB KNEELING DOWN? Encourage individual exploration on the bells until the children find sounds which move **down**. IF WE WANT TO MAKE A PATTERN OF SOUNDS WHICH GO DOWN, WHICH WAY WILL WE NEED TO MOVE ON THE BELLS? Help children discover that they must begin with the **high** bells, which are always to the right, and move to the left, toward the **low** bells. Notice differences in patterns which children develop: some may play patterns which use bells that are very close together; others may make up patterns that use bells which are far apart.

WHICH WAY WILL WE NEED TO MOVE TO FIND A PATTERN THAT SUGGESTS THE LARK FLYING UP? (To the right, from low to high.)

CAN YOU MAKE UP AN INTERESTING PATTERN THAT SOUNDS LIKE CHILDREN RUNNING? HOW CAN YOU "STAY THE SAME"? (By playing on the same pitch. Playing a pattern made up of short tones might suggest running.)

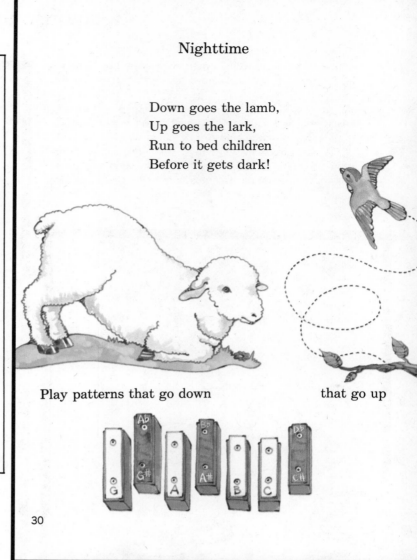

Nighttime

Down goes the lamb,
Up goes the lark,
Run to bed children
Before it gets dark!

Play patterns that go down   that go up

30

that stay the same.

31

Extend After children have experimented with patterns, plan a "performance." Some children may speak the poem as a choral reading; others may play the appropriate patterns at the end of each phrase of the poem. The remainder of the class may act out the parts of the lamb, the lark, and the children, and move appropriately.

The following poems may be used for similar activities. Chidren may improvise their own high or low melody patterns which move up and down at the appropriate times.

Here are the fireflies,   (High sounds that move
Last to remember   up and down to
The end of August   suggest fireflies
And first of September.   darting about.)

And here comes a caterpillar, (Low sounds with very
The last to creep   little up-down movement
Out of summer   to suggest a cater-
And into sleep.   pillar creeping along.)

Swinging

by Elizabeth Coatsworth

Up then and down with a bounce in the air,
Now the wind's making a fan of your hair.
When you go up, you have to go down,
But, oh! Did you count the steeples in town?

123

I'm Gonna Mail Myself

Words and Music
by Woody Guthrie

Key: D Starting Tone: A(5)
Autoharp Key: C Starting Tone: G(5)

Meter: $\frac{2}{4}$ ($\frac{2}{\downarrow}$)

DT/ **Record 5 Side B Band 3** VOICES: children's choir.
ACCOMPANIMENT: tenor banjo, tack piano, bass, percussion.
FORM: Introduction; Vocal, *v. 1;* Interlude; Vocal, *v. 2;* Coda.

Play the recording. Ask the class to guess what "myself" is. (A valentine!)

Concept DURATION: Patterns may be made of long and short tones which move in relation to an underlying beat.

Discover Play the recording. Enjoy the amusing words. LISTEN! I'M GOING TO TAP A PATTERN. CAN YOU FIND THE WORDS THAT MATCH THAT PATTERN IN THE SONG? Tap on a woodblock:

CAN YOU TAP THAT PATTERN WITH ME?

Children should imitate the pattern until they can tap it readily. NOW LISTEN AGAIN TO THE MUSIC! FIND THE WORDS THAT MATCH THE PATTERN. As children make suggestions, tap the original pattern and chant the words until they make the decision that this pattern is "Stick some stamps on top of my head." Follow a similar procedure and tap the other patterns, discovering that one pattern matches two sets of words. ("I'm gonna daub myself with glue" and "I'm gonna mail myself to you.")

Extend CAN YOU ADD AN ACCOMPANIMENT WHICH SOUNDS WITH EVEN, STEADY SOUNDS WHILE THE CLASS SINGS OUR PATTERNS? Choose four children, one for each two-measure phrase. To add to the fun, allow them to

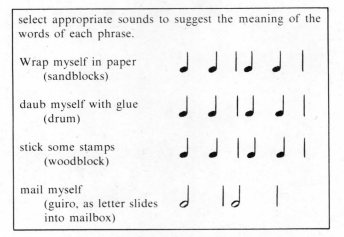

select appropriate sounds to suggest the meaning of the words of each phrase.

Wrap myself in paper (sandblocks)

daub myself with glue (drum)

stick some stamps (woodblock)

mail myself (guiro, as letter slides into mailbox)

Other Concept STRUCTURE: Sections of music may be the same or different.

Discover When children have discovered the three different rhythm patterns, call attention to the melodic similarities and differences among the four phrases. Sing phrase one on a neutral syllable, or play it on the bells. HERE IS OUR FIRST "VALENTINE." (Put a red heart on the flannel board.) NOW LISTEN CAREFULLY. SHOULD OUR NEXT VALENTINE BE THE SAME OR DIFFERENT? IS THE MELODY THE SAME OR DIFFERENT? Sing or play phrase two and discover that the melody is the **same.** (The rhythm is slightly altered.) The valentine should be the same, or almost the same. Follow the same procedure until four "valentines" are on the flannel board:

With spirit

1. I'm gon-na wrap my-self in pa-per, I'm gon-na daub my-self with glue,
2. I'm gon-na tie me up in a red string, I'm gon-na tie blue rib-bons, too;

Stick some stamps on top of my head, I'm gon-na mail my-self to you.
I'm gon-na climb up in ____ my mail-box, I'm gon-na mail my-self to you!

DT/ Record 5   Side B   Band 4   VOICES: children's choir.
ACCOMPANIMENT: accordion, bass, percussion.
FORM: Introduction; Vocal; Interlude; Vocal.

Dance of Greeting

Danish Folk Song

Key: D   Starting Tone: D(1)
Autoharp Key: C   Starting Tone: C(1)

Meter: $\frac{2}{2}$ $\left(\frac{2}{\text{♩}}\right)$

Concept DURATION: Rhythm patterns move in relation to an underlying beat.

Discover Help children respond to the basic **beat** by moving in a patterned dance. Play the recording and sing the words to the verse of the song. Ask children to stand beside their desks and do what the words indicate. Choose a leader to make up a motion during the refrain such as clap, tap, point toe, jump, or sway. The class follows the leader, maintaining a steady **beat**. Choose a different leader with a new motion each time the refrain is repeated.

Extend Clap and move on the verse of the song. During the refrain, ask individual children to make up rhythm patterns to play on classroom instruments while the rest of the group softly claps the basic beat.

A child might decide to play the tambourine in this manner:

shake   Tap!   Tap!

or claves (with the rhythm pattern of the melody):

Some children may choose to use several rhythm patterns rather than repeat the same one.

Clap, clap bow, ___ clap, clap bow. ___ Stamp! Stamp! Turn your-self a-round.

Clap, clap bow, ___ clap, clap bow. ___ Stamp! Stamp! Turn your-self a-round.

D.C. al Fine (after repeat)

Morningtown Ride

Words and Music by Malvina Reynolds

Key: C   Starting Tone: E(3)

Meter: 4/4 (♩)

DT/ Record 5   Side B   Band 5 VOICES: children's choir.
ACCOMPANIMENT: electric guitar, electric bass, piano, drums, percussion.
FORM: Introduction; *v. 1; v. 2;* Interlude; *v. 3* (fade out).

Concept: EXPRESSIVE TOTALITY: Musical elements can be combined to suggest a mood or feeling.

Discover   Play only the introduction of the recording. CAN YOU DECIDE WHAT THIS SONG IS GOING TO BE ABOUT? WHAT DO YOU HEAR THAT MIGHT HELP YOU DECIDE?

After children have made their suggestions, play the first verse. WERE YOU RIGHT?

As children talk about the reasons for their decisions, focus on the music: the choice of instruments, the steady, even rhythm of the low accompaniment.

Extend   Children may wish to dramatize this song. Some may pretend to be the train. CAN YOU MOVE WITH SHORT, SHUFFLING STEPS, IN THE RHYTHM OF THE ACCOMPAN-

IMENT? Other children may be Sarah, Tony, and John. Tony may ring the bell at the beginning of each phrase. Play a C bell or a triangle in this pattern:

The children may add their own train rhythm.

Sandblocks:

Bass xylophone:
Play in this rhythm   *or this*

1. Train   whis-tle   blow-ing   makes   a   sleep-y   noise;
2. Sa-rah's   at   the   en-gine,   To - ny rings the   bell,
3. May-be   it   is   rain-ing   where   our train will   ride;

Un-der-neath their blan-kets   go   all   the   girls   and   boys.
John__ swings the   lan-tern   to   show   that   all   is   well.
All   the   lit-tle   trav-elers   are   snug   and   warm in-side.

Head-ing   from   the   sta-tion,   out   a - long   the   bay,
Rock-ing,   roll-ing,   rid-ing,   out   a - long   the   bay,
Some-where there is   sun-shine,   some-where there   is   day,

All | bound for | Morn - ing - town, | man - y miles a - way.
All | bound for | Morn - ing - town, | man - y miles a - way.
Some-where | there is | Morn - ing - town, | man - y miles a - way.

Record 9   Side B   Band 4
National Orchestra and Choir of La
Radiodiffusion Francaise,
Ernest Bour, conductor.
TIME: 3:10

L'enfant et les Sortilèges
"La Chatte" and "Les Rainettes"

by Maurice Ravel
BORN 1875   DIED 1937

These two selections are from Ravel's opera *L'enfant et les Sortilèges* (The Bewitched Child). The opera is about a little boy who destroys every thing in his room and injures many of the plants and creatures in the garden. One night everything comes to life to scold and torment the bad boy. He finally redeems himself by performing an act of kindness. He helps a squirrel who has been injured and the animals forgive him. The first of these selections is a conversation between two cats. The second selection depicts the sounds of the creatures in the garden. Help children to hear how the composer used singing voices to imitate these sounds.

La Chatte (The Cat)

Concept   TIMBRE: Voices can be used to describe sounds.

Discover   Read the following lines to the children. Two cats meet. Their meeting begins with a "phist" which in cat language means "You'd better be careful." Then the cats begin a conversation. One cat says, "meow." The other cat answers with a long "mor-na-ow."

LISTEN TO THE CONVERSATION AND SEE IF YOU CAN TELL WHAT HAPPENS. (It sounds as though they get into a fight.) Ask questions to discover what happened in the music: DID WE HEAR REAL CATS ON THE RECORDING? (No.) WHAT WAS MAKING THE SOUNDS OF THE CATS? (Singing voices.)

WHAT DID YOU HEAR THAT MADE YOU THINK THE CATS WERE FIGHTING? (The cat sounds become louder and faster; the orchestra becomes louder.)

Extend   Children may make simple finger puppets. Place one puppet on each hand and dramatize what is happening in the music.

Les Rainettes (The Frogs)

Concept   TIMBRE: Voices combined with instruments may describe a scene.

Discover   Introduce the selection by telling the children that in this music voices are used with instruments to create a special mood and describe a certain place. LISTEN TO THE MUSIC. WHAT DO YOU THINK IT IS DESCRIBING? Play the recording.

Children will probably have ideas which are very close to the composer's intent. The scene is that of a quiet garden. A hoot owl calls out and a nightingale sings a high piping song. Soon, the croaking of frogs and the chirping of crickets are heard: the night is full of sounds. But the piece ends as it began, with the nightingale and hoot owl singing in the night.

Other Concept   EXPRESSIVE CONTROLS: Sounds may become gradually louder or softer.

Discover   Children may wish to make a group visual which represents the volume changes in this selection. Ask children to make small construction paper pictures of an owl, nightingale, frogs, and crickets. Use a large piece of white butcher paper. Play the selection and ask children to decide when it is **soft** and when **loud.** Draw a very large picture of the sound on the butcher paper:

Ask children to choose one of the hoot owls to depict the owl at the beginning of the piece. Paste this on the paper. Likewise select the nightingale. Paste on the frogs and crickets following the volume changes. Be certain that each child has something he has made on the chart. Select another owl and nightingale to place at the return of the soft music. The completed visual should look something like this:

127

Tommy Tamber (32–33)

Concept PITCH: A sequence of tones may move up, down, or stay the same.

Discover Before opening the children's books to pages 32-33, share the following activity with them. WE'RE GOING TO TAKE AN IMAGINARY WALK THROUGH THE PLAYGROUND! CLOSE YOUR EYES! CAN MY PIANO (BELLS) TELL YOU WHERE YOU ARE AND WHAT YOU ARE DOING? As you play the suggested patterns or improvise others, begin by describing the action and then playing the first pattern. Next, play the remaining patterns without previous description and invite children to make suggestions. Remind them that the "ups and downs" of the melody, as well as the rhythm, will help them know.
Here we go!

Through the hall, out the door . . .

down the front steps . . .

skipping across the playground. . .

up the steps of the slide. . .

swoo-oop down!

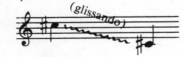

run to the swing!

back and forth, back and forth. . .

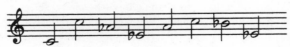

back to the schoolroom door. . .

Tommy Tamber

Sounds move up and down to make a melody.
Here is a picture of a melody.
Let's take a walk with Tommy Tamber.
Can you play Tommy's walk on the bells?

32

up the steps. . .

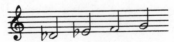

down the hall, into the classroom, sit down!

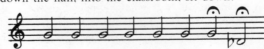

After children have listened and offered suggestions, play the patterns again, using the words as suggested. Invite children to show the movement as they take the pretended walk, stretching and bending to show the melodic direction.

CAN YOU DRAW A PICTURE OF OUR WALK? I CAN! Illustrate with a long line on the chalkboard, or use a long piece of wrapping paper. The picture will look something like the illustration on page 129.

128

UP

AND

DOWN.

TWISTING TURNING.

Take your own melody for a walk.
Draw your melody.
Play it on the bells.

33

Read the instructions and give individu-
al children time to "take Tommy's walk on the bells" while
the class chants the poem. Arrange the bells in various
groupings so that children have an opportunity to experiment and explore different pitch combinations. (See
below.)

Extend Invite children to make up other walks—through
the park, around the house, a beetle crawling along a side-
walk, an airplane, a bird soaring in the sky, and others.
A child might sketch his "walk" and invite a classmate
to express the walk with bell patterns.

This is a good activity for small groups to work on
independently. Put bells and drawing materials in the
Music Learning Center. Invite children to work in pairs
to plan a "melody walk," to draw it, to improvise the melody, and to play it for the class.

Whole-tone scale:

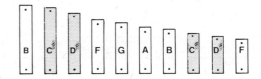

Pentatonic scale:

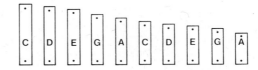

Chromatic scale:

Picture of a walk

Up and Down the Hill (34–35)

34

Concept PITCH: A series of tones may move up, down, or remain the same.

Discover Invite the students to look at the picture in the pupil's book. WHICH NURSERY RHYME IS SHOWN IN THIS PICTURE? (Jack and Jill.)

Review the poem and chant it with the children:

Jack and Jill went up the hill
To fetch a pail of water.
Jack fell down and broke his crown
And Jill came tumbling after!

Ask a child to play a pattern which describes Jack and Jill climbing **up** the hill (step by step) and falling **down** (perhaps a glissando or a rapid step-wise motion down). Use step-bells, a xylophone, or song bells suspended vertically.

COUNT THE NUMBER OF STEPS JACK AND JILL TOOK AS THEY CLIMBED. Let one child play this pattern again.

YOU PLAYED EIGHT BELLS! CAN YOU SING THE NUMBERS AS SARAH PLAYS THAT PATTERN AGAIN? CAN YOU SING THE NUMBERS "BACKWARDS" AS SARAH PLAYS BACK DOWN THE STAIRS?

Extend Cut dime-sized disks from construction paper. Make enough so that each child may have his own packet. CAN YOU MAKE UP A NEW PATTERN BY PUTTING DISKS ON THE STEPS IN YOUR BOOK? CAN YOU PLAY YOUR NEW PATTERN ON THE STAIRSTEPS? BE SURE YOU ARE PLAYING THE RIGHT NUMBERS!

Another time, ask one child to play a pattern on the bells, starting on the first bell. The other children must put their disks on the stairsteps to match the pattern the leader played.

As children use numbers to identify pitch patterns, it is important that they realize that these numbers describe relationships between one pitch and another within a scale. For this reason, it is essential that a variety of keys other than C be used.

Children may enjoy singing the song "Jack and Jill." Listen to the melody; draw attention to the fact that this melody does not "go up and down" like our melody did, "to match the words." Add a bell accompaniment made up of the scale pattern while the class sings the traditional melody.

Build Stairsteps for the Classroom

Steps may be made from styrofoam or plywood. Styrofoam has the advantage of lightness. The steps can be dismantled for easy storage and portability. Children themselves can assemble and take down the steps. The dimensions shown in the diagram on page 131 will be adequate to support the bells. Six strips of styrofoam two inches thick and two strips one inch thick are needed. *(See diagram, top of page 131.)*

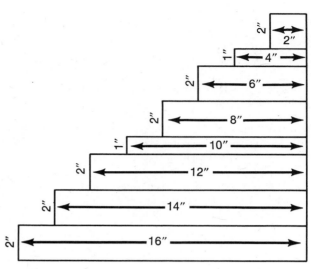

35

Jack and Jill

Mother Goose Rhyme

Key: C   Starting Tone: C(1)

Meter: $\frac{6}{8}$ $\left(\begin{smallmatrix}2\\ \end{smallmatrix}\right)$

Record 5 Side B Band 6 VOICE:
woman.
ACCOMPANIMENT: woodwind quartet,
percussion.
FORM: Instrumental; Vocal; Instrumental;
Vocal; Coda.

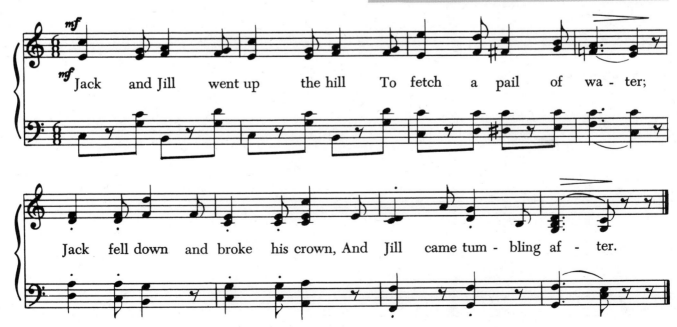

mf

Jack   and Jill   went up   the hill   To fetch   a   pail   of   wa - ter;

Jack   fell down   and broke   his crown, And   Jill   came tum - bling af - ter.

Dance in the Circle

Louisiana French Folk Song

Key: C   Starting Tone: C(1)

Meter: $\frac{3}{4}$ ($\frac{3}{\downarrow}$)

DT/ Record 5   Side B   Band 7 VOICES: children's choir.
ACCOMPANIMENT: string quartet.
FORM: Instrumental; Vocal; Instrumental; Vocal; Coda.

Concept PITCH: A melody can be based on a specific group of tones such as a major scale.

Discover Play the song for the children. DOES THE MELODY START AT THE TOP OF OUR STAIRSTEPS AND MOVE DOWN, OR DOES IT BEGIN AT THE BOTTOM AND MOVE UP?

When children have listened to and learned the words of the song, help them become aware that the melody outlines a scale by asking them to move in the following fashion. (They should make each movement on the first beat of each measure.)

8 hands on head

7 hands on shoulder

6 hands on chest

5 hands on waist

4 hands on thighs

3 hands on knees

2 hands on calves

1 hands on toes

Extend WHO CAN PLAY THE BELLS AS WE SING? Guide children to sense that they are playing only the "outline" of the melody, not every tone in the melody. To help, draw a line picture of the song, circling the tones they will play.

Put the picture in the Music Learning Center. Place the resonator bells for the C scale on stairsteps or use step bells so that children can practice individually. Some children will be able to learn to play the complete melody.

Ask children to show the pattern with disks on the stairsteps in the pupil's book, page 34-35.

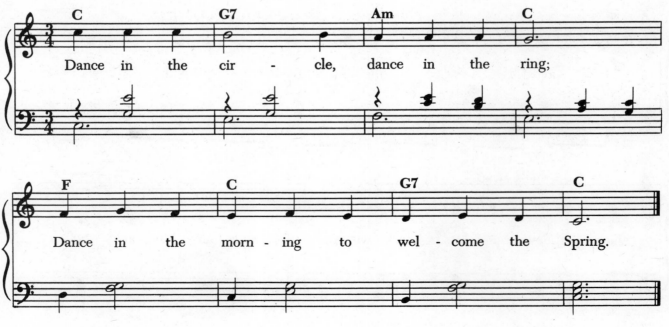

Dance in the cir - cle, dance in the ring;

Dance in the morn - ing to wel - come the Spring.

DT/ Record 5 Side B Band 8 VOICE:
male folk-singer.
ACCOMPANIMENT: percussion.
FORM: Introduction; Vocal; Interlude;
Vocal.

Happiness

African Folk Song

Key: F   Starting Tone: C(5)

Meter: $\frac{2}{2}$ $\left(\frac{2}{\text{♩}}\right)$

Concept EXPRESSIVE TOTALITY: Rhythms, melodies, dynamics, and tempo help suggest moods in music.

Discover Play the recording. WHAT IN THE MUSIC HELPS US KNOW THIS IS A HAPPY SONG? (The tempo, the melody that skips about.)

After children have learned to sing the song, invite them to plan their own musical expression. The class sings: "He's such a happy (sad, angry, grumpy) fellow." One child must answer, "I have a brand new bike, oh!" or "I lost my candy bar, oh!"

HOW WILL YOU SING DIFFERENTLY TO EXPRESS EACH WAY YOU FEEL? (Change dynamics and tempo.)

Extend Children may add an accompaniment, playing with the beat. WHICH INSTRUMENTS CAN MAKE "HAPPY" SOUNDS? (Bells, finger cymbals, etc.) WHICH MIGHT YOU USE FOR A "GRUMPY" SOUND? (Guiro or sand blocks.)

Listen to Melody (36)

This lesson is based on "Bath of Graces," from *The Adventures of Mercury*, page 15. Before introducing this lesson, give the class an opportunity to listen to the music several times.

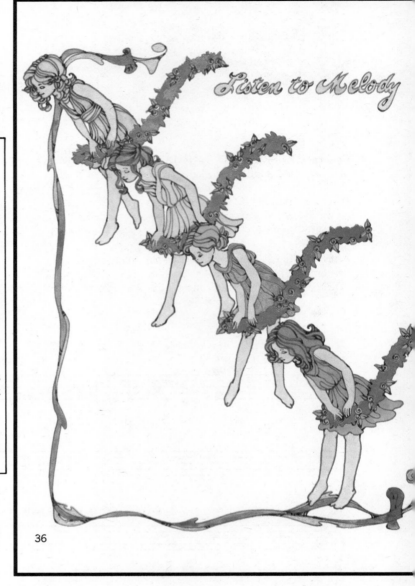

Concept   PITCH: Tones within a melody create a contour which moves up and down.

Discover   LOOK AT THE PICTURE IN YOUR BOOKS. THIS IS A PICTURE OF A MELODY. HOW DO YOU THINK THE MELODY WILL MOVE? Guide children to notice, in addition to the general direction, that the picture suggests four groups of patterns. Each pair of patterns begins a little **lower**.

LET'S LISTEN TO THE MUSIC THAT THIS PICTURE DESCRIBES. Use the Jumbo Book and follow the picture as the first phrase is played. (The first phrase is made up of the four groups of patterns shown in the book.) Continue to play the composition to its end.

DID YOU HEAR THAT SAME MELODY AGAIN? MORE THAN ONCE? Help children recognize that the entire melody is stated four times. (Phrases two and four begin on a different pitch.)

Extend   Children may draw their own pictures as they listen again. Then invite children to move to the music as shown on page 37 of the pupil's book.

Other Concepts   TEXTURE: Two rhythm patterns may be sounded simultaneously.

Discover   To help children hear the two melodies played simultaneously, tap the two rhythms:

Small sticks

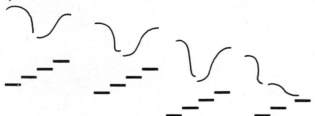

Finger cymbals

Two children may accompany the music, using instruments such as those mentioned above.

   PITCH: Two melodies may be combined to create harmony.

Discover   Some children may be able to hear the contrasting melody played by the lower strings. Its general direction is upward. Each pattern lasts for two of the melody patterns.

Ask a few children to show this pattern while others dance the melody. To show that it is lower, ask them to sit on the floor. They should begin with their hands on the floor to the left and move them gradually upward to the right.

Move to Melody (37)

Concept PITCH: Tones within a melody create a contour which rises and falls.

Discover After children have completed the discovery activity on page 36 of the pupil's book, draw attention to the illustrations on this page. THESE CHILDREN ARE SHOWING THE SHAPE OF THE MUSIC AS THEY MOVE. CAN YOU SHOW IT WITH MOVEMENT?

Divide the class into groups of four. They should stand in a line with arms extended upward to the left. The first child (the one to the left) begins. He shapes the first pair of patterns with his arms, then "hands" the melody to the second child as the second pair of patterns begins. Continue through the third and fourth children to the end of the phrase. Repeat this sequence three more times. The addition of colored scarves will add interest to the children's movements.

Another time, children may wish to work alone. They might shape the melody with their arms while stepping to the rhythm of the melody with their feet.

Extend Invite children to draw or move to other melodies they know. Some appropriate examples would be:

Good Night, page 18

Gavotte, page 5

Shoheen Sho, page 188

Sleep, Baby, Sleep, page 8

"Entreating Child,"
    from *Scenes from Childhood,* page 156.

See-Saw, Margery Daw (38)

Music by J. W. Elliott
Mother Goose Rhyme

Key: G   Starting: G(1)

Meter: $\frac{6}{8}$ $\left(\frac{2}{\text{♩.}}\right)$

Concept   PITCH: The tones of a melody may move by steps or skips.

Discover   Have the class turn to page 38 of the pupil's book. Read the poem together and talk about how one moves on the see-saw. WHEN YOU GO UP AND DOWN ON THE SEE-SAW, DO YOU MOVE JUST A LITTLE WAY, OR DO YOU MOVE QUITE FAR—FROM LOW TO HIGH? (Quite far.) Invite children to show the movement of the see-saw with their arms while you chant the poem.

Read the suggestions in the pupil's book. Arrange the four bells shown in a row, or use stairsteps. Invite someone to find a pattern that moves back and forth from **high** to **low,** just as the see-saw moves.

Extend   Play the recording of "See-Saw, Margery Daw." CAN YOU HEAR THE PATTERN YOU PLAYED? (It is the melody for the first phrase, "See-saw, Margery Daw.")

Learn to sing the song. Then invite one child to play the pattern over and over while others sing the melody.

DT/ Record 6   Side A   Band 1 VOICES: children's choir.
ACCOMPANIMENT: string quartet.
FORM: Introduction; Vocal; Interlude; Instrumental; Interlude; Vocal; Coda.

See-Saw Margery Daw

See-saw, Margery Daw,
Jack shall have a new master;
He shall have but a penny a day,
Because he won't work any faster.

Play a pattern that sounds like the see-saw going up and down

Play it on the bells.
Play bells that are far apart.
Play the pattern over and over!

38

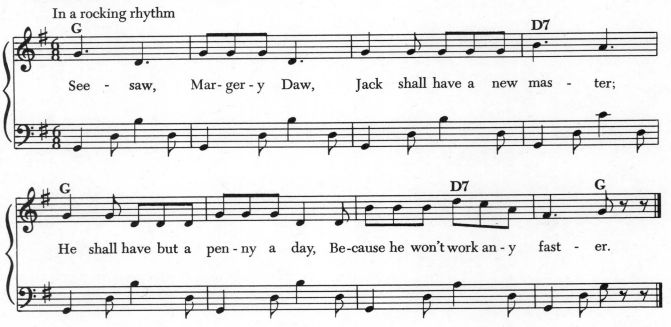

In a rocking rhythm

See - saw,   Mar - ger - y   Daw,   Jack   shall   have   a   new   mas - ter;

He   shall   have   but   a   pen - ny   a   day,   Be - cause   he   won't   work   an - y   fast - er.

136

Hippity Hop to the Barber Shop

Hippity hop to the barber shop.
To buy a stick of candy,
One for you and one for me,
And one for Jack a-dandy!

Play a pattern that sounds like "hip-hop."
Play it on the bells.
Play bells that are close together.

Play the pattern over and over.

39

Hippity Hop to the Barber Shop (39)

English Nursery Song

Key: F   Starting Tone: F(1)

Meter: $\frac{6}{8}$ ($\,.$)

Concept   PITCH: The tones of a melody move up and down by steps or skips.

Discover   Read the poem with the children and look at the illustration in the book. These boys are "hippity hopping" along, with one foot on the curb and one foot in the street. WHEN YOU HIP-HOP ALONG, DO YOUR FEET STAY CLOSE TO THE GROUND, OR DO YOU SORT OF BOUNCE UP AND DOWN? (Bounce up and down.) COULD YOU MAKE UP A PATTERN ON THE BELLS THAT HIP-HOPS UP AND DOWN? WILL YOU PLAY BELLS THAT ARE FAR APART OR CLOSE TOGETHER? (**Close together,** because you don't hop very far up or down.)

Place the C and D bells on stairsteps and ask one child to play the **up-down pattern** while others chant the poem. Then play the recording and learn to sing the song. This pattern may be played over and over as an accompaniment.

Extend   Compare the sounds of the two patterns played to accompany "See-Saw, Margery Daw" and "Hippity Hop to the Barber Shop." WHEN WE PLAYED A "SEE-SAW" PATTERN, WE HAD TO "SKIP" BELLS, DIDN'T WE—BECAUSE OUR PATTERN WENT WAY UP AND WAY DOWN. WHEN WE PLAYED A "HIP-HOP" PATTERN, WE PLAYED BELLS THAT WERE NEAR TOGETHER, SO WE JUST "STEPPED" UP AND DOWN.

DT/ Record 6   Side A   Band 2   VOICE: child.
ACCOMPANIMENT: recorder, bassoon, harpsichord.
FORM: Introduction; Vocal; Instrumental; Vocal; Instrumental (fast version).

Go to Sleep *Fais ton Dodo*

Louisiana French Folk Song

Key: F   Starting Tone: A(3)

Meter: $\frac{3}{4}$ $\left(\begin{smallmatrix}3\\ \end{smallmatrix}\right)$

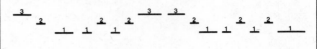

Record 6   Side A   Band 3   VOICE: woman.
ACCOMPANIMENT: string quartet.
FORM: Introduction; Vocal (English); Instrumental; Vocal (French); Coda.

Concept   PITCH: The tones of a melody move up and down by steps and skips.

Discover   Show the picture of the first phrase of this melody in line notation.

I BELIEVE YOU CAN LEARN TO PLAY THIS MELODY BEFORE YOU HEAR IT! LET'S LOOK AT OUR PICTURE AND SEE WHAT IT TELLS US ABOUT THE WAY THIS MELODY SOUNDS. WILL IT BEGIN HIGH OR LOW? (High.) WHICH WAY DOES IT MOVE NEXT? (Down.) Ask similar questions about the directional movement throughout. Then observe the movement again, this time emphasizing the distance between the pitches. WHEN THIS SONG BEGINS, IT MOVES DOWN BY STEPS. CAN YOU DECIDE WHAT HAPPENS NEXT? (**Stays the same,** then moves by **steps**—up, down, up, up.)

Put out three bells: F G A. As one child plays, the rest of the class may instruct him as to which bell he should use. Help control the rhythmic duration of each pitch by pointing to the tones. You may want the children to chant the rhythm first: long short—long short—short short short—lo-ong.

When the melody has been played in rhythm, ask the class to sing along on a neutral syllable. Then play the recording. LISTEN NOW TO THE SONG. CAN YOU FIND THE MELODY YOU PLAYED? ("Go to sleep, my dear little one" and "Go to sleep, Papa is upstairs.")

Extend   Ask children to draw their own pictures for phrase two of the song. They should discover that phrase two is the same except for the last tone. Determine that this song always moves in **steps.**

Give children additional experience with numbers by put-

ting the melody on a chart with numbers. Put the chart in the Music Learning Center for children to use when they wish to work alone.

Other Concept   PITCH: Tones may be combined to form harmony.

Discover   Play the autoharp accompaniment for the class as they sing. Ask them to decide when you should change chords. RAISE YOUR HAND WHEN YOU THINK THE "SOUND OF THE AUTOHARP" SHOULD CHANGE.

Invite one child to help you play. Hold down the chord button while he strums on each accented beat. Two children may also work together, with one holding down the appropriate buttons while another strokes the strings. A chart such as the one below will show the child which buttons to press down.

F	F	C7	F
F	F	C7	F

The pronunciation for the French follows. Because the "n" and "r" sounds cannot be represented adequately in English, be sure to listen to the recording for the most accurate pronunciation.

feh to^n doh-doh moh^n ptee frehr

feh to^n doh-doh moh^n ptee pee-eh-roh
(repeat both lines)

Quietly

Go to sleep, my dear lit - tle one, Go to
Fais ton do - do, mon ___ p'tit frère; Fais ton

sleep, Ma - ma is be - low. Go to sleep, Pa -
do - do, mon p'tit Pier - rot. Fais ton do - do,

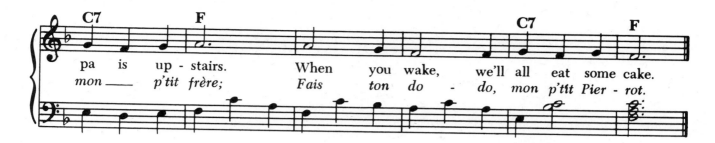

pa is up-stairs.　When you wake, we'll all eat some cake.
mon —— p'tit frère;　Fais ton do - do, mon p'tit Pier - rot.

Record 6 Side A Band 4 VOICES: children's choir.
ACCOMPANIMENT: percussion.
FORM: Instrumental; Vocal; Instrumental.

It's Raining

Traditional

Pentatonic Starting Tone: G

Meter: $\frac{4}{4}$ ($\frac{4}{\text{♩}}$)

Concept PITCH: The tones of a melody move up and down by steps and skips.

Discover Put out three bells: E, G, and A. WHO CAN MAKE UP A MELODY THAT USES ONLY THREE TONES? CAN YOU MAKE A MELODY THAT SOMETIMES SKIPS, SOMETIMES STEPS, AND SOMETIMES STAYS THE SAME? Give children freedom to explore. Encourage them to use interesting rhythms. As children experiment, they may realize that these three tones are often used in their own playground chants.

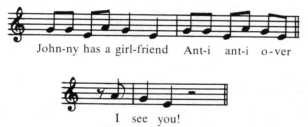

John-ny has a girl-friend Ant-i ant-i o-ver

I see you!

After children have experimented, play "It's Raining" for them. DO YOU HEAR ANYTHING THAT SOUNDS LIKE SOMETHING

YOU'VE ALREADY DONE? Help children realize that this song uses only three tones, just as the chants do.

Extend Some children may wish to practice until they can play the complete song. Put the bells in the Music Learning Center where they can work individually.

Other Concept PITCH: Tones may be combined to create harmony.

Discover When a child can play the complete melody in the correct rhythm, suggest that he ask another child to work with him to add an accompaniment. Put these bars on the soprano glockenspiel.

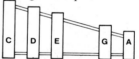

Suggest that the accompanist play in a rhythm that is different from the melody.

Play this on the bass xylophone:

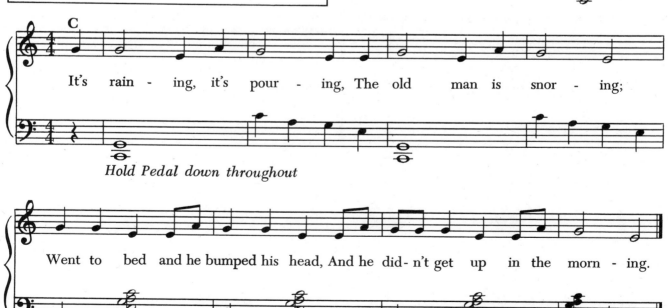

It's rain - ing, it's pour - ing, The old man is snor - ing;

Hold Pedal down throughout

Went to bed and he bumped his head, And he did-n't get up in the morn - ing.

Small Group Event No. 3

Concept   PITCH: Sounds may be relatively high or low.

Discover   Provide opportunities for children to improvise simple melodies and accompaniments. They should work in small groups. When other learning activities are in progress, experiment by "dampening" the sound. When using resonator bells, wrap the end of the mallet in felt and secure it with a rubber band. Later, when children perform for the class, the felt may be removed. Provide resonator bells (C D E G A C) and mallets. Place the bells in scrambled fashion in the Music Learning Center.

Invite two children to explore the bells to find the highest and lowest sounds in this group. Provide instructions so that one child will organize these sounds into an accompaniment as the other child plays a melody on the remaining bells.

Make the following chart and place it with the bells in the Music Learning Center. Read the chart with the two children to be sure they understand the instructions.

FIND THE LOWEST BELL.
FIND THE HIGHEST BELL.

PLAY OVER AND OVER AGAIN:

LET'S CALL THIS PART I OF THE PIECE.
USE THE REST OF THE BELLS AND MAKE UP A MELODY.
LET'S CALL THIS PART II OF THE PIECE.
CAN YOU AND YOUR PARTNER PLAY PART I AND PART II AT THE SAME TIME?
PLAY YOUR PIECE FOR THE CLASS.
CAN YOU GIVE YOUR PIECE A NAME?

Extend   Involve the rest of the class as active listeners by asking the following questions:
DID THE PERFORMERS FIND THE LOWEST AND HIGHEST SOUND FOR PART I? DID YOU LIKE THE PIECE? CAN YOU THINK OF OTHER WAYS TO PLAY THIS PIECE? (The piece may need to be played more than once as children find answers to the questions.)

Record 6 Side A Band 5 VOICE: woman.
ACCOMPANIMENT: string quartet.
FORM: Instrumental; Vocal; Coda.

Baa, Baa, Black Sheep

Mother Goose Rhyme

Key: C   Starting Tone: C(1)

Meter: $\frac{4}{4}$ $\left(\frac{4}{\text{♩}}\right)$

Concept DURATION: Rhythm patterns are made up of long and short tones.

Discover CAN YOU READ THE RHYTHM OF THIS NEW SONG? Show the pattern with lines. Chant with **long, short,** and **lo-ong.**

When children can chant and tap the pattern, chant with words. YOU LEARNED THAT SO WELL! LISTEN NOW TO THE RECORDING AND LEARN THE MELODY!

Other Concept PITCH: Tones within a melody move up and down by steps or skips.

Discover Show the melody pattern for the first measure on a chart with lines and numbers. Put the melody pattern for measures three and four on another chart.

WHICH PATTERN MOVES BY SKIPS? WHICH BY STEPS? CAN YOU SING THE PATTERNS WITH NUMBERS? WHICH WORDS OF OUR SONG MATCH THESE PATTERNS? ("Baa, baa, black sheep" and "Yes sir, yes sir, three bags full.")

141

Play and Sing (40–41)

Concept PITCH: The tones of a melody move up and down by steps and skips.

Discover Look at the pupil's book with the class. The pictures help to describe the poem and also show how the melody will move.

Learn to chant the poem in rhythm before determining the melody.

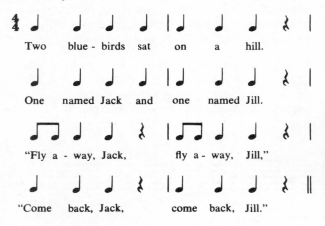

Two blue - birds sat on a hill.

One named Jack and one named Jill.

"Fly a - way, Jack, fly a - way, Jill,"

"Come back, Jack, come back, Jill."

Put the bells shown in the first picture on the stairsteps. WHO THINKS HE CAN PLAY THE MELODY FOR "TWO BLUE BIRDS SAT ON A HILL"? THE PICTURE HELPS YOU KNOW HOW THE MELODY SHOULD MOVE. Decide that it begins with the **lowest** bell, moves **up,** then **down:**

Practice playing, then singing the melody. HOW WILL "ONE NAMED JACK AND ONE NAMED JILL" MOVE? (It begins a little **higher,** then goes **up** and **down** by steps.)

Add bells G and A to the stairsteps. Practice playing and singing the two phrases, one after the other.

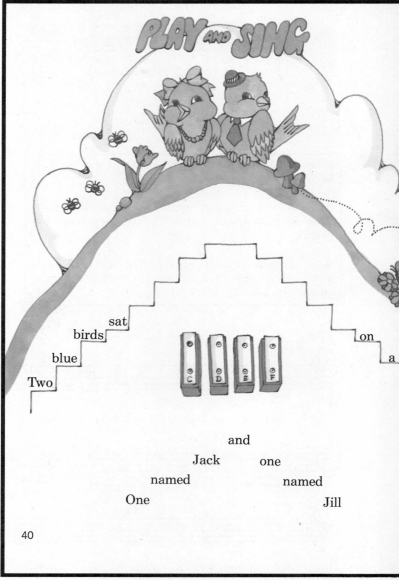

sat
birds
blue
Two on a

and
Jack one
named named
One Jill

40

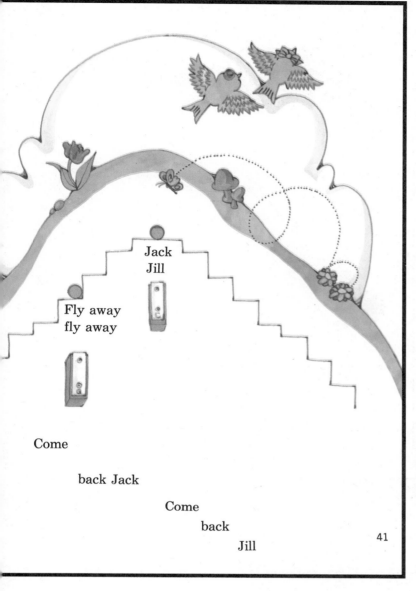

LOOK AT OUR STAIRSTEPS ON THE NEXT PAGE AND DECIDE
HOW THE MELODY WILL MOVE FOR "FLY AWAY JACK, FLY
AWAY JILL." WILL IT MOVE BY STEPS OR SKIPS? (By **skips**.)
Add the high C bell and practice this pattern.

Study the picture for "Come back, Jack, come back, Jill."
Help the class decide that it begins high, **skips down, skips**
again, then moves down by **steps.** Help the children find
this pattern.

CAN WE PLAY AND SING THE WHOLE SONG? YOU ARE SUCH
GOOD MUSICIANS THAT YOU HAVE LEARNED TO PLAY AND
SING A SONG BY LOOKING AT ITS PICTURE!

Extend Help children determine the numbers for the
complete song by observing the position of the bells on
the stairsteps. As they count, remind them that when patterns **skip**, numbers will need to be omitted; when patterns
step, they will use every number, one after the other. The
numbers will be:

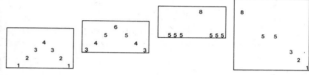

DT/ Record 6 Side A Band 6 VOICES:
children's choir.
ACCOMPANIMENT: flute, bassoon, violin,
cello, percussion, trumpet, trombone.
FORM: Instrumental; Vocal; Instrumental;
Vocal; Coda.

Two Bluebirds

Traditional

Key: C   Starting Tone: C(1)

Meter: $\frac{4}{4}$ $\left(\frac{4}{\stackrel{}{\downarrow}}\right)$

Two blue-birds sat on a hill.   One named Jack and one named Jill.

"Fly a-way, Jack,   fly a-way Jill,"   "Come back, Jack,   come back, Jill."

143

Ding, Dong, Bell

Mother Goose Rhyme
Traditional

Key: F   Starting Tone: F(1)

Meter: $\frac{4}{4}$ ($\frac{4}{\;}$)

DT/ Record 6   Side A   Band 7   VOICES:
children's choir.
ACCOMPANIMENT: trumpets, clarinet, viola,
trombone, percussion.
FORM: Introduction; Vocal; Instrumental;
Vocal.

Concept   PITCH: Melodies move by steps and skips within a scale.

Discover   A chart showing the melody of phrase one of "Ding, Dong, Bell" can be prepared.

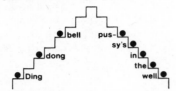

Remind children of their experience with "Two Blue Birds." Put out the bells F G A B♭ C and ask them to play the melody from its "picture." Remind them that determining the number of each tone to be played may also help them.

When children have learned to play and sing the first phrase, play the recording. LISTEN TO THE COMPLETE SONG.

DID YOU LEARN YOUR PART OF THE MELODY CORRECTLY? CAN YOU HEAR THAT SAME MELODY AGAIN? (Yes, "Who put her in, Little Johnny Green" has the same melody; the rhythm is slightly changed.) YOU ALREADY KNOW HALF THE SONG! LISTEN CAREFULLY AND SEE IF YOU CAN LEARN THE WHOLE SONG!

Sing the song as a dialogue:

Group 1: measures 1-2   Group 2: measure 5

Group 2: measure 3   Group 1: measure 6

Group 1: measure 4   All: measures 7-10

Other Concept   PITCH: Tones may be combined to create harmony.

The following pattern may be played as an accompaniment on bass xylophone or metallophone, to suggest the sound of the bell:

Record 6 Side B Band 1 VOICES: woman, man.
ACCOMPANIMENT: English horn, clarinet, flute, harp.
FORM: Introduction; Vocal, *v. 1;* Interlude; Vocal, *v. 2;* Interlude; Vocal, *v. 3;* Coda.

David Dillie Dow

Words and Music by John Jacob Niles

Key: D minor   Starting Tone: A(5)

Meter: $\frac{4}{4}$ ($\frac{4}{\downarrow}$)

When children have heard the song, discuss the various things David did. When they know the song, they may act out David's chores. End each verse with a big bow.

Concept PITCH: Melodies are made up of tones that move by step or skip.

Discover LISTEN CAREFULLY. CAN YOU HEAR A MELODY PATTERN THAT MOVES DOWN BY STEPS? ("David Dillie Dow".) Scramble the D E F G A bells and put them out.

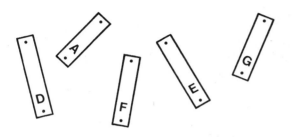

Ask the class to help one child put them in order from low to high so the melody pattern can be played. As the class works, ask leading questions to help them. ARE ALL THE BELLS THE SAME SIZE? DO YOU SUPPOSE THE FACT THAT SOME ARE BIGGER MAKES ANY DIFFERENCE IN THEIR SOUND? WHICH BELL SEEMS TO BE THE LOWEST—THE BIGGEST BELL OR THE SMALLEST?

Children may play up and down these five bells as an introduction and as an interlude between each verse.

Other Concept PITCH: Melodies are made up of a specific group of tones such as a major or minor scale.

Discover Some children may notice that this song sounds "different." Play the D E F G A pattern of the minor scale on which this song is based. Then play D E F♯ G A (the beginning of the major scale). Ask children to describe the difference between the two patterns. (Avoid trying to convince the children that minor is "sad!")

To extend children's awareness of the differences, return to "Two Blue Birds." Put out the bells for the C minor scale (C D E♭ F G A♭ B♭ C). Ask children to play the song using this new scale, and invite their comments about the differences they hear.

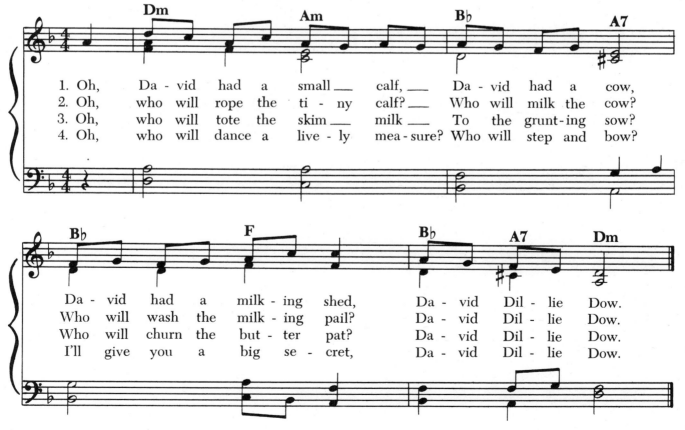

1. Oh,   Da - vid   had   a   small ___ calf, ___ Da - vid   had   a   cow,
2. Oh,   who   will   rope   the   ti - ny   calf? ___ Who   will   milk   the   cow?
3. Oh,   who   will   tote   the   skim ___ milk ___ To   the   grunt - ing   sow?
4. Oh,   who   will   dance   a   live - ly   mea - sure? Who   will   step   and   bow?

Da - vid   had   a   milk - ing   shed,   Da - vid   Dil - lie   Dow.
Who   will   wash   the   milk - ing   pail?   Da - vid   Dil - lie   Dow.
Who   will   churn   the   but - ter   pat?   Da - vid   Dil - lie   Dow.
I'll   give   you   a   big   se - cret,   Da - vid   Dil - lie   Dow.

Two Bluebirds (42–43)

Piano accompaniment on page 143.

> **Concept** PITCH: Melodies may move by steps or skips.
>
> **Discover** This song is an introduction to staff notation. children should have learned the song "Two Blue Birds" and completed all the activities suggested on pages 142–3 before proceeding to this activity.
>
> As children look at pages 42-43 of the pupil's book, encourage them to comment on this new "picture of melody." DO YOU KNOW THIS SONG? WHAT HELPS YOU TO KNOW? (The words and illustrations.)
>
> WE CAN ALSO TELL WHICH MELODY IT IS BY LOOKING AT ITS PICTURE. DO YOU REMEMBER WHEN THE MELODY FOR "TWO BLUE BIRDS" MOVED UP AND DOWN BY STEPS? ("Two bluebirds sat on a hill.") WHEN DID IT MOVE UP BY SKIPS? ("-way, Jack," and "Come back.") CAN YOU REMEMBER WHERE IT STAYED THE SAME? ("fly away.")
>
> Guide children to compare the "pictures" of these three patterns and to talk about the differences. As they do so, give them the new vocabulary they need. The five lines seen in the picture are called a **staff**. The black dots are **notes**. Notice that some notes are **on lines** (that is, the line goes through the middle of the note). Other notes are **in the spaces** between the two lines.
>
> Choose a child to play the melody again while the class follows this new "picture of the melody." Suggest that the children follow the up-down curve of the note picture by sliding a finger along the page as they listen or sing.

Extend Write some patterns from previously learned songs on a chart so that children may use them in various ways.

Sleep, Baby, Sleep

Stretching Song

(Now tall, now small)

Ding, Dong, Bell

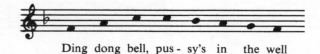

Ding dong bell, pus - sy's in   the well

See-Saw, Margery Daw

Two Bluebirds

Here is another way to show a picture of melody.
Where does the melody go up and down? Stay the same?

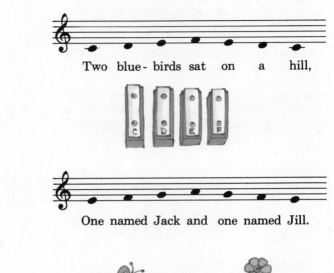

Two blue - birds sat   on   a   hill,

One named Jack and one named Jill.

42

Hey, Betty Martin

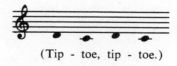

(Tip - toe, tip - toe.)

Examine each picture and decide how the tones will move: **up-down**, by **steps**, or by **skips**. As children make observations, play the patterns for them. DOES IT SOUND THE WAY YOU THOUGHT IT WOULD? SING EACH SONG AS IT IS IDENTIFIED.

Another time, show two patterns only. Play the recording of one of the songs and ask the children to choose the appropriate "picture."

Put the charts in the Music Learning Center. Write the names for the bells they need below the notes so that children may play the patterns.

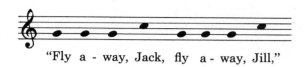

"Fly a - way, Jack, fly a - way, Jill,"

"Come back, Jack, come back, Jill."

43

Exploring the Staff

Children are ready to investigate staff notation when they can:

show the contour of melodies with lines;

describe melodic movement using the terms **up-down** and **step-skip**;

identify familiar melodies from numbers;

learn new melody patterns from numbers.

After children have been introduced to the idea that melodies may be "pictured" on a staff with notes, plan additional activities. Draw a staff on a flannel board. Cut note heads from construction paper or felt. Invite children to make up their own "melody pictures" following certain instructions:

MAKE A MELODY THAT MOVES UP AND DOWN BY STEPS.

MAKE A MELODY THAT MOVES UP AND DOWN BY SKIPS.

MAKE A MELODY THAT MOVES UP BY SKIPS AND DOWN BY STEPS.

As individual children put notes onto the flannel board, play each new melody on the piano. Ask the class to decide whether the instructions have been followed. DOES HER MELODY MOVE UP AND DOWN BY STEPS? WHAT DOES SHE NEED TO DO TO HER PICTURE SO THAT IT WILL SOUND THIS WAY?

Help the children realize that:

In music notation, the "empty spaces" are just as important as the lines: notes can go **on lines** (line through the middle of the note), or **in spaces** (note inserted "between" two lines).

When we want to make a melody move by **steps,** the notes must be on every line and in every space, one after another. When the melody moves by **skips,** lines or spaces are omitted.

Magic Tom-Tom

from the Congo
Words and Arrangement by Carol Hart Sayre

Tonality: Pentatonic   Starting Tone: E

Meter: $\frac{4}{4}$ $\left(\frac{4}{\text{♩}}\right)$

DT/ Record 6   Side B   Band 2   VOICES: children's choir.
ACCOMPANIMENT: percussion.
FORM: Introduction; Vocal; Interlude; Vocal.

TODAY WE'RE GOING TO TAKE A TRIP ON A MAGIC CARPET TO A FAR-AWAY LAND. LISTEN TO FIND OUT WHERE YOU ARE GOING. THERE IS SOMETHING MAGIC THERE, ALSO! CAN YOU FIND OUT WHAT IT IS? Play the recording as often as needed to decide that the song takes place in a jungle (as suggested by the presence of the monkey and birds). There is a magic tom-tom. Determine that a tom-tom is a type of drum.

Concept   DURATION: Rhythm patterns include long and short tones.

Discover   HERE IS A PICTURE OF ONE OF THE PATTERNS THE MAGIC DRUM SINGS. Put this pattern on the chalkboard or on a chart.

— — — — —

HOW WILL THIS PATTERN SOUND? (Long, long, short short long.) In this song, the half note will be considered the "long" tone, the quarter note "short." The terms "long" and "short" describe relationships, not absolutes. Be careful that the children do not get the idea that the half note is always "long," the eighth note always "short," but rather that sounds are longer and shorter in relation to each other.

Tap the pattern. LISTEN TO THE SONG AGAIN. CAN YOU FIND WORDS THAT MATCH THIS PATTERN? ("Boom, boom, boom, boom, boom.") HERE IS ANOTHER PATTERN. HOW WILL IT SOUND?

— — — —

(Long short short lo-ong.) The words are "Oh, dance and sing."

LISTEN TO THE INTRODUCTION. DO YOU HEAR ONE MAGIC TOM-TOM OR MORE THAN ONE? HOW WILL YOU DECIDE? (By listening for different "sounds" [timbres] and hearing more than one pattern at a time.) Tap with the recording. Tap first one tom-tom pattern, then the other. Write each pattern on the chalkboard.

Give the two drums to two children; ask them to accompany as the class sings.

Extend   Review rhythmic notation with the children to prepare them for combining the rhythmic notation with melodic notation on the staff. Show them the note pictures for the two drums.

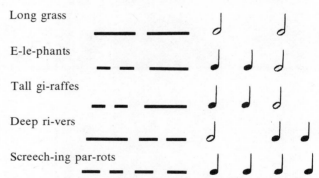

PRETEND YOU HAVE A MAGIC TOM-TOM. CAN YOU MAKE IT TELL ABOUT THE JUNGLE? WHAT MIGHT YOU SEE IN A JUNGLE THAT YOUR DRUM COULD DESCRIBE? As children suggest word patterns and play them on a drum, show each with lines, then with notes. A few might be as follows.

Long grass

E-le-phants

Tall gi-raffes

Deep ri-vers

Screech-ing par-rots

The patterns the children develop may be placed on 3" by 5" cards so that each child has his own packet. Individuals may then organize their cards into a sequence to make up their own "magic tom-tom" compositions. WHEN YOU HAVE A PLAN FOR YOUR COMPOSITION, PRACTICE IT. PLAY IT FOR THE CLASS.

Strongly accented, steady rhythm

Boom,   boom,   boom,   boom,   boom,   Boom,   boom,   boom,   boom,   boom.   Oh,

lis - ten to my mag- ic tom- tom, Lis - ten to its mag - ic beat! All the

birds hov - er near to chirp and sing, All the mon- keys swing down with

danc - ing feet. Oh, dance and sing! Oh, dance and sing!

Let's Make Long Sounds

Concept RHYTHM: Patterns are made up of long and short sounds.

Discover The purpose of this activity is to extend the awareness of sound duration to accommodate additional relationships (the relationships of whole, half, and quarter notes to each other). The notation shown on this page is for the information of the teacher, not the boys and girls.

To help children sense the longer sounds, show them how to make swishing sounds with their hands:

1. Make a table-top with one hand.

2. Make circles on the "table-top" hand with the other hand to produce swishing sounds.

When chanting the patterns, the voice may provide the underlying pulse. (Stress each pulse vocally while sustaining sound with hands.)

SAY WHAT I SAY—DO WHAT I DO.

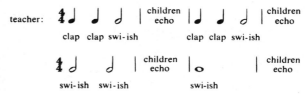

Extend Make up other rhythm patterns to "dictate" to the children. Invite them to respond by speaking the appropriate word as they clap or make swishing sounds. The youngsters should be challenged, but the teacher should pay close attention to the level of ability of the students so that they will be successful in their responses.

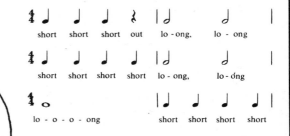

149

On a Monday Morning

Polish Folk Song
English version by Edmund Lakaszewski

Key: D Starting Tone: D(1)
Autoharp Key: C Starting Tone: C(1)

Meter: $\frac{3}{4}$ $\left(\frac{3}{\,\lrcorner}\right)$

DT/ Record 6 Side B Band 3 VOICES: children's choir.
ACCOMPANIMENT: flute, bassoon, violin, cello, percussion, trumpet, trombone.
FORM: Introduction; v. 1; Interlude; v. 2; Interlude; v. 3; Interlude; v. 4; Interlude; v. 5; Interlude; v. 6; Coda.

Listen to the recording; talk about different things that "tatús" (father, pronounced tah-toosh) and "I" did on this farm long ago. If possible, find pictures to illustrate various farming activities so children will grasp the meaning of the song.

Concept DURATION: Rhythm patterns may be made up of tones that are longer and shorter.

Discover After the song has become familiar to the children, divide the class into two groups. The first group chants each phrase; the second group echoes immediately by tapping the rhythm.

Group 1 chant: Group 2 tap:

On a Monday morning

Sunny Monday morning

Sowed our seed, tatús and I

DID ANY OF YOUR PATTERNS SOUND THE SAME WHEN YOU CLAPPED THEM EVEN THOUGH THE WORDS WERE DIFFERENT? Help the children discover that there are only two different rhythm patterns in the entire song. Phrases one and two have the same rhythm. The remaining phrases all have the same rhythm as phrase three.

Extend CAN WE SHOW OUR RHYTHM PATTERNS WITH LINES? CAN WE DESCRIBE THEM WITH WORDS?

First pattern:
(Short short long long lo-ong long.)

━━ ━━ ━━ ━━ ━━━━ ━━

Second pattern:
(Short short long long short short lo-ong.)

━━ ━━ ━━ ━━ ━━ ━━ ━━━━

HERE ARE THREE KINDS OF NOTES. Hold up eighth, quarter, and half notes cut from felt or construction paper. CAN YOU DECIDE WHICH NOTE WE CAN USE TO SHOW EACH PART OF OUR PATTERN?

First pattern:

Second pattern: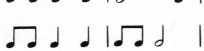

Other Concept PITCH: Melody patterns move by steps or skips. Use this song as an opportunity to show children how rhythm and melody combine in a "picture of music."

Show the picture of melody for phrase one on a chart:

WHO CAN TELL ME WHICH SONG I AM SHOWING? As children make suggestions, sing their answers until they decide which is correct. Decide whether each song suggested moves by steps or skips. Compare its motion with the movement shown in the picture.

THIS IS A PICTURE OF THE MELODY. LOOK! WE CAN ADD RHYTHM TO OUR PICTURE! While children watch, add the stems to each note head. THE "HEAD" TELLS US ABOUT THE MELODY; WE NEED THE "HEAD" AND THE "STEM" TO FIND OUT ABOUT THE RHYTHM.

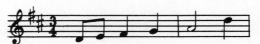

1. On a Mon - day morn - ing, sun - ny Mon - day morn - ing,
2. On a Tues - day morn - ing, sun - ny Tues - day morn - ing,
3. On a Wednes - day morn - ing, sun - ny Wednes - day morn - ing,
4. On a Thurs - day morn - ing, sun - ny Thurs - day morn - ing,
5. On a Fri - day morn - ing, sun - ny Fri - day morn - ing,
6 On a Sat-ur - day morn - ing, sun - ny noon and eve - ning,

Sowed our seed, ta - tuś and I, Sowed it when the sun was high.
Mowed our hay, ta - tuś and I, Mowed it when the sun was high.
Dried our hay, ta - tuś and I, Dried it when the sun was high.
Raked our hay, ta - tuś and I, Raked it when the sun was high.
Hauled our hay, ta - tuś and I, Hauled it till the dusk was nigh.
Sold our hay, ta - tuś and I, Sold it when the night was nigh.

Sowed our seed, ta - tuś and I, Sowed it when the sun was high.
Mowed our hay, ta - tuś and I, Mowed it when the sun was high.
Dried our hay, ta - tuś and I, Dried it when the sun was high.
Raked our hay, ta - tuś and I, Raked it when the sun was high.
Hauled our hay, ta - tuś and I, Hauled it till the dusk was nigh.
Sold our hay, ta - tuś and I, Sold it when the night was nigh.

Little White Duck

Music by Bernard Zaritsky
Words by Walt Barrows

Key: F   Starting Tone: C(5)

Meter: C $\left(\begin{smallmatrix}2\\ \mathbf{d}\end{smallmatrix}\right)$

DT/ Record 6   Side B   Band 4   VOICES: children's choir.
ACCOMPANIMENT: harp, oboe, French horn, cello.
FORM: Introduction; v. 1; Interlude; v. 2; Interlude; v. 3; Interlude; v. 4; Interlude; v. 5.

Children should have a number of opportunities to hear and enjoy this song informally before they attempt to learn it. Keep reviewing the story until children are sure of the sequence of the animals' appearances. After the children have listened once or twice, they may join in with the animal sounds at the end of each verse while they continue to listen to the remainder of the song.

Concept   DURATION: Music moves in relation to an underlying beat.

Discover   Invite children to plan actions to describe the movements of each animal. Suggest to the "animals" that they "swim" with the **rhythm of the beat.** (The half note sounds with the beat in this song, so the rhythm of the beat will be: $\mathbf{2\atop2}$ ♩ ♩ | .) Play an autoharp accompaniment, strumming on each beat.

Choose appropriate instruments to accompany the sound of each animal.

  Duck—guiro

  Frog—deep drum

  Bug—finger cymbals

  Snake—sandblock

  Child crying—C E F bells

Help children hear the difference between the "long" sounds of the beat played on the autoharp, and the short—rest sounds of the pattern played on the percussion instruments.

HERE IS A PICTURE OF OUR BEAT.

HERE IS A PICTURE OF THE PATTERN.

Discuss the differences; review the function of the ⅛ sign. (Rest, be quiet.)

Extend   Review other songs with the children, talking about the difference between the rhythm of the beat and the rhythm of the melody. Show the differences in lines and in notes.

HERE IS A PICTURE OF "IF YOU'RE HAPPY." (page 68)

rhythm of melody:

rhythm of beat:

"Trot, Pony, Trot" (page 86)

rhythm of melody:

rhythm of beat:

THE RHYTHM OF THE BEAT IS ALWAYS THE SAME; EACH NOTE IS JUST LIKE THE OTHERS. THE RHYTHM OF THE MELODY CHANGES; SOMETIMES THE NOTES SHOW LONGER SOUNDS, SOMETIMES SHORTER SOUNDS.

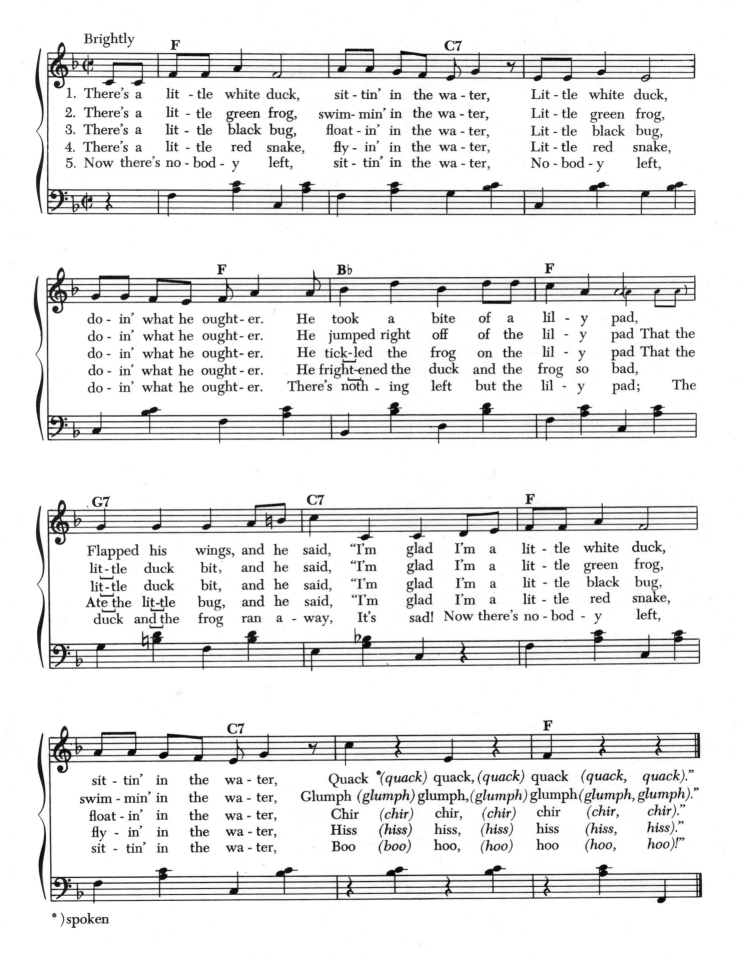

Ha Ha This-A-Way

American Folk Song

Key: F   Starting Tone: F(1)

Meter: $\frac{2}{4}$ ($\frac{2}{\textdownbarredflat}$)

DT/ Record 6   Side B   Band 5   VOICES: children's choir.
ACCOMPANIMENT: guitar, double bass, percussion, banjo.
FORM: Instrumental; Vocal; Interlude; Vocal, Coda.

Concept   DURATION: Rhythm moves with steady beats, some of which are accented.

Discover   Ask children to move as they listen to the refrain of this song. CAN YOU MOVE WITH THE STEADY BEAT? Observe the different ways children move.

THIS TIME, LET'S ALL DO THE SAME MOVEMENT WHILE I PLAY THE DRUM. REPEAT YOUR MOVEMENT OVER AND OVER.

Drum:

YOU ALL MOVED WITH MY BEAT. HERE IS A PICTURE OF THE PATTERN I PLAYED. Use two shades of construction paper to show the accent.

Ask children to comment on differences in the picture.

Extend   As children repeat the movement, play the drum again, changing it to move in threes.

DID YOU STILL WANT TO MOVE THE SAME WAY? WHY DID YOU NEED TO CHANGE? HERE IS A PICTURE OF THE NEW BEAT I PLAYED. HOW IS IT DIFFERENT?

Notice that now a **strong beat** comes in after every two lighter beats instead of after every one. Play "The Farmer," page 157. WHICH PICTURE MATCHES THE BEAT RHYTHM OF THIS SONG? (The one that shows movement in threes.)

When I was a lit-tle boy, When I was a lit-tle boy,
I went to a lit-tle school, Lit-tle school, __ lit-tle school,

When I was a lit-tle boy, six years old.
I went to a lit-tle school, I've been told.

Refrain

Ha, ha, this-a-way; Ha, ha, that-a-way;

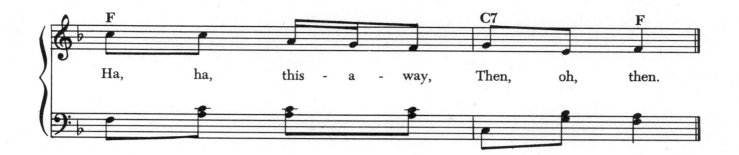

Ha,   ha,   this - a - way,   Then,   oh,   then.

Response to Patterns of Sound

Concept DURATION: Rhythm patterns are made up of sounds and silences that are long and short.

Discover Children will be responding to rhythmic patterns which include tones of different lengths (as represented by quarter notes, half notes, whole notes, and rests) long before they actually see notation. Even after notation has been introduced, provide children with many opportunities to respond to a variety of rhythmic patterns. Echo games provide an excellent means of giving children the repeated experiences necessary for gaining understanding and control of rhythm.

Most girls and boys clap with a horizontal motion of "in—pull apart—back in." This often causes tension and may prevent the child from performing with rhythmic accuracy.

LET'S DISCOVER A NEW WAY TO CLAP. Hold one hand, palm up, like a table top. This hand remains still, to receive the claps.

The other hand moves up and down like a yo-yo and initiates the clapping sound.

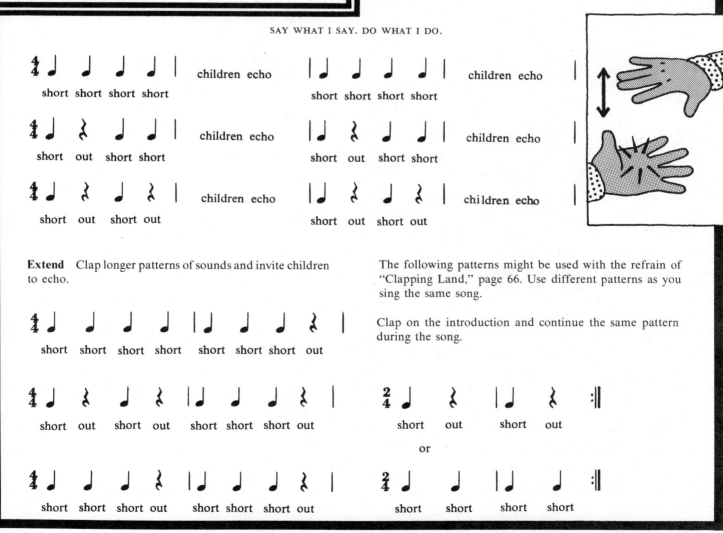

SAY WHAT I SAY. DO WHAT I DO.

Extend Clap longer patterns of sounds and invite children to echo.

The following patterns might be used with the refrain of "Clapping Land," page 66. Use different patterns as you sing the same song.

Clap on the introduction and continue the same pattern during the song.

or

155

Scenes from Childhood, Excerpts

by Robert Schumann
BORN 1810   DIED 1856

Record 9   Side B   Band 5
Walter Gieseking, pianist.
TIME: 6:35

Introduce each of the following movements from *Scenes from Childhood* at a different time. Each composition may be heard in many different ways. When children are familiar with each piece, play several and compare the different moods. Help children expand their musical vocabulary as they talk about melodies, rhythms, and designs. Encourage children to show their musical awareness through movement as well as verbally.

Catch Me

Concept   DURATION: Rhythm is made up of patterns of longer and shorter sounds.

Discover   THE TITLE OF THIS MUSIC IS "CATCH ME." WHY IS THIS A GOOD TITLE? (The "running" rhythm of the melody is often interrupted, as though something such as a ball or person is being caught.)

WHEN DOES IT SOUND LIKE THE BALL IS BEING TOSSED AND CAUGHT? DOES THE MUSIC TELL YOU? (On the long, louder tones, at the beginning of each short pattern.)

Children may work in pairs: one "tosses" on the first long tone and the other "catches" on the next long tone.

Entreating Child

Concept   PITCH: A melody has a shape which rises and falls.

Discover   Play the recording. Show the contour of the three melodies on charts.

(A)   **(B)**   **(C)**

Talk about how each moves. "Scramble" the order and ask children to decide which chart should be first, which second, which third.

Extend   Make enough charts of each melody (four of the first one, two of each of the others) so that children can show the melodic shape of the entire phrase sequence. (A A B B C C A A)

Dreaming

Concept   STRUCTURE: Music is made up of phrases.

Discover   This lovely melody should be used many times for quiet listening before asking children to listen for its design.

CAN YOU SHOW OUR PHRASES WITH YOUR BODY AND ARMS? Have the children begin by bending to the right, with both hands almost touching the floor. As the phrase is sounded, they could gradually straighten up, moving their arms in an arc overhead, then bending again, this time to the left. Repeat for each long phrase. (There are eight phrases, all based on the same melodic shape.)

Knight of the Hobby Horse

Concept   DURATION: Music can move in threes; rhythm patterns may be even or uneven.

Discover   Tell children the title of this music. Invite them to pretend they are riding a rocking horse. With one foot in front, they may "rock" back and forth, using a slow galloping step.

Concept   MUSICAL CONTROLS: Music may become louder and softer.

Discover   As children move to the "rocking" rhythm, some may also respond to the changes in dynamic level. Cut different shapes to reflect the contrasting dynamic levels. Have six shapes, one for each phrase. Ask children to put the shapes in order, to show the changes in dynamics.

Frightening

Concept   MUSICAL CONTROLS: Music may be loud and soft, fast and slow, smooth (legato) and "jerky" (staccato).

Discover   IF YOU WERE MAKING UP RESTFUL MUSIC, WOULD IT BE LOUD OR SOFT? (Soft.) WOULD IT BE FAST OR SLOW? (Slow.) SMOOTH OR "JERKY"? (Smooth.) IF YOU WERE MAKING UP EXCITING MUSIC, HOW WOULD IT MOVE? (Fast, loud, "jerky.") CAN YOU DRAW A DESIGN THAT SHOWS SOUNDS THAT ARE RESTFUL? DRAW ANOTHER DESIGN THAT SHOWS SOUNDS THAT ARE EXCITING? Give children two pieces of construction paper on which to draw their designs. When they have completed the two designs, play the music. IF YOU HEAR RESTFUL MUSIC, HOLD UP YOUR "RESTFUL" DESIGN. IF YOU HEAR EXCITING MUSIC, HOLD UP YOUR "EXCITING" DESIGN. Play the recording. Children will quickly discover that they must change from one picture to another because the music alternates between restful and exciting.

Exploring Music: the Fourth Quarter

DT/ Record 6 Side B Band 6 VOICES: children's choir.
ACCOMPANIMENT: string quartet.
FORM: Introduction; *v. 1;* Interlude; *v. 2;* Interlude; *v. 3;* Interlude; *v. 4;* Coda.

The Farmer

English Singing Game

Key: F   Starting Tone: F(1)

Meter: $\frac{3}{4}$ $\left(\frac{3}{\quarternote}\right)$

Concept DURATION: Beats may be grouped by accents.

Discover CAN YOU SHOW HOW THE FARMER SOWS HIS BARLEY AND WHEAT? THIS FARMER LIVED LONG AGO. HE SOWED HIS GRAIN BY HAND, TOSSING IT OVER THE PLOWED GROUND. (Demonstrate: start with right hand in left, as though reaching for a handful of grain, then move right hand outward in an arc as though tossing grain.)

Children may work in pairs, as suggested by the words of the song. One child "shows" the movement during verse one; the other member of the pair imitates him during verse two.

Extend Remind children of the pattern they observed when learning "Ha Ha This-a-way." WHICH PICTURE WILL MATCH THIS MUSIC? To help them decide, put both pictures up. (Use chalk, construction paper in the chalk tray, or felt lines on a flannel board.) Ask children to tap first one pattern, then the other, as they listen to the recording. WHICH PATTERN SEEMS TO "MATCH"? (The second one.)

157

Taffy

Traditional

Key: C Starting Tone: C(1)

Meter: $\frac{4}{4}$ $\left(\frac{4}{\quarternote} \right)$

Record 6 Side B Band 7 VOICE: man.
ACCOMPANIMENT: woodwind quartet,
percussion.
FORM: Introduction; Vocal; Instrumental;
Vocal; Coda.

Play the recording and enjoy the amusing words. Help children understand the meaning. TAFFY WAS A WELSH-MAN; YOU ARE AN AMERICAN. HE CAME FROM A COUNTRY CALLED WALES. THE MARROW BONE IS WHAT IS LEFT AFTER ALL THE MEAT IS GONE FROM THE LEG OF BEEF. WHAT DO YOU SUPPOSE HAPPENED TO THE MEAT? (Taffy ate it!)

Concept PITCH: Melodies are based on a specific group of tones such as a major scale.

Discover Play the recording one more time, enjoying the song, then put this pattern on the stairsteps:

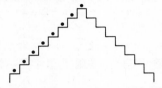

CAN YOU SING OUR PATTERN WITH NUMBERS? Sing up and down the scale, pointing at each disk. THIS TIME, SING IN THE RHYTHM I SHOW YOU AS I POINT. SOMETIMES YOU NEED TO REPEAT NUMBERS. Point at the stairsteps, in the rhythm of the first four measures of "Taffy."

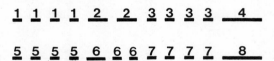

WHO KNOWS THE MELODY WE SANG? IT IS FROM A SONG WE HAVE LISTENED TO AND ENJOYED! If children do not name "Taffy," guide them more specifically. IT IS PART OF THIS SONG. CAN YOU FIND THE WORDS THAT MATCH? Play the recording again. CAN YOU SING THAT MELODY WITH WORDS? CAN YOU PLAY THAT MELODY ON THE BELLS?

Extend Line up eight children in front of the room; hand out the C bells in this order.

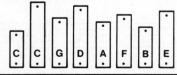

HERE ARE THE BELLS FOR OUR SONG. WILL YOU PLAY THE MELODY WE SANG? Ask children to play one after another. They will soon discover that the bells are "all mixed up." OH DEAR, OUR BELLS AREN'T IN THE RIGHT ORDER! CAN SOMEONE HELP ME FIX THEM? As the class makes suggestions, ask the first child to play his bell. Compare it with the second child's bell. WE NEED TO BEGIN WITH THE LOWEST BELL. WHICH ONE WILL BE OUR FIRST BELL? When children have selected the proper bell (the low C), ask the child holding that bell to stand at the beginning of the line. Now ask him and the third child to play. WHICH IS THE LOWEST? (The one at the beginning of the line.) Continue in similar fashion until all the bells are in order from low to high.

NOW WE CAN PLAY OUR MELODY! BUT FIRST LET'S COUNT OUR BELLS. Count and sing: 1 2 3 4 5 6 7 8. Write these numbers on the chalkboard. Point to them in the appropriate rhythm as the bell players perform the first half of the song.

GOOD! WHO KNOWS WHICH BELLS WE NEED TO PLAY "I WENT TO TAFFY'S HOUSE"? WILL THE BELLS MOVE DOWN OR UP? BY STEPS OR SKIPS? (A big skip down.) Find the appropriate bells and write the numbers on the chalkboard.

8 8 8

1 1 1

Follow a similar sequence of questions and experimentation until the entire song has been played on the bells.

Other Concepts DURATION: Rhythm patterns are made up of long and short tones.

Discover Show these two rhythm patterns in notes.

WHO KNOWS THE NAME OF THE SONG I AM SHOWING? I HAVE SHOWN YOU THE FIRST TWO RHYTHM PATTERNS WE SANG! CAN YOU DECIDE HOW THEY SOUND? TELL ME WHEN THE SOUNDS WILL BE SHORT AND WHEN THEY WILL BE LONG.

The class should chant:

short short short short long long

short short short short lo-ong

Help them to name the song "Taffy."

EXPRESSIVE TOTALITY: Rhythm, melody, tempo, volume, and timbre combine to communicate musical ideas or extra-musical feelings.

Discover As children enjoy the recording, draw attention to accompaniment which helps describe the words of the song.

Notice the pattern that moves down by steps during the instrumental and at the end of the song. It might suggest going to Taffy's house (or hurrying away). Listen for the "thump" and decide what it might be describing.

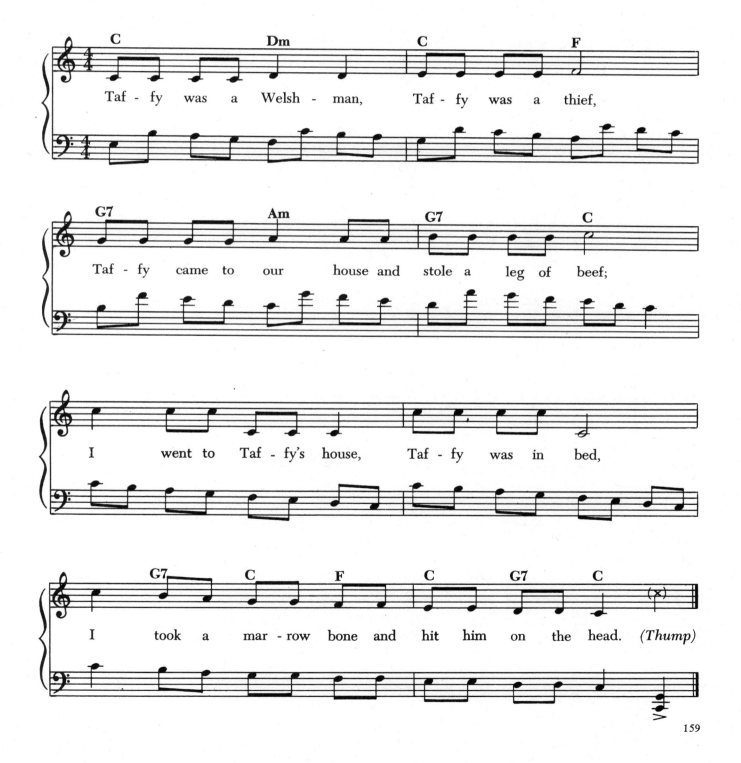

159

Little Red Caboose

American Folk Song

Key: D Starting Tone: A(5)
Autoharp Key: C Starting Tone: G(5)

Meter: $\frac{2}{4}$ $\left(\frac{2}{\text{♩}}\right)$

Concept MUSICAL CONTROLS: The tempo of music may become faster or slower.

Discover Listen to the recording. Discuss the overall movement of the train as described in the music (**slow-fast-slow**). Invite children to use their own symbols to draw a picture of how the music changed.

DT/ Record 7 Side A Band 1
ACCOMPANIMENT: electric guitar, electric bass, piano, percussion.
FORM: Introduction; Vocal; Interlude; Vocal (fade out).

Extend Girls and boys may wish to dramatize this music through movement. Encourage children to select appropriate instruments for an accompaniment based on ideas heard in the recording. They might use sandblocks, bells, and whistles.

160

DT/ Record 7 Side A Band 2 VOICE: male folk-singer.
ACCOMPANIMENT: percussion.
FORM: Introduction; Vocal; Interlude; Vocal; Coda.

Lullaby

Chinese Folk Song

Pentatonic Starting Tone: G

Meter: 4/4 (♩)

Concept TIME AND PLACE: The ways in which the elements of music are combined in a piece can reflect the time and place of its origin.

Discover Review previously learned songs from other countries. These might include "Trot, Pony, Trot," page 87 (China), "Happiness," page 133 (Africa), and "My Twenty Pennies," page 184 (Latin America).

BOYS AND GIRLS EVERYWHERE LIKE TO SING AND PLAY. SOMETIMES WE CAN TELL WHERE THE BOYS AND GIRLS LIVE BY THE SOUND OF THEIR MUSIC. WHAT KINDS OF THINGS DO YOU NOTICE IN THESE THREE SONGS THAT MIGHT HELP US DECIDE THAT THEY MIGHT BE SUNG BY BOYS AND GIRLS IN DIFFERENT PARTS OF THE WORLD? Children may make a variety of suggestions. One important difference is the choice of instruments. Draw attention to the accompaniments in each selection.

Trot, Pony, Trot: bells, wood block

Happiness: percussion

My Twenty Pennies: trumpets, guitar

NOW LISTEN TO A NEW SONG. CAN YOU DECIDE WHERE THE BOYS AND GIRLS WHO LIKE TO SING THIS SONG LIVE? IT IS FROM THE SAME PLACE AS ONE OF THE SONGS WE JUST LEARNED!

Help children decide by listening to the instruments that this song comes from the same land as "Trot, Pony, Trot."

Play the melody for "Lullaby" on the bells for the children. Ask them to count the different bells you use. (Six.) Draw attention to the letter names; observe that only five dif-

ferent letter names are used. Play "Trot, Pony, Trot" and discover that only three different letter names are used in this song. THIS IS ANOTHER CLUE. SONGS THAT BOYS AND GIRLS SING IN CHINA OFTEN USE ONLY A FEW TONES.

Other Concept PITCH: Harmony is created by combining tones.

Discover Help children use harmony by learning several instrumental parts to accompany the song. Ask children to clap the rhythm of the pattern in each instrumental part shown below. Discover that Part I and Part II keep the steady beat, while Part III has a pattern of long and short sounds and silences. Choose one child to play each pattern. Play his pattern several times as he listens carefully, noting steps and skips. Then ask him to practice his patterns over and over.

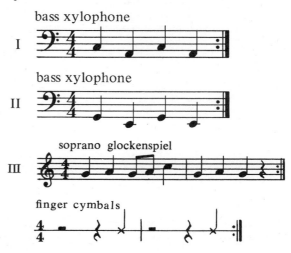

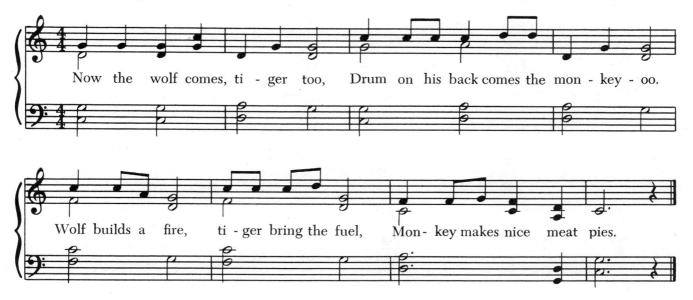

My Pony (44–45)

German Folk Song

Key: G   Starting Tone: G(1)

Meter: $\frac{2}{4}$ $\left(\frac{2}{\downarrow}\right)$

Concept   PITCH: Tones of a melody move up and down by steps and skips.

Discover   Look at the picture on page 44 of the pupil's book. Decide how the pattern will move: **up by skips,** then **down by steps.** Listen to the recording. Discover that on the word "Trot, trot, trot! Trot, my pony, trot!" the melody moves in the way illustrated by the picture on page 44.

Play the recording again and ask children to mirror the movement of this melody with their hands as they listen. CAN YOU SHOW THE MELODY FOR THE LAST PHRASE TOO? Then challenge children to sing the melody without assistance.

Look at the pictures on page 45. Help the children recall that this is another way to show pictures of melody. Look at each picture. Decide what the picture tells about the melody. DOES IT MOVE UP OR DOWN? DOES IT MOVE BY STEPS OR SKIPS?

Determine that the melody for "Go and never stop!" moves **up:** "Trot, my pony, trot" moves **down;** "Trot, trot, trot" moves **up by skips.**

My Pony

Listen to this song.
When does the melody move like this?

44

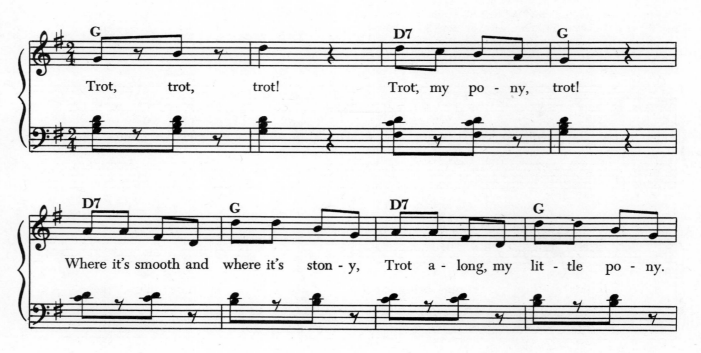

Trot,   trot,   trot!   Trot, my po - ny, trot!

Where it's smooth and   where it's   ston - y,   Trot a - long, my lit - tle po - ny.

When does the melody move up?

When does the melody move down?

When does the melody move like this?

Play these melody patterns on the bells.

45

Put the bells shown in the pupil's book on the stairsteps and ask one child to play these patterns. When he can play them in the appropriate rhythm, help him to combine them in the proper sequence so that he can accompany the class during phrases one and four as the class sings the entire song.

Extend Write short melodic patterns on individual charts, as shown below.

Ask the class to learn to play and sing each pattern, then invite the children to put the charts in sequence to plan a complete melody. One child may be the "conductor" and point to the appropriate chart. He may also point at the individual notes to indicate rhythm. The rhythm pattern might also be planned ahead of time and indicated on each chart by adding either lines or the appropriate stems.

DT/ Record 7   Side A   Band 3   VOICES: children's choir.
ACCOMPANIMENT: harp, oboe, French horn, cello.
FORM: Instrumental; Vocal; Interlude; Coda.

Pussy Cat, Pussy Cat

Music by J.W. Elliott
Mother Goose Rhyme

Key F   Starting Tone: C(5)

Meter: $\frac{6}{8}$ ($\frac{2}{\text{♩.}}$)

Record 7 Side A Band 4 VOICES: children's choir.
ACCOMPANIMENT: woodwind quintet.
FORM: Introduction; Vocal; Instrumental; Vocal; Coda.

Concept PITCH: Tones within a melody may move up or down by steps or skips, or they may remain the same.

Discover Put the following patterns on four separate charts.

After children have listened to the recording and enjoyed the music, put the four charts up in the order shown above. HERE IS A SCRAMBLED PICTURE OF OUR SONG! DO YOU THINK YOU CAN PUT OUR PICTURE IN ORDER? WHO CAN

FIND THE PICTURE THAT MATCHES THE FIRST PART OF OUR SONG? Sing "Pussy cat, pussy cat, where have you been?" As children make suggestions, ask leading questions. WHERE DOES THE MELODY BEGIN, HIGH OR LOW? DOES IT MOVE UP OR DOWN? BY STEPS OR SKIPS? OR DOES IT REMAIN THE SAME? Help children decide that the last chart shown is really the first pattern of the song. Sing the second phrase "I've been to London to visit the Queen" and ask similar questions. Proceed throughout until children have the four phrases in correct order.

Sing the song, as one child points to the notation on each chart.

Other Concept TIMBRE: Instruments have distinctive sounds. Draw attention to the accompaniment played by a woodwind quintet. The pictures of these instruments may be found in the pupil's book, pages 56-57.

Some children may be able to hear individual instruments during the instrumental interlude. The **oboe** plays the melody on phrase one while the **flute** plays a contrasting melody. The **clarinet** plays the melody on phrase two, and the **bassoon** can be heard playing a low accompaniment.

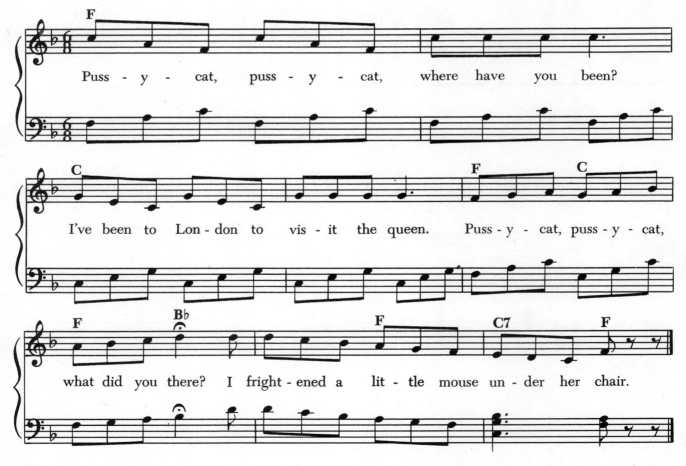

Puss - y - cat, puss - y - cat, where have you been?

I've been to Lon - don to vis - it the queen. Puss - y - cat, puss - y - cat,

what did you there? I fright - ened a lit - tle mouse un - der her chair.

Music of Other Times and Places

The selections on this page should not only help children to become aware of music of other times and places but also to expand their sensitivity to musical organization through movement. The following information describes musical features which may be obvious to children as they hear and respond to the music. Encourage the children to improvise appropriate movements as they listen to these selections.

Viva Autlan, excerpt

Mexican Mariachi Music

by Peters-Amaya

After the trumpet fanfare, the Mariachis play a happy melody. The form of the excerpt is A A B B. Invite children to respond to the steady beat which moves in groups of four.

African Drumming, excerpt

Children will hear many exciting percussion sounds. Invite them to respond to the repeated rhythm in the background.

HOW WILL YOU MOVE WITH THIS SOUND? The pattern is **uneven;** a skip or gallop would be appropriate.

Limbo Dance

Trinidad Steel Band Music

Children will discover that some instruments are playing even rhythms as others play uneven rhythms. Divide the class into three groups. Each group makes up a movement appropriate for one of the rhythms.

Even—low drums

Even—fast "shac-shac" (maraca-type shakers)

Uneven—high steel drums

Ocho (Ancient Court Days), excerpt

by Shiko Ozaki

Invite the children to move to this dignified Japanese music. Divide the class into two groups. Let Group I respond to the sustained sounds of the flute and Group II move to the sharp, quick sounds of the drum. The instruments are heard in the following order in the excerpt: flute; drum; combination of flute, plucked strings, and percussion.

Villancico

By Juan del Enciña
BORN C. 1468   DIED 1530

Help children hear the contrasting instrumental combinations and rhythms as they respond through movement to the following sequence of sounds.

1. Quartet of recorders, tambourine (moves in threes);

2. Soprano recorder and tambourine alternating with quartet of recorders and tambourine (quicker tempo, moves in twos);

3. Quartet of recorders, tambourine (moves threes);

4. Soprano recorder and tambourine alternating with quartet of recorders and tambourine (quicker tempo, moves in twos).

Branle de Poictou

Anonymous

Listen to this French dance from the sixteenth century played on ancient wind and string instruments. Help children to decide whether the music moves in an **even** or **uneven** rhythm. (Uneven.) Children may decide to sway or skip to the music.

Bourrée
from *Fireworks Music*

by George Frideric Handel
BORN 1685   DIED 1759

As children listen to the music they will become aware that some sections are loud, others soft. Move appropriately to the music following this design.

Design:	A	A	B	B	coda
Volume:	soft	loud	soft	loud	loud

Instruments: woodwinds strings woodwinds strings strings

I Wish I Was a Little Bird

American Folk Song

Key: F Starting: C(5)

Meter: $\frac{2}{2}$ $\left(\frac{2}{\text{♩}}\right)$

DT/ **Record 7 Side A Band 5** VOICES: children's choir.
ACCOMPANIMENT: flute, bassoon, violin, cello, percussion, trumpet, trombone.
FORM: Instrumental; *v. 1;* Instrumental; *v. 2;* Coda.

Enjoy the amusing song. Invite children to think of things they wish they were. What would they do?

Concept PITCH: Melodies move up and down by steps or skips.

Discover Show these four patterns on separate charts.

CAN YOU FIND ANYTHING THAT IS THE SAME IN EVERY PICTURE? WHAT IS THE DIFFERENCE? (The first three begin on the same tone; the last one ends on that tone; each picture shows a skip, but each skips a different distance.)

DO YOU THINK YOU COULD PUT THESE IN ORDER TO SHOW THE BEGINNING OF EACH PHRASE OF OUR SONG? DO WE BEGIN WITH THE SMALLEST SKIP OR THE BIGGEST? (The smallest.) Put the first three patterns in order. (3 2 1) Help the children discover that the fourth pattern shows the skip for "little song." Find the correct bells and invite someone to play while the class sings. (C F G A B♭ C)

Extend DID YOU NOTICE THAT THE LAST PHRASE DOESN'T HAVE A MELODY? POOR LAST PHRASE! COULD WE MAKE UP OUR OWN MELODY? Invite children to experiment with different patterns, using the bells placed in the order for the preceding activity. As children explore, talk about how the melody might move—by steps or skips. WHERE SHOULD IT END? Experiment; it should come "home" to the F bell.

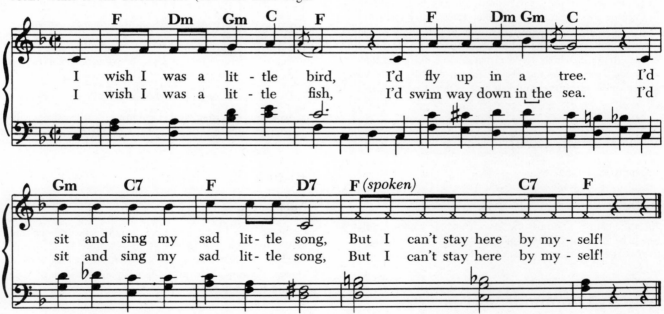

I wish I was a lit-tle bird, I'd fly up in a tree. I'd
I wish I was a lit-tle fish, I'd swim way down in the sea. I'd

sit and sing my sad lit-tle song, But I can't stay here by my-self!
sit and sing my sad lit-tle song, But I can't stay here by my-self!

Welcome Spring

Tyrolian Folk Song
Collected by W.S. Haynie

Key: F Starting Tone: C(5)

Meter: $\frac{2}{4}$ $\left(\frac{2}{\text{♩}}\right)$

DT/ **Record 7 Side A Band 6** VOICES: children's choir.
ACCOMPANIMENT: harp, cello, oboe, French horn.
FORM: Introduction; *v. 1;* Interlude; *v. 2;* Coda.

Concept DURATION: Rhythm patterns move with long and short tones.

Discover HERE IS THE RHYTHM OF A NEW SONG. I THINK YOU CAN LEARN IT ALL BY YOURSELVES! Write the rhythm of the song on a chart or on the chalkboard.

Review the relative lengths of the two kinds of notes shown. The ♩ is "long;" the ♫ sounds "short short." Chant the rhythm of the phrases with "long" and "short," then chant the words in rhythm.

Listen to the recording. DID YOUR RHYTHM SOUND LIKE THE RHYTHM ON THE RECORDING? CAN YOU DECIDE NOW WHAT THE RHYTHM IS FOR THE REST OF THE SONG? Help children realize that phrases one and two have the same rhythm.

Extend Play a game with the class. Show the rhythm of the first phrase of familiar songs on the flannel board with notes. Some that might be used are:

The Farmer

It's Raining

Go to Sleep

Ding Dong Bell

Ask children to guess the titles.

Other Concept PITCH: Melodies move up and down by steps or skips.

Discover: Invite children to draw melody pictures for these patterns:

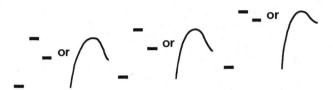

"Gone the ice"   "Gone the snow"   "Flowers bloom"

Discover that each pattern **skips up.** Guide children to realize that each pattern begins a little higher and skips a little higher. To reinforce this awareness, one child may play the following pattern as the class sings.

1. Gone the ice,   gone the snow,   Flow-ers bloom in   fields be-low.
2. Come with me,   we will go   Where the pret-ty   cow-slips grow.

Green the grass,   blue the sky,   White the clouds that   drift on   high.
We will walk,   we will sing,   All in wel-come to the   Spring.

167

If I Were a Flower

Words and Music
by Joseph and Nathan Segal

Key: D   Starting Tone: D(1)
Autoharp Key: C   Starting Tone: C(1)

Meter: 4/4 (4/♩)

DT/ Record 7   Side A   Bands 7A and 7B
VOICES: children's choir.
ACCOMPANIMENT: harp, French horn, oboe, percussion.
FORM: 7A - Introduction; Vocal.
      7B - Instrumental.

Concept PITCH: High, low, and "middle" sounds may be combined to create harmony.

Discover After children are familiar with the words to the song, play the first "question and answer" (measures 1-4) of the instrumental. Notice that the melody of the "flower" is played by an **oboe** in the children's own range. CAN YOU HEAR SOMETHING THAT SUGGESTS THE SNOW AND RAIN AND CLOUDS? ARE THEY ABOVE THE FLOWER OR BELOW? (Above, as suggested by the sound of the **harp,** above the melody.) Listen for high, middle, and low sounds in the remainder of the song. Cut pictures from felt and invite children to place them on the flannel board to show the relative **highness** and **lowness** of melody and accompaniment as they listen.

Record 7 Side B Band 1 VOICES: children's choir.
ACCOMPANIMENT: organ.
FORM: Instrumental; Vocal, *vv. 1 and 2.*

All Things Bright and Beautiful

Music by William Tyndale
Words by Cecil F. Alexander

Key: C   Starting Tone: C(1)

Meter: $\frac{4}{4}$ ($\frac{4}{\downarrow}$)

You may wish to introduce this song at Easter time. Play the recording. Discuss the words of the song with the children. Encourage them to suggest things that they think are "bright and beautiful" in nature.

Concept PITCH: Melodies move up and down by steps and skips.

Discover Ask children to "mirror" the shape of the melody with their hands as they listen. Discover that the over-

all contour of the melody goes from **high** to **low.**

Give one bell each to eight children. Let them play the following pattern as an accompaniment.

The pattern may also be used in ascending order as an introduction and interlude between verses.

1. All things bright and beau - ti - ful, All crea - tures great and small,
2. Cold wind in the win - ter, The pleas - ant sum - mer sun,

All things wise and won - der -ful, The Lord God made them all.
Ripe fruits in the gar - den; He made them ev - ery one.

It Rained a Mist

Virginia Folk Song

Key: E♭ Starting Tone: G(3)
Autoharp Key: C Starting Tone: E(3)

Meter: $\frac{3}{4}$ ($\frac{3}{\text{♩}}$)

DT/ Record 7 Side B Band 2 VOICES: children's choir.
ACCOMPANIMENT: trumpet, clarinet, viola, trombone, percussion.
FORM: Introduction; *v. 1;* Interlude; *v. 2;* Interlude; *v. 3;* Interlude; *v. 4;* Coda.

Concept DURATION: Rhythm patterns move with long and short sounds.

Discover Ask children to plan an introduction for the song that suggests the idea of mist. Use a glockenspiel with these bars in place: D E F G A. Sing in C.

WHAT KIND OF PATTERN MIGHT YOU PLAY TO SUGGEST RAIN FALLING? Allow children to make up a pattern that moves down in threes. It might be something such as the following.

ADD RAINDROPS

Fingertips
on drum:

AND FEET SLOSHING IN PUDDLES.

Sand blocks

HOW WILL YOU CHANGE YOUR PATTERN WHEN THE SUN COMES OUT?

Sunshine sparkling:

Finger cymbals

Heels clicking on dry sidewalks:

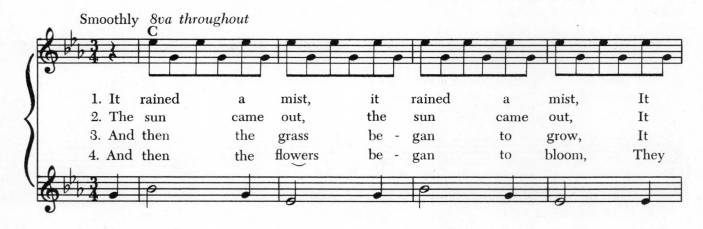

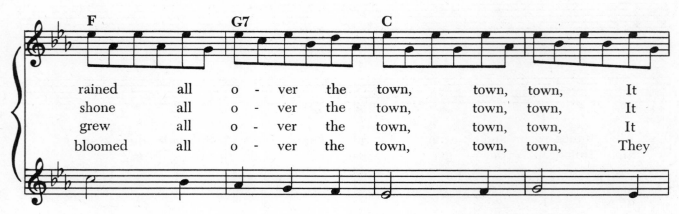

Smoothly *8va throughout*

1. It rained a mist, it rained a mist, It
2. The sun came out, the sun came out, It
3. And then the grass be-gan to grow, It
4. And then the flowers be-gan to bloom, They

rained all o - ver the town, town, town, It
shone all o - ver the town, town, town, It
grew all o - ver the town, town, town, It
bloomed all o - ver the town, town, town, They

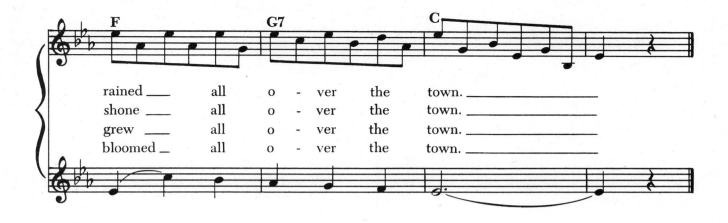

rained ___	all	o - ver	the	town. _____
shone ___	all	o - ver	the	town. _____
grew ___	all	o - ver	the	town. _____
bloomed _	all	o - ver	the	town. _____

Record 10   Side A   Band 8
Ensemble conducted by Buryl Red.

Bunny Hop

by Ray Anthony and Leonard Auletti

Concept DURATION: Rhythm patterns may be made up of sounds and silences.

Discover This is a patterned dance which children will enjoy performing. Sing the song and learn the dance as described in the words of the song. Add the sounds of instruments to the dance. Use a guiro and a bongo drum.

After the children have enjoyed the dance, write the following rhythm pattern on the board. Review the fact that the **notes** represent **sound** and the **rests** represent **silence.** Tell children that the notes represent what their feet did when they danced. Ask them to clap what their feet did. Point to the chalkboard.

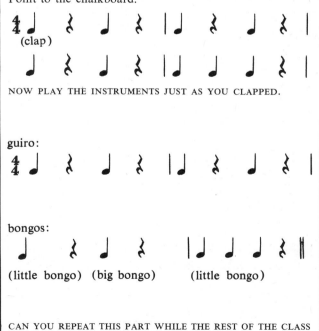

(clap)

NOW PLAY THE INSTRUMENTS JUST AS YOU CLAPPED.

guiro:

bongos:

(little bongo)   (big bongo)   (little bongo)

CAN YOU REPEAT THIS PART WHILE THE REST OF THE CLASS SINGS AND DANCES THE BUNNY HOP?

Extend You may wish to perform this dance for another class or for a school program. Easy costumes which add fun to the dance may be made from white paper bags and pink and blue construction paper.

Directions:

1. Cut hole for face and semicircles for shoulders.

2. Attach pink ears and a blue bow with a stapler.

3. Add black whiskers if you wish.

Summer Morning (46–47)

Music by William S. Haynie
Words by Barbara Young

Pentatonic   Starting Tone: F(1)

Meter: $\frac{3}{4}$ ($\frac{3}{\quarternote}$)

Concept PITCH: High, low, and middle sounds may be combined to create harmony.

Discover Have the children open their books to pages 46–47. Read the title with them. IF YOU WENT FOR A WALK ON A SUMMER MORNING, WHAT MIGHT YOU SEE? WHAT MIGHT YOU HEAR? As children make suggestions, encourage the observation that some things one saw or heard would be **high** (birds, clouds); other things would be **low** (frog, dog); some would be **in the middle** (himself, other children).

After the song has been heard, read the instructions on page 47. Suggest that children listen this time to find out what makes the high sounds and the low sounds. WHO MAKES THE SOUNDS IN THE MIDDLE? (The voices.) LOOK AT THE PICTURE OF THE PICCOLO, THE SMALL INSTRUMENT WHICH PLAYS THE HIGH SOUNDS. LISTEN FOR THE LOW SOUNDS OF THE CELLO.

Divide the class into three groups: one for the low sounds, one for high sounds, and one to be "in the middle." STAND UP EACH TIME YOU HEAR YOUR SOUND! BE SURE YOU SIT DOWN WHEN YOU NO LONGER HEAR YOUR SOUND! Play the complete recording. Discuss what happened. Discover that the low sounds continued throughout the music, but the high and middle sounds were sometimes silent.

Record 7   Side B   Band 3   VOICES: children's choir.
ACCOMPANIMENT: string quartet, piccolo.
FORM: Introduction; Vocal; Interlude; Instrumental; Interlude; Vocal; Coda (vocal and instrumental fade-out).

Summer Morning

Sum - mer morn - ing bright and ear - ly,

Winds are wak - ing, clouds are cur - ly,

Ev - ery - thing is ros - y pearl - y,

Sum - mer morn - ing bright and ear - ly.

46

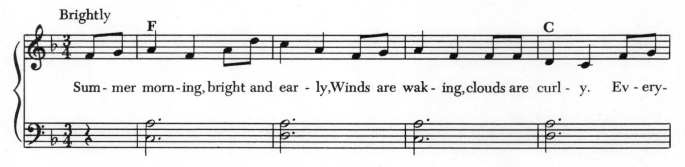

Brightly

F   C

Sum - mer morn - ing, bright and ear - ly, Winds are wak - ing, clouds are curl - y.   Ev - ery-

172

Listen for high sounds.

Can you be the sounds in the middle?

Listen for low sounds.

47

Extend Invite children to add high and low sounds by playing accompaniments. They may improvise patterns of their own or use patterns such as the following.

Bass xylophone:

Soprano glockenspiel (Play as an introduction, then continue throughout song.):

The pattern given above may be played on the black keys of the piano if the melody is sung a half step higher. (Start the melody on F♯.)

thing is ros - y, pearl - y, Sum - mer morn - ing, bright and ear - ly.

Expressive Movement, No. 2

Concept EXPRESSIVE TOTALITY: Timbres, pitches, durations and dynamics may be combined to express musical ideas.

Discover Help children to express their ideas through movement by engaging them in activities such as the following.

Suggest movements with word cues; then as children express the ideas through movement, add the interpretive sounds of the instruments. The teacher might play the instruments at first, but two children should take over the accompaniment as soon as possible.

Use two sizes of drums to help express the following idea.

GO INTO A DARK PLACE.

FEEL THE SIDES OF YOUR DARK PLACE. . .

ARE THEY SMOOTH? (Rub drum head.) **(drum roll)**

OR LUMPY? (Short sounds on drum.)

IS IT DEEP? (Big drum.)

OR SHALLOW? (Smaller d r u m.)

IS IT WIDE? **(big drum)**

OR NARROW? **(small drum)**

COME OUT OF YOUR DARK PLACE. IS IT HARD TO SEE?

FIND ANOTHER WAY TO GET INTO YOUR DARK

PLACE. (Repeat sound ideas in appropriate ways as the children pretend to re-enter and explore this or another dark place.)

Use two sizes of triangles to help express the following idea.

GO INTO A BRIGHT PLACE.

FEEL THE SIDES OF YOUR BRIGHT PLACE.

ARE THEY SMOOTH? (Rub triangle.) (triangle roll)

OR LUMPY? (Short sounds.)

ARE YOU IN A HIGH PLACE? (Small triangle.)

OR A LOW PLACE? (Larger triangle.)

STEP OUT OF YOUR BRIGHT PLACE.

FIND ANOTHER WAY TO GET INTO YOUR BRIGHT PLACE. (Repeat the sounds in appropriate ways as children pretend to re-enter and explore this or another bright place.)

DT/ Record 7   Side B   Band 4   VOICES: children's choir.
ACCOMPANIMENT: string quartet.
FORM: Introduction; Vocal; Interlude; Vocal.

The Day

Music by Ronald Lo Presti
Words by William English

Modal (Dorian on A)   Starting Tone: A(1)

Meter: $\frac{3}{4}$ $\left(\begin{smallmatrix}3\\ \end{smallmatrix}\right)$

Concept PITCH: Melody patterns may be combined to create harmony.

Discover Play the recording. When children are familiar with the melody, they may add accompaniments to the song.

Part I Alto metallophone: Repeat the sound of "A" four times softly as an introduction. Then continue throughout the song.

Part II Alto glockenspiel: Play only during the first phrase of the song:

Part III Soprano metallophone: Play only on the second phrase of the song:

Night is a place where there is not a trace of

light. _____ I like the day 'cause the

games that I play take sight. _____

175

Whole-Part (48–49)

Hot Cross Buns

Mother Goose Rhyme

Key: F Starting Tone for First Melody: A(3)
Key: F Starting Tone for Second Melody: C(5)

Meter: $\frac{4}{4}$ ($\frac{4}{\downarrow}$)

Concept STRUCTURE: A "whole" piece of music is made up of smaller parts.

Discover Talk about the pictures found on page 48 of the pupil's book. Notice that each pair of pictures shows a **whole** and a **part.** CAN YOU THINK OF OTHER WHOLE THINGS THAT HAVE PARTS? Look around the room and find examples. If possible, choose things that can actually be taken apart so that children can see that the parts, when combined, make a whole: a fountain pen, strings of beads, pages in a loose-leaf notebook.

When children have explored this idea, look at page 49 in the book. CAN WE SING THIS WHOLE SONG? Sing the melody for the class, play the recording, or invite them to show you that they can learn to sing it themselves, discovering first the rhythm (use short, long, lo-ong to chant the rhythm), then the melody (based on three tones, 1-2-3, or the F scale).

48

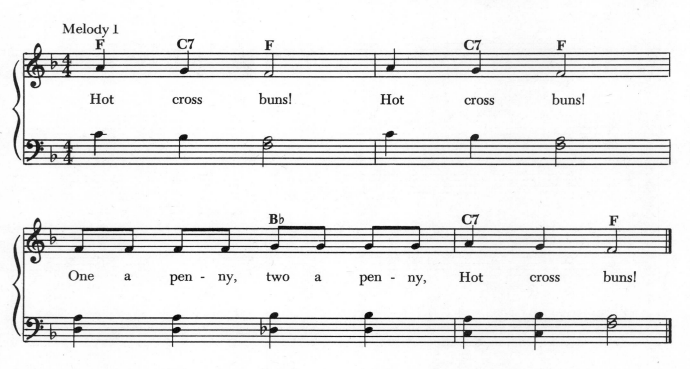

176

Sing this whole song.

Hot   cross   buns!   Hot   cross   buns!

One a pen-ny, two a pen-ny, Hot   cross   buns!

Here is a part of the song.
Where does this part belong?

49

When children can sing the song, look at the bottom of the page. CAN YOU PUT OUR POOR SONG BACK TOGETHER AGAIN? Decide that the part shown by itself belongs to the empty space on the bottom staff.

Extend Another day, put each measure on a separate chart. "Scramble" the order of the charts and ask children to put them together again. The left and right edges of the charts might be cut so that the edges fit together. This could reinforce the idea of putting parts together to make a whole.

This same activity may be extended by putting other familiar songs such as "Pussycat, Pussycat" and "Welcome Spring" on similar charts. Put the charts in the Music Learning Center and invite children to put the "musical jigsaw puzzle" together. Sing what they have organized. IS THIS THE WAY THE PARTS SHOULD BE PUT TOGETHER?

Other Concept TEXTURE: Two melodies may be sounded simultaneously.

Discover When children know the melody, introduce them to the second melody shown on this page by singing it lightly as the class sings the familiar tune.

DID YOU HEAR TWO TUNES? COULD SOMEONE SING WITH ME? Choose a few children with independent singing voices and ask them to join in the new melody.

Extend Put out the needed bells. (C F G A B♭ C) Guide one child to practice until he can play the new melody. He may then play it as an accompaniment while the class sings.

Record 7 Side B Band 5 VOICES: woman, man.
ACCOMPANIMENT: autoharp, bells.
FORM: Introduction; Vocal; Instrumental; Vocal; Vocal.

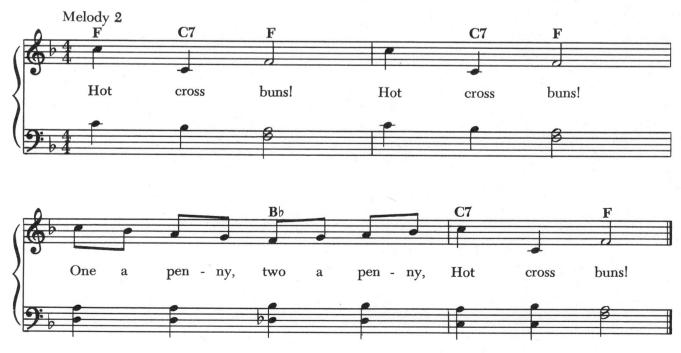

Melody 2

Hot   cross   buns!   Hot   cross   buns!

One a pen-ny, two a pen-ny, Hot   cross   buns!

Same-Different (50-51)

Concept STRUCTURE: Sections of music can be the same or different.

Discover Look at the pictures shown in the pupil's book. WHAT PARTS ARE THERE IN A HAMBURGER? (Bun and meat.) HOW MANY PARTS? (Three: top of bun, bottom of bun, meat patty.) ARE ANY TWO PARTS THE SAME, OR ALMOST THE SAME? (Yes, the top and bottom are both made of bread; they are almost the same.) Follow with similar questions as children look at the cookie, the ice-cream cone, and the hot cross buns.

Follow the suggestion at the bottom of the pupil's page. Sing the song. Help children decide first that there are four parts.

1. Hot cross buns!

2. Hot cross buns!

3. One a penny, two a penny,

4. Hot cross buns!

Next, guide them to discover that parts one, two, and four are the **same;** part three is **different.**

Look at the picture at the top of page 51. WHY IS THIS A GOOD PICTURE OF "HOT CROSS BUNS"? (Because it shows four parts; three are the same and one is different.)

Cut figures out of construction paper to match those shown in the pupil's book. Give one each to four children. Ask each child to hold up his picture when his part is sung.

SAME DIFFERENT

Sing "Hot Cross Buns."
Which parts are the same?
Which part is different?

Parts can be the same or different.

50

Here is a picture of the parts of "Hot Cross Buns."

Make your own music.
Each person may make a different part.
Plan when each one will play.
Some parts may sound the same.
Some parts may sound different.

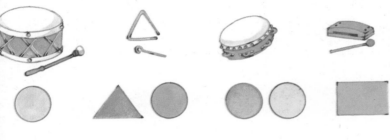

Make another plan for your music.
Use as many parts as you like.

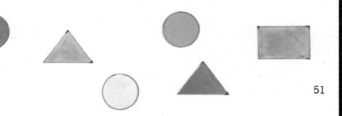

51

Extend   Read the suggestions in the pupil's book and plan music made up of different parts. At first, work together as a class. Later, give small groups an opportunity to work independently and plan their own compositions.

Draw attention to the geometric shapes below the picture of the instruments. Decide that the circle will stand for the drum part, the triangle for the triangle part, the rectangle for the wood block or triangle. HOW MANY TIMES WILL THE DRUM PLAY ITS PART? (Four times.) THE TRIANGLE? (Once.) THE WOOD BLOCK OR TAMBOURINE? (Once.)

Cut geometric figures from construction paper so that children may organize their own musical parts. Remind them that each person must remember the part he plans so that when it is repeated it sounds exactly the same as the first time he played it.

Review familiar songs. Help children to find the number of parts (phrases), then decide whether parts are the same or different. Show the design with geometric shapes.

The Day (two parts)

○   △

I'm a Little Teapot (four parts)

○   △   ○   □

One Misty, Moisty Morning (four parts)

□   □   △   ○

179

I Love My Shirt

Words and Music by Donovan Leitch

Key: C   Starting Tone: C(1)

Meter: $\frac{4}{4}$ $\left(\begin{array}{c}4\\ \natural\end{array}\right)$

DT/ **Record 7**   **Side B**   **Band 6**   VOICES: children's choir.
ACCOMPANIMENT: tenor sax, trumpet, French horn, trombone, percussion, guitar, bass, piano, drums.
FORM: Introduction; *v. 1*; *v. 2*; *v. 3*.

Concept   STRUCTURE: Music is made up of sections which may be the same or different.

Discover   Sing the refrain for the class, "I love my shirt, I love my shirt, my shirt is so comfortably lovely." LISTEN CAREFULLY TO THE WHOLE SONG! HOW MANY TIMES DID YOU HEAR THAT PHRASE? (Six times, twice in each verse.)

DOES THAT MELODY SOUND THE SAME EACH TIME? (Yes, the words may change a little, but the music is always the same.)

LET'S SHOW THAT MELODY WITH THIS CIRCLE:

CAN WE BEGIN OUR PICTURE OF THIS MUSIC WITH THE CIRCLE? (No, there is another part first.) GOOD. THEN WE'LL SHOW IT WITH A SQUARE. LISTEN CAREFULLY. BE READY TO TELL ME WHEN WE NEED TO ADD ANOTHER PART TO OUR PICTURE. YOU WILL NEED TO DECIDE WHETHER WE NEED A CIRCLE, A SQUARE, OR ANOTHER SHAPE. The final order should be as follows:

CAN YOU SING THE REFRAIN EACH TIME IT RETURNS? LISTEN TO THE PART THAT TELLS THE STORY. This song is longer and more complex than many the children will have sung in class. Some may only learn to sing the refrain; others will pick up the entire song, and may wish to add new verses describing other parts of their wardrobes.

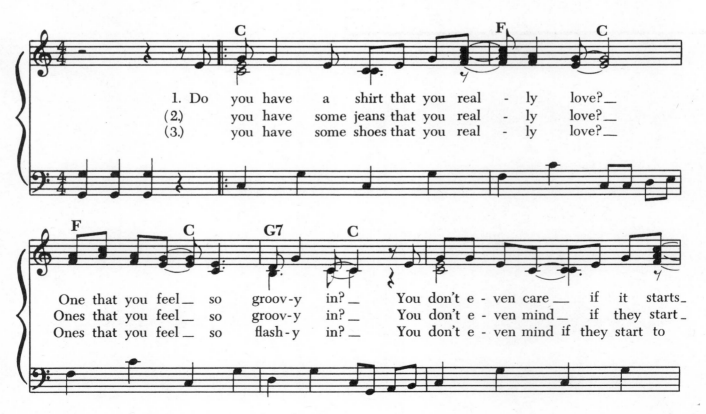

1. Do you have a shirt that you real - ly love?_
(2.) you have some jeans that you real - ly love?_
(3.) you have some shoes that you real - ly love?_

One that you feel_ so groov-y in?_ You don't e - ven care_ if it starts_
Ones that you feel_ so groov-y in?_ You don't e - ven mind_ if they start_
Ones that you feel_ so flash-y in?_ You don't e - ven mind if they start to

Small Group Event, No. 4

Concept EXPRESSIVE TOTALITY: Timbre, tempo, and dynamics may be combined to suggest extra-musical ideas.

Discover Have available a variety of percussion instruments such as rhythm sticks, guiros, sandblocks, wood blocks, and finger cymbals. If possible, provide pictures of a bee and a frog. CAN YOU MAKE A CONVERSATION BETWEEN A BEE AND A FROG?

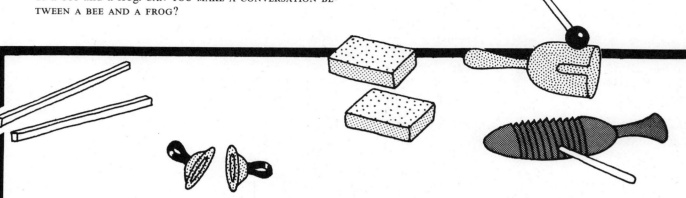

Invite two children to be the bee and the frog. Let each child experiment with sounds until he finds the appropriate one for his character.

Have the bee and the frog carry on a conversation. There must be:

1. Times when one of them repeats what the other has said.

2. Times when they speak slowly . . . very fast . . . softer . . . louder.

3. A time when they do not speak at all.

LET THE CLASS HEAR YOUR CONVERSATION. Decide whether the performers used the ideas suggested.

Extend Review Ravel's "La Chatte," from *L'enfant et les Sortilèges*, page 127. LISTEN AGAIN TO THE CONVERSATION BETWEEN TWO CATS. HOW COULD YOU TELL WHEN A DIFFERENT CAT WAS TALKING? HOW COULD YOU TELL WHEN THEY WERE TALKING ABOUT DIFFERENT THINGS? DID YOU USE SOME OF THESE SAME WAYS WHEN YOU PLANNED YOUR COMPOSITION? WHAT HELPS US KNOW WHEN DIFFERENT PEOPLE ARE TALKING? (Different voice sounds, different instruments.) WHAT HELPS US KNOW WHEN THEY STOP TALKING ABOUT ONE THING AND BEGIN TO TALK ABOUT SOMETHING ELSE? (A new musical idea such as a change in rhythm, pitch, loudness, speed.)

My Twenty Pennies

Venezuelan Folk Song
Translated by Olcutt Saunders

Key: F   Starting Tone: F(1)

Meter: 3/4 (3/♩)

DT/ Record 7   Side B   Band 7 VOICES: boy's choir.
ACCOMPANIMENT: 2 trumpets, guitar, bass, drums, percussion.
FORM: Introduction; *v. 1;* Interlude; *v. 2;* Interlude; *v. 3;* Interlude; *v. 4;* Interlude; *v. 5;* Interlude; *v. 6;* Coda.

To help children learn the meaning of the Spanish words, prepare pictures of the six different animals (turkey, cat, goat, monkey, parrot, cow) with the Spanish names.

Concept TIME AND PLACE: The melodies, rhythms, and instruments used in music can reflect the music's time and place of origin.

Discover After children have learned the song and learned to pronounce the Spanish words for familiar animals, listen again to the music. THIS MUSIC COMES FROM A FARAWAY COUNTRY IN LATIN AMERICA. THE SOUND OF THE WORDS HELP US KNOW THAT. SO DOES THE SOUND OF THE MUSIC! LISTEN AGAIN AND FIND SOME INTERESTING SOUNDS.

Some of the instruments used in the accompaniment are similar to those found in the classroom. Show children the **maracas,** the **claves** (or rhythm sticks), the **cowbell.** THESE ARE INSTRUMENTS THAT PEOPLE IN LATIN AMERICA USE TO ACCOMPANY THEIR SONGS. WE LIKE TO USE THESE INSTRUMENTS TOO!

*Repeat this section in verses 2-6, naming all previous animals.

But now I still have my twen- ty pen- nies.

Record 10 Side A Band 9
Philadelphia Orchestra,
Eugene Ormandy, conductor.
TIME: 2:30

Dance of the Little Swans and Galop
from *The Swan Lake,* Op. 20

by Peter Ilyich Tchaikovsky
BORN 1840   DIED 1893

Dance of the Little Swans

Introduce this piece by explaining that the music is from a ballet called *Swan Lake.* In the ballet a group of little swans perform a dance.

Concept STRUCTURE: Music is made up of parts which are the same or different.

Discover Play the recording. HOW DO YOU THINK THE LITTLE SWANS MIGHT BE MOVING? (In two ways: with a walking movement and with a smooth, gliding movement.) Listen to the piece again and decide whether the swans are walking or smoothly gliding. SHOW ME WHEN YOU THINK THE SWANS ARE WALKING BY MOVING YOUR FINGERTIPS IN THE PALM OF YOUR HAND; RUB YOUR PALMS TOGETHER WHEN THEY SEEM TO BE GLIDING.

Play the recording. Children will discover that the swans seem to walk during the first section. (The bassoon plays a basic "walking" pattern under a melody played by woodwinds.) In the second section, the strings play a slightly smoother melody. The first section is then repeated.

Extend Reinforce the children's discovery by placing a picture on the board. Make several capital S's.

As each section is heard, turn the S's into swans. The completed visual might look like this.

Galop

Concept DURATION: Sounds may be arranged in even or uneven patterns.

Discover Here is another dance from the ballet *Swan Lake.* CLOSE YOUR EYES AND LISTEN TO THE MUSIC. CAN YOU IMAGINE HOW YOU MIGHT DANCE TO THE FIRST PART OF THIS MUSIC? WOULD YOUR FEET MOVE IN AN EVEN OR UNEVEN RHYTHM? (Gallop or skip in an uneven rhythm.)

■ ▬ ■ ▬

WOULD IT BE A FAST OR SLOW DANCE? (Fast.) MAKE THE SOUND OF THE RHYTHM BY PATTING YOUR KNEES. Play the recording through the first section of the music as children do this.

The second part of the music has heavily accented steady beats. (▬ ▬ ▬ ▬) HOW WOULD YOU CHANGE YOUR MOVEMENTS IN THIS SECTION? Children may decide to use both hands, patting both knees at the same time to show how the rhythm has changed to a **heavy beat.** Play the recording. Help children discover that the first and second section of the music are repeated throughout the piece.

Extend DANCE WITH THE MUSIC. MOVE FREELY AS YOU DANCE. DO NOT USE THE SPACE THAT YOUR NEIGHBOR IS IN. WILL YOUR MOVEMENTS CHANGE WHEN THE SECTIONS OF THE MUSIC CHANGE? As this is a rather boisterous movement which needs space, arrange the room to accommodate the movement and limit the number of children who will participate at a given time.

185

Same Train

Spiritual

Tonality: Pentatonic   Starting Tone: F

Meter: $\frac{4}{4}$ ($\frac{4}{4}$)

DT/ Record 8   Side A   Band 1 VOICES: children's choir.
ACCOMPANIMENT: electric guitar, electric bass, piano, drums, organ.
FORM: Introduction; *v. 1;* Interlude; *v. 2;* Interlude; *v. 3;* Interlude; *v. 4;* Coda.

Concept   RHYTHM: Music moves in relation to a steady, underlying beat.

Discover   As children listen to the music, invite them to tap the beat softly. Later, children might enjoy doing the following motions to the **accented beats** (♩ 𝄾 ♩ 𝄾).

1	2	3	4	1	2	3	4
clap knees		hand clap		hands out		hand clap	

Point out the interesting **rhythm of the melody** which doesn't always sound **with the beat.**

Other Concept   PITCH: Tones may be combined to create harmony.

Discover   Play (or have a child play) this pattern as an accompaniment.

The following pattern might be used as an introduction and coda. Allow two children to practice it; one might play the top two notes, the other the bottom one.

Rhythmically

Same train,— same train,—
Same train,— same train,—
Same train,— same train,—
Same train,— same train,—

same train — car-ry my moth-er, Same train,— same train,—
same train — car-ry my fa-ther, Same train,— same train,—
same train — car-ry my sis-ter, Same train,— same train,—
same train — car-ry my broth-er, Same train,— same train,—

186

same train _ car-ry my moth-er. Same train _ be back to-mor-row,
same train _ car-ry my fa-ther. Same train _ be back to-mor-row,
same train _ car-ry my sis-ter. Same train _ be back to-mor-row,
same train _ car-ry my broth-er. Same train _ be back to-mor-row,

Same train, _ same train. _
Same train, _ same train. _
Same train, _ same train. _
Same train, _ same train. _

Record 10 Side A Band 10
Orchestra conducted by Lehman Engel.
TIME: 2:16

March of the Siamese Children
from *The King and I*

by Richard Rodgers
BORN 1902

This march is from the musical *The King and I,* which takes place in a palace in the faraway land of Thailand. In the story, this music is played when all the king's children march in to meet their new teacher.

Concept Music may be organized into same and different sections.

Discover Play the selection. Invite children to plan a march to the music. The design of the music should be reflected by the design of their march.

A The parade opens with a melody played softly on the flute, accompanied by a few percussion instruments and answered by the oboe.

B Low brass instruments, answered by low strings, in-troduce a new tune. The oboe suggests the opening theme.

A The first tune returns, now louder, played by the strings and accompanied by other instruments.

C Listen for the solemn third tune, played on trumpets and other brass instruments. The strings provide a bridge to the return of A.

A The repetition of the first melody brings the march to a happy close.

Extend Children may wish to add a few appropriate instrumental sounds to the march: an occasional sound of finger cymbals or triangle; alternating clicks of two sizes of wood blocks; a gong to announce the special event; a cymbal played softly with a mallet. Help children decide when and how often each instrument should play.

Shoheen Sho (52-53)

Welsh Folk Song

Key: G   Starting Tone: G(1)

Meter: $\frac{2}{4}$ ($\frac{2}{\text{♩}}$)

Concepts STRUCTURE: Music is made up of patterns that are the same or different.

PITCH: Melodies move up and down by steps or skips.

Discover Ask the children to follow the instructions and answer the questions in the pupil's book, page 53. HOW CAN YOU TELL WHICH PARTS OF THE MUSIC WILL SOUND THE SAME? Decide that if the **notes on the staff** look the **same,** they should sound the same. Observe that all the notes on the first staff are exactly the same as those on the third staff, so these two melodies will sound exactly alike. All the notes on the second staff look the same as those on the fourth staff, so these two patterns will sound the same. The first pattern (first three notes) on each staff looks the same, so every staff will begin the same way, but end differently.

Discover Follow the second set of instructions in the pupil's book. Look at the pattern. Decide that it moves up by steps. Ask one child to play it. WILL YOU BEGIN ON THE LOWEST BELL OR THE HIGHEST BELL? (Lowest.)

To answer the last question, ask the children to find a picture in notes that moves up by steps, like the "line picture" (the first three notes on each staff).

Decide that this pattern must be played four times.

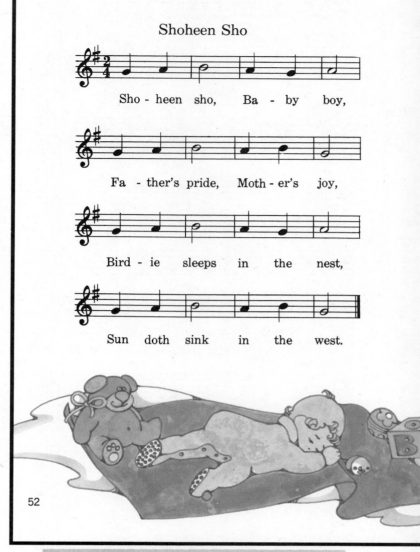

Shoheen Sho

Sho - heen sho,   Ba - by   boy,

Fa - ther's pride,   Moth - er's   joy,

Bird - ie   sleeps   in   the   nest,

Sun   doth   sink   in   the   west.

52

DT/ Record 8   Side A   Band 2 VOICES: children's choir.
ACCOMPANIMENT: harp, oboe, French horn, cello.
FORM: Instrumental; Vocal; Instrumental; Vocal; Coda.

Tenderly

Sho - heen   sho,   Ba - by   boy,
Bird - ie   sleeps   In   the   nest,

188

Look at the music.
Which parts will sound the same?
Listen to the music. Were you right?

Play the pattern that sounds like this.

Play it on these bells.

How many times will you play it?

53

(Sho-heen sho, Ba-by boy)

Ask a child to play this pattern on the bells. Observe that all parts of the melody move up or down by steps. HOW MUCH OF OUR SONG CAN YOU PLAY NOW? (The first staff and third staff.)

Who can draw a picture of "Father's pride, Mother's joy"? As someone draws, point out that this melody has a **skip** at the end.

(Fa-ther's pride, Moth-er's joy)

NOW HOW MUCH OF OUR SONG CAN YOU PLAY? (All of it.) Ask one child to play; then ask the class to sing the melody, first on a neutral syllable, then with words, as someone points to the two pictures.

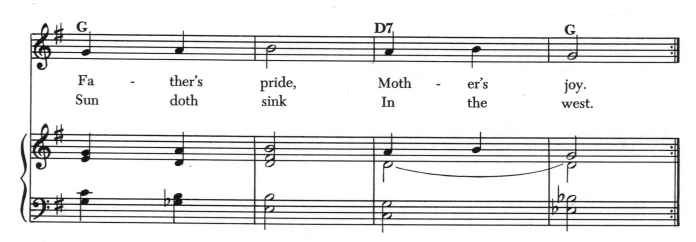

Fa - ther's pride, Moth - er's joy.
Sun doth sink In the west.

Shake the Papaya Down

Calypso Song
Collected by W. S. Haynie

Key: F   Starting Tone: A(3)

Meter: 4/4 (4/♩)

DT/ Record 8   Side A   Band 3   VOICES: children's choir.
ACCOMPANIMENT: banjo, electric piano, electric bass, drums, percussion, rhythm guitar.
FORM: Introduction; Vocal; Interlude; Vocal; Interlude; Vocal; Coda.

Concept   TIMBRE: Different sound sources have distinctive qualities.

Discover   Put a variety of percussion instruments on the table. Include among them a **bongo drum** (or high-pitched small drum), **guiro**, **cowbell.** You might add instruments such as **triangle**, **wood block**, or **maracas** as well.

Ask several children to play instruments. Invite comments on the sound of each, encouraging children to think of words to describe the quality of sound (crisp, bright, scratchy).

LISTEN TO THIS MUSIC. WHICH OF OUR INSTRUMENTS CAN YOU HEAR? Children should be able to identify the sounds of the **guiro**, the **drum**, and the **cowbell.**

Extend   Play a game. Hide the instruments in a closet or behind a screen. Ask one child to go behind the screen and play one instrument. A second child must then go behind the screen, choose the same instrument, and play it. The class decides whether or not he has chosen the right one.

Other Concept   DURATION: Rhythm patterns are made up of long and short sounds.

Discover   Show this pattern in line notation.

■ — ■ — ■ —

Chant the pattern with "short" and "long" while you keep a steady beat on a small drum.

LISTEN TO OUR SONG. CAN YOU FIND THAT INTERESTING RHYTHM? HOW MANY TIMES DO YOU HEAR IT? Help children realize that the entire song is made up of this same pattern; it is heard seven times.

To emphasize the interesting "short-long" rhythm that begins each pattern, ask one child to play it on the guiro, using a down-up motion (♪ ♩).

Ma - ma   says   no   play;   This   is   a   work - day.

Up   with   the   bright   sun;   Get   all   the   work   done.   If   you   will   help   me,

Climb   up   the   tall   tree,   Shake   the   pa - pa - ya   down.

190

DT/ Record 8 Side A Band 4 VOICES: boy's choir.
ACCOMPANIMENT: string quartet.
FORM: Introduction; *v. 1;* Interlude; *v. 2;*
Interlude (German verse); Coda.

Piep, Piep, Mäuschen

German Folk Song
Words adapted

Key: E♭   Starting Tone: E♭(1)
Autoharp Key: F   Starting Tone: F(1)

Meter: $\frac{4}{4}$ ($\frac{4}{\text{♩}}$)

Concept STRUCTURE: Music is made up of sections that are the same or different.

Discover Sing the first phrase (two measures) on a neutral syllable. WHEN DO YOU HEAR THIS PATTERN? DO YOU HEAR IT MORE THAN ONCE? Play only the first verse of the recording. Decide that the phrase is heard at the beginning and end of the song. Show these two patterns with identical shapes, or with pictures that illustrate the song. HOW MANY OTHER PARTS DO WE HAVE TO OUR SONG? DO WE NEED A NEW SHAPE, OR CAN WE USE THE SAME ONE FOR THE WHOLE SONG? (There is one more part which should be shown with a different shape.)

Other Concept PITCH: Melodies move up and down by steps or skips.

Discover This melody uses only five tones. Some children may be able to learn to play the complete melody on the bells. Put the E♭ F G A♭ B♭ bells and a chart showing the numbers in the Music Learning Center so that children may practice individually.

Pronunciation for the German follows.
First and third phrases: peep peep moy-schen
                               blahyb in dahy-nem hoy-schen
Middle phrase: ah-leh klahy-nen moy-seh-lahyn
                     zind in eeh-rem hoy-seh-lahyn

1. Peep, peep, lit-tle mouse, do not leave your lit-tle house.
2. Tick, tock, tick,___ tock, keep on tick-ing lit-tle clock.
1. Piep, piep, Mäus - chen, bleib in dei - nem Häus - chen.

All the oth-er lit-tle mice stay in-side and are so nice,
All the chil-dren sleep to-night as the stars are shin-ing bright,
Al - le klein-en Mäu- se - lein sind in ih - rem Häu - se - lein,

Peep, peep, lit-tle mouse, do not leave your lit-tle house.
Tick, tock, tick,___ tock, keep on tick-ing lit-tle clock.
Piep, piep, Mäus - chen, bleib in dei - nem Häus - chen.

191

Aunt Hessie's White Horse (54-55)

South African Folk Song
English version and piano arrangement
by Elizabeth Poston

Key: D   Starting Tone: D(1)
Autoharp Key: C   Starting Tone: C(1)

Meter: $\frac{2}{4}$ ($\frac{2}{\downarrow}$)

Read the title of the new song to the children. Look at the picture. WHAT KIND OF HORSE DOES AUNT HESSIE HAVE? Decide that it is a rocking horse.

Concept   PITCH: Melodies move up and down by steps and skips.

Discover   Compare the stairstep picture on page 55 of the pupil's book with the note picture on page 54. The melody moves **up** five **steps** at the beginning of each phrase. It moves **down** five **steps** at the end of the song. WHAT HAPPENS THE REST OF THE TIME? (The melody stays the same; it repeats the same tone.)

Give the five bells shown in the pupil's book to five children. Ask the children to "put themselves in order" from low to high. Let the class help them decide on the correct order. CAN YOU PLAY THE FIRST FIVE TONES OF OUR SONG? WHO WILL PLAY NEXT? (The highest bell.) After reviewing the rhythm of the melody, help the five children play the complete song as it appears in the pupil's book.

Aunt Hessie's White Horse

Can't you   see   Aunt Hes - sie's white horse,

Aunt Hes-sie's white horse, Aunt Hes-sie's white horse,

Oh   can't you   see   Aunt Hes - sie's white horse,

And   gee - up   a   trot   for   me?

54

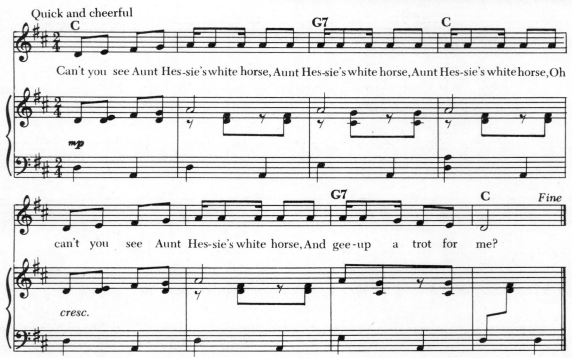

Quick and cheerful

Can't you see Aunt Hes-sie's white horse, Aunt Hes-sie's white horse, Aunt Hes-sie's white horse, Oh

can't you   see   Aunt Hes-sie's white horse, And gee-up   a   trot   for   me?

When does the melody move like this?

When does the melody move like this?

Here are the bells for the first five sounds of the song.
The bells are all mixed up.
Put them in order from low to high.
Play the first part of this song.

Can you find this uneven pattern in the song?

55

Later, put the five bells in the Music Learning Center. The melody might be shown with numbers or the children may follow the note picture in the book. Give individuals the opportunity to practice the entire melody.

Other Concepts DURATION: Rhythm patterns may be even or uneven.

Discover Clap the uneven pattern shown at the bottom of the pupil's page 55 (short long short long long). CAN YOU FIND THE NOTE PICTURE FOR THIS RHYTHM? WILL THE NOTES ALL BE THE SAME, OR WILL SOME BE DIFFERENT? (Decide that some will be different.) Guide children to find the places where two different kinds of notes are shown. ("Aunt Hessie's white horse.") Chant the rhythm over and over: "Hessie's white horse, Aunt Hessie's white horse . . ." Then chant the text in rhythm. HOW WILL THE FIRST PART SOUND? (Even, because all the notes look the same.) Challenge children to play and sing the complete melody.

PITCH: Tones may be combined to create an accompaniment. One child may add a rocking accompaniment, using these three bells:

He may improvise a pattern that moves up and down to suggest the movement of the rocking horse. For example:

DT/ Record 8 Side A Band 5 VOICES: children's choir.
ACCOMPANIMENT: trumpet, clarinet, viola, trombone, percussion.
FORM: Introduction; Vocal; Interlude; Vocal.

Don't you call him slow, Aunt Hes-sie will make him go; He'll gal-lop a-long so fine, He'll make the whole world mine. Oh

193

Peter and the Wolf (56-57)

by Serge Prokofiev (proh-kohf'-yehf)
BORN 1891   DIED 1933

Concept EXPRESSIVE TOTALITY: Timbres, melodies, rhythms, and expressive controls may be combined to help music "tell a story."

Discover Recall the musical story of "The Three Bears" that the children enjoyed earlier in the year. TODAY WE ARE GOING TO LISTEN TO ANOTHER MUSICAL STORY ABOUT A BOY NAMED PETER AND A WOLF!

Open the pupil's book to pages 56–57 (or use the Jumbo Book). Have the children look at the pictures of animals and people. Identify each. WE ARE GOING TO LISTEN TO SOME MUSIC THAT HELPS TO TELL A STORY. EACH CHARACTER HAS HIS OWN MELODY AND HIS OWN SPECIAL INSTRUMENT.

Call attention to the pictures of the instruments. Help children recall the names of each. Most have been heard before in accompaniments for songs they have learned. As each instrument is named, you may wish to show the name on a card.

Have the class listen to the opening section of the recording which describes the different characters and introduces the instrumental melodies (the first band). Ask children to discuss what they have heard and to give reasons why they think each instrument is a good choice for that character. Draw attention to the lilting melody, played by the **strings,** which represents a happy boy. Notice the bird-like sound of the **flute.** The nasal quality of the **oboe** imitates the quack of a duck. Emphasize the stealthy sound of the **clari- net** melody which represents the cat. The grumpy sound of the **bassoon** represents the grandfather. The dark quality of the **French horns** suits the scary wolf and the roar of the **timpani** sounds like guns.

Listen again to this opening section; give the cards with the names of the instruments to seven children. Each should hold up his card when his instrument is heard.

Listen to the remainder of the record and enjoy the story. Draw children's attention to the other aspects of the music which help to tell the story, such as:

the duet between flute and strings after Peter and the bird have been introduced;

the argument between bird and duck as flute and oboe are heard;

the stealthy sound of the cat creeping toward the bird;

the sound of the bird flying upward into the tree;

the sound of the gate closing with finality behind Peter and grandfather;

the cat scampering up the tree when the wolf appears;

the sad music when the duck is swallowed;

Peter and the Wolf

56

Record 10   Side B
Cyril Ritchard, narrator;
Philadelphia Orchestra,
Eugene Ormandy, conductor.
TIME: 23:18

57

the sound of the wolf snapping at the bird as she circles his head;

the sound of the strings as the rope is slowly let down and the tug on the rope as the wolf tries to get away;

the marching tune of the hunters as they leave the woods;

Peter's melody played on brasses instead of strings as the triumphal march begins;

the fragment of the oboe melody at the end when the duck is discovered alive inside the wolf!

Extend Tell the story of "Jack and the Beanstalk" with musical sounds. Ask children to use resonator bells or a xylophone and make up a melody for Jack. JUST AS IN PETER AND THE WOLF, EACH TIME WE TELL ABOUT JACK WE WILL HEAR HIS MELODY.

The student who makes up the melody will need to keep it simple enough so that he can repeat it. He might use the following sounds:

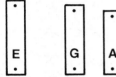

Allow ample time for discussion of appropriate instruments to describe other characters and actions in the story. The children may offer the following suggestions:

cow—two sizes of wood blocks, coconut shells

beans—maraca

climbing up and down beanstalk—slide whistle

giant—big drum

goose (laying golden egg)—drum roll ending with finger cymbals

magic harp—autoharp or guitar

chopping down the beanstalk—claves

crash of the giant falling—cymbals

As some children play the sounds, another child may act as the narrator. The voice of the giant may be supplied by the remaining children so that everyone participates in the story. Each time the giant appears on the scene, he says:

Fee Fie Foe Fum
I smell the blood of an Englishman.
Be he live or be he dead,
I'll grind his bones to make my bread.

Have children chant these lines in rhythm. A large drum can supply the basic beat for the chant.

WILL THERE BE TIMES WHEN SEVERAL THINGS ARE HAPPENING AT ONCE? (Yes, for example, when Jack comes down the beanstalk we will hear Jack's melody, the giant chasing him, the harp's strumming.) HOW DID THE INSTRUMENTS HELP US EXPRESS THE STORY? (They help to describe what was happening.) WOULD THE STORY HAVE BEEN JUST AS EXCITING IF TOLD USING WORDS ALONE? (Probably not.)

The Moon Is Coming Out (58-59)

Japanese Folk Song

Pentatonic   Starting Tone: B♭(5)

Meter: $\frac{2}{4}$ ($\frac{2}{♩}$)

Listen to the song as children look at the illustrations in the book. THIS IS A SONG FROM A FARAWAY LAND, JAPAN. BOYS AND GIRLS WHO LIVE IN JAPAN LIKE TO SING IT.

Concept   PITCH: Tones may be combined to create harmony.

Listen again and point out the sounds of the accompaniment. Let children follow the suggestions in the book and plan an accompaniment. WHICH INSTRUMENT SHOULD WE CHOOSE TO ACCOMPANY A SONG FROM JAPAN? Listening to the accompaniment on the recording may give children ideas about which instruments would be appropriate. Bells, finger cymbals, and tone blocks would all be suitable. Ask one child to make up an accompaniment using the bells E♭ F G B♭ C.

The Moon Is Coming Out

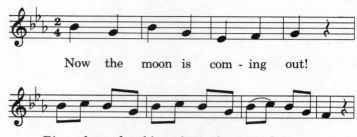

Now the moon is com - ing out!

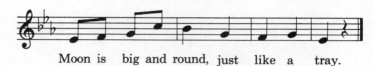

Big and round, so big and round, as round as a tray.

Moon is big and round, just like a tray.

58

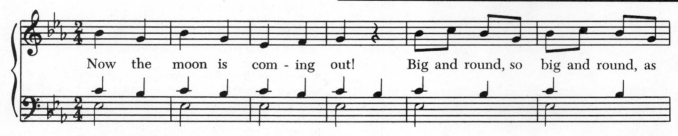

Now the moon is com - ing out!   Big and round, so   big and round, as

What sounds will you choose to accompany this song?

Plan a part to begin the song.

What can you do while you are singing?

Plan a part to end the song.

59

Other Concept STRUCTURE: Music is made up of parts that are the same or different.

Invite some children to plan movements to describe the words of the song. They may sit on the floor with feet tucked under them. CAN YOU PLAN MOTIONS TO MATCH THE PHRASES? HOW MANY DIFFERENT MOTIONS WILL YOU MAKE? (Three.) HOW DO YOU KNOW WHEN TO END A MOTION? (The music comes to rest at the end of each phrase.) WILL ANY OF YOUR MOTIONS BE THE SAME, OR SHOULD EACH BE DIFFERENT? (Each should be different, because each phrase is different.) The motions might be as follows:

Phrase 1: Begin with hands crossed in lap, head down, gradually bring arms up in a curve till they are touching above head, tracing the shape of a moon.

Phrase 2: Fingertips still touching, move "tray" back and forth.

Phrase 3: Beginning with fingertips above head, gradually move arms in an arc downward until hands are back in lap, crossed as at beginning.

DT/ Record 8   Side A   Band 6 VOICES: children's choir.
ACCOMPANIMENT: harp, recorder, percussion.
FORM: Instrumental; Vocal; Instrumental; Vocal; Coda.

The Lion Game (60-61)

Zulu Game Song

Key: D   Starting Tone: A(5)

Autoharp Key: C   Starting Tone: G(5)

Meter: $\frac{2}{4}$ ($\frac{2}{\downarrow}$)

Concept   TIME AND PLACE: The instruments used in music can reflect the time and place of origin of a piece.

Discover   Review "The Moon Is Coming Out." Recall that this song was sung by children who lived in Japan. Compare the sound of the Japanese song with the sound of "The Lion Game" which is from Africa. WHERE DO YOU THINK THE BOYS AND GIRLS WHO LIKE TO SING THIS MUSIC LIVE? WHAT HELPS YOU KNOW? (The subject of the song, the lion, may be one clue. Also, this kind of drum accompaniment is typical of much African music.)

Extend   Follow the suggestions in the pupil's book and add an accompaniment. Children might base their introduction and accompaniment on word patterns from the song.

Way, way, o
(deep drum)

Oh, the li-(on)
(higher drum)

one and one and
(tone block)

The Lion Game

Way,   way,   oh   way,

Oh   the   li -   on,

One and one and one and one and

Put   a   peb - ble   here.

60

C

Way,   way,   oh   way,   Oh the li - on,
We,   we,   o,   we,   I - ngo - nya - ma,

198

What sounds will you choose to accompany this song?
Plan a part to begin the song.
What can you do while you are singing?
Plan a part to end the song.

61

One child might improvise an introduction using the notes of the song. He might play it on a xylophone.

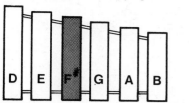

Other Concept MUSICAL CONTROLS: A steady beat may begin slowly and gradually become faster.

Discover "The Lion Game" is similar to the American game "Button, button, who's got the button?" Sitting in a circle, the children begin singing slowly, then gradually increase the tempo to the end of the verse. As they sing, a pebble is passed from hand to hand. Whoever is holding the pebble at the end of the verse must drop out of the circle. The children must pass the pebble on in response to the increasing speed of the beat. The song is repeated (each time starting slowly and getting faster) until only one child is left. He is the lion.

As the class plays the game, one person may sit in the center and play the drum to set the tempo. Begin with a slow, steady beat; gradually increase the speed while the class sings and passes the pebble.

Pronunciation for the African words follows.

way, way, oh, way
een-gohn-yah-mah
moon-yeh, moon-yeh, moon-yeh, moon-yeh
fah-kay moon-yeh lah.

DT/ Record 8 Side A Band 7 VOICE: male folk-singer.
ACCOMPANIMENT: percussion.
FORM: Introduction; English verse; Interlude; African verse.

One and one and one and one and Put a peb - ble here.
Mu - nye, mu - nye, mu - nye, mu - nye, Fa - ka mu - nye la.

America

Music Attributed to Henry Carey
Words by Samuel Francis Smith

Key: F Starting Tone: F(1)

Meter: $\frac{3}{4}$ ($\frac{3}{4}$)

Concept STRUCTURE: Music is made up of sections which may be combined into larger forms.

Discover Plan a performance for a patriotic holiday by combining "America" with "An Amer-I-can." Begin by singing and performing "An Amer-I-can" as suggested in the lesson on page 20. Follow this with group singing of "America," then repeat "An Amer-I-can." The three parts may be connected by a "bridge" using drum and cymbal.

An Amer-I-can Bridge America Bridge An Amer-I-can

Record 8 Side A Band 8 VOICES: boy's choir.
ACCOMPANIMENT: brass ensemble.
FORM: Introduction; Vocal, *v. 1;*
Interlude; Vocal, *v. 2.*

Point out that the class has created a **long piece of music** made up of three main parts. Parts one and three are the **same,** part two is **different.** The sections might be represented in the following way.

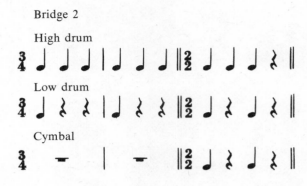

Stately

My coun-try, 'tis of thee, Sweet land of lib - er - ty,

Of thee I sing; Land where my fa - thers died, Land of the

pil - grims' pride, From ev - er - y__ moun - tain-side Let__ free - dom ring.

200

Classified Index of Music and Poetry

Classified Index of Musical Skills

203

Alphabetical Index of Music and Poetry